ANCIENT
CIVILIZATIONS

ANCIENT
CIVILIZATIONS
GREAT EMPIRES AT THEIR HEIGHTS

TIMOTHY R. ROBERTS

SMITHMARK
PUBLISHERS

a division of U.S. Media Holdings, Inc.
115 West 18th Street, New York, NY 10011

FRIEDMAN GROUP BOOK

This edition published in 1997 by SMITHMARK Publishers, a division of U.S. Media Holdings, Inc., 115 West 18th Street, New York, New York 10011.

SMITHMARK books are available for bulk purchase for sales promotion and premium use. For details write or call the manager of special sales, SMITHMARK Publishers, 115 West 18th Street, New York, New York 10011; (212) 532-6600

ISBN 0-7651-9328-0

ANCIENT CIVILIZATIONS
was prepared and produced by
Michael Friedman Publishing Group, Inc.
15 West 26th Street
New York, New York 10011

Editor: Celeste Sollod
Art Director: Jeff Batzli
Designer: Jonathan Gaines
Photography Editor: Deidra Gorgos

Color separations by Fine Arts Repro House Co., Ltd.
Printed in the United Kingdom by Butler & Tanner Limited

Frontispiece: The entrance to the second temple of the mortuary temple of Rameses II (1279–1213 B.C.) at Thebes features statues of Osiris, the god of the underworld, with whom the dead Rameses is identified. The tombs for some of Rameses's minor officials were built into the cliffs behind the temple and are visible between the temple pillars.

Page 6: Archaeologists found thousands of clay tablets, the diplomatic archives of the Mari kings between 1810 and 1760 B.C., in the ruins of the palace of Zimri-Lim (1782–1759 B.C.), at Mari on the Euphrates River in modern-day Syria. Zimri-Lim was a contemporary king of Hammurabi.

In Memory of Henry E. Buchholz

Special thanks to Ben Boyington and Celeste
Sollod for their advice and expertise.

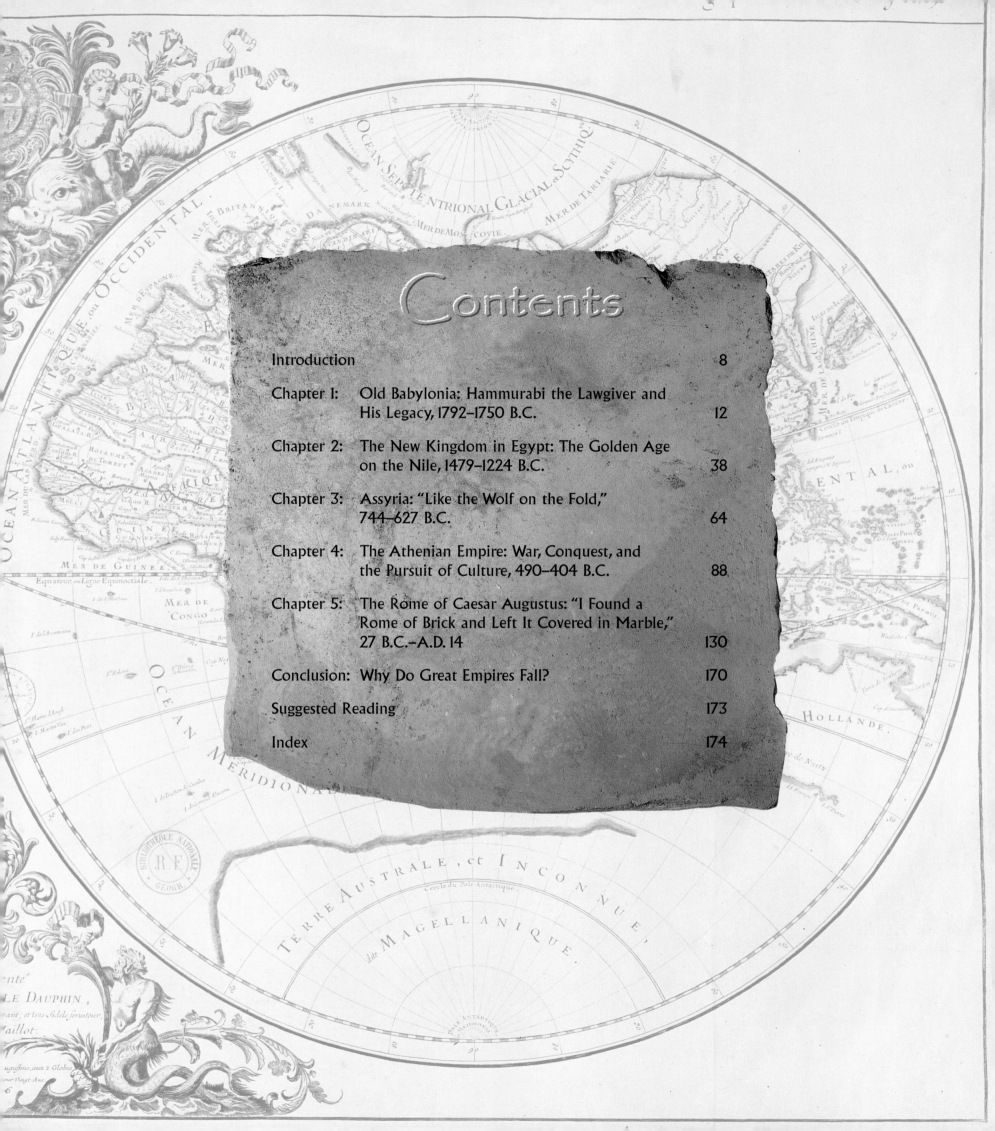

Contents

Introduction

About suffering they were never wrong,
The Old Masters: how well they understood
Its human position; how it takes place....
Anyhow in a corner, some untidy spot
Where the dogs go on with their doggy life and the
torturer's horse
Scratches its innocent behind on a tree....

—W.H. Auden, "Musée des Beaux Arts"

Few people can look at the ruins at Rome, Athens, Khorsabad (about 12½ miles [20km] north of Mosul, Syria), or Karnak without realizing that they are viewing the remnants of great empires. Visitors to Athens who view the Parthenon, atop the Acropolis, realize that this building is a reflection of a dynamic civilization. The same is true for the Forum and Pantheon in Rome or the Pont du Gard near Nîmes, in southern France.

Architecture and art, however, are not the only markers of a great civilization—most grand societies match their achievements in art and architecture with great literature, whether it is the poetry of Virgil, Horace, or Akhenaten; the plays of Euripides or Aeschylus; or the *Epic of Gilgamesh*. That is not to say that great works of art and literature do not occur among people who are barbaric or uncivilized. The isolated, bright literary lights of the *Iliad* and the *Odyssey*, for example, illuminate one of the darkest ages of Greece, but accomplishments such as these are the exception, not the rule.

The achievements listed here, when they have all been attained at the same time, have resulted in "golden ages" for their civilizations. This book presents a survey of those ancient civilizations that achieved—for however brief a time—success in all aspects of society. For example, when Hammurabi ruled Babylon (c. 1792–1750 B.C.), his scribes, artists, and architects were producing unique literature and law, dynamic art, and monumental buildings at the same time that his armies and administrators were subjecting much of present-day Syria and Jordan to his political control. Similarly, sometime later, between roughly 490 and 404 B.C., the great city of Athens not only ruled and administered the Aegean world but also sheltered the literary efforts of Aeschylus, Sophocles, Euripides, Herodotus, Aristophanes, and Thucydides. It also recognized and used the artistry of the sculptor Phidias, the architectural skill of Ictinus and Callicrates, and the illustrative power of the painter Polygnotus. During the same period, the city even played host—albeit grudgingly—to the great philosopher Socrates, the mentor of Plato.

At the same time that these successful ancient civilizations were engaged in impressive intellectual and artistic endeavors, their armies and, sometimes, navies were expanding their spheres of influence through military efforts. This connection between the fine arts and the art of war is probably no coincidence. The greatness of Athens followed that city's defeat of Persia, just as the golden age of Assyria (744–627 B.C.) followed hard on the heels of the military triumphs of that nation's kings—Tiglath-Pileser III, Sargon II, and Sennacherib. The glories of Rome followed the victories of Caesar Augustus, the first emperor of the Roman Empire, which left him master of the whole Mediterranean Basin. And during the greatest and most artistically sophisticated period of ancient Egypt, which begins with the rule of Thutmose III (1479–1425 B.C.) and ends with the death of Rameses II (1224 B.C.), Egyptian armies were expanding the empire's borders from the Euphrates in the north to Nubia in the south. It is popular to decry war and to praise the blessings of peace, but, ironically, it often seems that a successful war (the winning of which may be its own creative experience) results in a flowering of art, architecture, and literature. It seems that war, which often brings out the worst in man, can also create an energy that continues beyond the conflict and allows for a burst of creativity within the societies that play a part.

Our interest in these societies, however, is not so much their history-changing successes as their more "regular" activities. However important the political, military, and intellectual accomplishments of a particular civilization may be, it is the mundane elements of an ancient culture that are most interesting, for it is those with which we identify. Few readers today have made major military or political decisions, written weighty legal decisions, or created great masterpieces of art, but they have gotten drunk, been married, spent money, gone to the doctor, and had troubles with friends and family. How, when, and how often the Mesopotamians drank beer, where Athenians carried their small change, what Egyptians used for makeup, and how Romans dealt with unruly children—these are the ordinary things that make up these ancient societies, and things that we can all understand and with which we can all identify. These are the elements that paint true pictures of societies as vibrant as our own.

The Porch of the Maidens on the west end of the Erechtheum was built between 421 and 407 B.C. to house various small Athenian religious cults. The pillars that support the roof are called caryatides and were common elsewhere in Greece. Similar pillars sculpted in a male form were called atlantides. These caryatides were so popular in the ancient world that Roman Emperor Augustus had copies made for his forum in Rome.

The Pont du Gard near Nîmes in Provence, France, is the most famous surviving Roman aqueduct in the world. Three tiers of arches rising to a height of nearly 160 feet (49m) carried water across the river valley of the Gard.

Chapter One

Old Babylonia

Hammurabi the Lawgiver and His Legacy, 1792–1750 B.C.

Civilization began in Mesopotamia, in that corridor between the sluggish Euphrates and the fast-flowing Tigris. In this magical spot, there came together, quite suddenly, all the elements that are necessary for a culture to pull itself up from wandering tribalism to an artistic, economic, and urban level that we define as "civilization." Agriculture, urban living, writing, public art, monumental architecture, literature, centralized states—all of these things occurred first in Mesopotamia and then spread to the rest of the world. Egypt would not have been Egypt without the influence from the Middle East, and the earliest European cultures have roots that go back to this same place. Even Chinese civilization seems to be younger than the Mesopotamian, and the Chinese appear to have borrowed the basic building blocks of civilization from Mesopotamia rather than developing them on their own.

Opposite: The crowning of Zimri-Lim, king of Mari from 1782 to 1759 B.C. He was a contemporary of Hammurabi, and the two kings corresponded. In this portion of a wall painting, the king stands before the goddess Ishtar and receives from her the symbol of justice—an important aspect of kingship. Although she is usually depicted as the goddess of love, Ishtar in this picture is presented as a warrior goddess, carrying two war clubs slung over her back.

When Hernán Cortés first beheld the Aztec city of Tenochtitlán in A.D. 1519 and both marveled at its culture and was repulsed by its brutality, it is possible that he was seeing the palest reflection of his own origins. We can believe this because, while Mesopotamian culture influenced the earliest European civilizations in Crete and Greece—which later shaped the civilization of Rome, which in turn spawned the early modern European world—another branch of that same Mesopotamian tree was spreading to earliest China. From China, basic artistic and religious elements probably crossed the Pacific to influence the Olmec culture of southern Mexico, which in turn spawned the great civilizations of the Maya and Aztecs which Cortés saw.

All this makes for wonderful speculation, and we may never truly understand how civilization got its start, but one thing is certain: after developing the building blocks of civilization, Mesopotamia became a bewildering world of tiny city-states that for nearly three thousand years were constantly fighting one another to control this or that patch of fertile ground along a stretch of one of the mighty rivers. Nor is this surprising; it is, after all, the potential fertility of the soil, the climate of the region, and the seasonal activities of the Tigris and Euphrates that explain nearly everything about early Mesopotamia.

The soil of Mesopotamia is deep and rich, but there is hardly any rain to exploit the land's potential to grow crops. This problem is partially solved by an annual flood that occurs from April through June, when both rivers swell past their banks and deposit a layer of water and nutrient-rich sediment. Unfortunately, this annual flooding is a double-edged sword: the floodwaters of the two rivers come at the same time that the young crops of barley (*Hordeum vulgare*), emmur wheat (*Triticum dicoccum*), and einkorn wheat (*Triticum monococcum*) are beginning to grow. If nothing were to be done, the floodwaters would drown the young plants. Successful cultivation requires dikes to protect the fields from the onslaught and

D oor plaques, such as this one, which portrays the figure of Ur-Nanshe (2494–2465 B.C.), a king of Lagash, and his retainers, were common throughout Mesopotamia on buildings from earliest times to the fourth century B.C. They were affixed to door jambs to help support a wooden peg on which a timber door hung, and they usually commemorate the ruler who built the temple or palace.

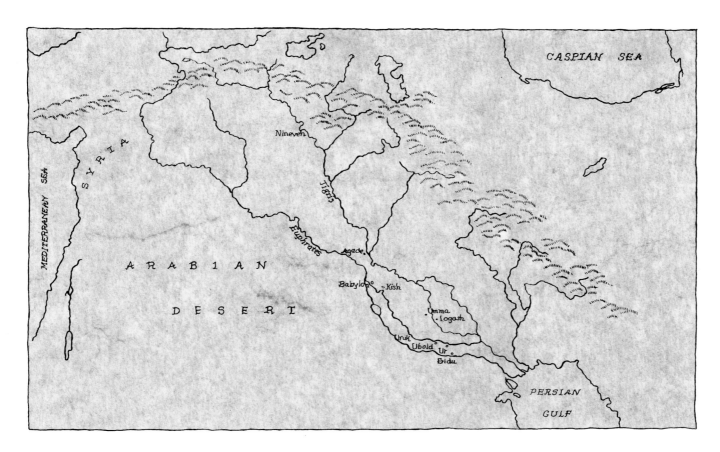

reservoirs to hold the floodwater and allow it to be released gradually into the fields throughout the growing season. In years of especially high water, the rivers can change course and a previously rich area be left arid and barren.

From a very early date, therefore, the inhabitants of Mesopotamia had to band together in some kind of order to protect their agricultural potential from the very thing that made it possible. This banding together resulted in the development of the first city-states. In the course of two millennia, dozens of tiny cities grew up in Mesopotamia, each with its own small area of farmland. Often these cities were within sight of one another. How small these city-states were is readily apparent today: a tourist can stand on the site of ancient Ur and clearly see the mound that marked the site of Ur's enemy Eridu, then turn around to see the mounds of two other rival cities, Uruk and Larsa.

These little states carried on constant miniwars. Occasionally, one city might gain dominance over weaker neighbors. In about 2340 B.C., Lugal Zagesi of Umma conquered Lagash and everything south to the Persian Gulf. Even at their largest, though, these "empires" were small—Lugal Zagesi probably controlled an area of about 150 miles (240km) in diameter—and their control over any area was fleeting, lasting only until another city-state conquered one or more of its neighbors. Conquered aggressors might end their days immobilized in a "neck stock" outside the gates of the conqueror's city. For Lugal Zagesi, the city of his shame was Nippur. When people entered the city to petition his conqueror, Sargon of Akkad, they threw insults at Lugal Zagesi. As bad as this punishment may seem, it was much worse for the loyal armies of a leader who lost a battle. The usual fate of captured soldiers was wholesale slaughter on the battlefield; a "favored" few were allowed to live—they were blinded and then taken back to the conqueror's city to move a grinding stone or haul water from the canals, wells, or reservoirs to the fields.

Sargon of Akkad was born the illegitimate son of a barmaid. The legend goes that as an infant he was in danger of being killed. His mother placed him in a basket and sent him downstream along the Euphrates, and a royal princess rescued him. The princess's father was king of Kish. The princess adopted Sargon, who grew up to kill his "grandfather"; then Sargon succeeded to the throne. Sargon went on to create a united Mesopotamia, from Brak, in extreme southern Turkey, down to the head of the Persian Gulf—quite a large "empire" for the time.

Sargon's reign, which lasted from 2334 to 2279 B.C., was not a peaceful one; constant revolts plagued his reign, and the empire did not survive his death.

The truly amazing thing about this period of constant, and no doubt bitter, warfare was that the third millennium B.C. was the most dynamic period in the development of the facets of what we call "civilization." Humankind developed writing, sculpture, building, and art—skills that mark and define a certain sophistication. Some unknown Mesopotamian invented the arch, another figured out the wheel, and still another created the ziggurat, a high-stepped pyramidal tower with a temple at the top. People began to create monumental sculpture and art for the purpose of glorifying and identifying their nation. To defend the successes of the early city-states and protect the cropland that supported them, the first organized armies and fortified cities were developed.

The goal of warfare at this time was not to conquer your enemy's town but rather to destroy his cropland and, at the same time, prevent him from destroying yours. If an invading army could destroy the food-producing capability of an enemy city, then that city would starve. To prevent this, each city-state periodically formed its citizens into a loosely disciplined rabble, outfitted them in leather caps and square hide shields, gave each soldier a copper-pointed spear, and sent them out to fight. On the battlefield, these troops would form long lines, with the edges of each man's shield overlapping the shield of the man next to him. These formations were held as the lines advanced across an open field. A famous sculpture called the Stele of the Vultures, made in Lagash in about 2450 B.C., shows such a phalanx advancing over the dead bodies of their foes. Nobody on this stele has a sword, because at this early date, tempering metal into a piece long enough to have a usable blade with a sharp edge was not possible. Bows existed but had not been adapted to warfare. Chariots also existed, but they were too cumbersome to maneuver on a battlefield; they had four solid wooden wheels and a flat wooden bed and were drawn by four onagers (small wild asses).

Unfortunately, our understanding of early Mesopotamian tactics is based mostly on speculation and deduction; historians have not yet found any formal descriptions of battles from this time. From what we do know, it seems that the only discipline involved was in getting the soldiers to a battlefield and motivating them to engage the enemy. These battles were, it seemed, incredibly chaotic—the two masses came together in a pushing, shoving mass with every man attempting to maneuver his spear around the edge of an opponent's shield and stab him. It seems a haphazard way to make war, and if early Mesopotamian generals were like their later Greek counterparts, who practiced this same kind of warfare, they gave their troops enough wine before a battle to get them to go boldly forward, oblivious to the dangers. The outcome was generally decided by one side's line crumbling, and the troops running for their lives. To move past this haphazard style of conflict and develop an edge that would allow one particular faction to gain lasting control within the region, Mesopotamia needed a ruler who could impose some kind of order and create at least a nucleus of professional soldiers.

The excavated and partially reconstructed ziggurat of Ur dedicated to the moon god was probably built by Ur-Nammu (2112–2095 B.C.). Ur was the most famous of many ancient Sumerian cities that dotted the Mesopotamian landscape before the arrival of the Semitic invaders, from whom Hammurabi descended.

Hammurabi and the Rise of Babylonia

s it turned out, that leader was the famous Hammurabi, who by 1764 B.C. had led the previously insignificant city-state of Babylon, on the Euphrates, to its position as the central unifying power in all Mesopotamia. Indeed, so powerful was Hammurabi's stamp on this period of time that even after his death the whole area was collectively called Babylonia, and the previously minor town of Babylon became the civil and religious center of the region until the Greeks, under Alexander the Great, conquered the area a millennium and a half later.

At the beginning of his reign, however, there was nothing to distinguish Hammurabi from any of the other local rulers. He was an Amorite, a race of Semitic barbarians whose ancestors had wandered out of the Arabian peninsula sometime in the third millennium B.C. and hired themselves out as mercenaries to various petty rulers in Sumer, the southern part of Mesopotamia. By about 1900 B.C., the Amorites were ruling the cities where they had previously done military service and the people had spread north, gaining enough power to become a factor in the politics of Akkad, the northern part of Mesopotamia.

Like its leader, there was nothing remarkable about the city of Babylon when Hammurabi first came to power. Founded around 2700 B.C., this city had a small temple complex and, after 2112 B.C., a royal governor from Ur, located 175 miles (280km) to the southeast. Apparently, the name Babylon derived from the word *babilani*—the "gate of the gods"—but there really was nothing to justify the town's having such a grandiose name at that early date.

Hammurabi was the sixth king of a dynasty that went back to 1894 B.C., to a king named Sumu-abum. According to archaeologists and historians, this dynasty marks the "Old" Babylonian period of Mesopotamian history, as opposed to the "New" or Neo-Babylonian period, whose most successful ruler was the great Nebuchadrezzar II (reigned 604–562 B.C.), justly famous in his own right as the king who built the famous Hanging Gardens of Babylon, took Jerusalem in 586 B.C., and conquered the Jews in what came to be known as the Babylonian Captivity. Although Hammurabi was the most important ruler of the Old Babylonian period, his first thirty years in power seem to have been spent quietly watching from the sidelines as a couple of other local strongmen struggled for control: Rim-Sin of Larsa (r.1822–1763 B.C.), a city about 125 miles (200 km) southeast of Babylon, and Shamshi-Adad (r.1813–1781 B.C.) of Assur, located about 200 miles (320 km) to the north in present-day northern Syria.

The diplomatic and military exploits of these two leaders can be followed in great detail because their diplomatic correspondence has been preserved—the clay

The relief at the top of the famous law code of Hammurabi shows the sun god giving Hammurabi the law code that is inscribed on the pillar underneath.

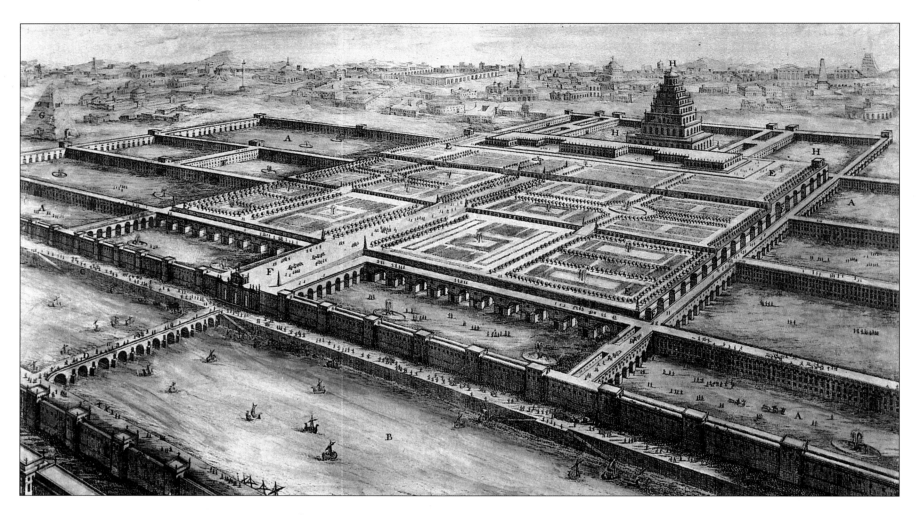

A reconstruction of the Babylon of Nebuchadrezzar II (r. 604–562 B.C.). Over 1100 years after Hammurabi ruled Babylon, another great king, Nebuchadrezzar, would build his capital on the very site where Hammurabi's stood. Unfortunately the grandeur of Hammurabi's capital is now forever buried, and archaeologists can only speculate on its extent.

tablets on which they corresponded were baked into solid bricks when the library at Mari, a town under Shamshi-Adad's rule, burned. The two men were at war not only with one another but also with other chieftains to the east and west. In the early part of Hammurabi's reign, the two frequently asked him for a levy of Babylonian infantry, a request he filled for one or the other, as the political climate dictated. The young Hammurabi, it seems, was an astute politician who was able to weave his city's fortunes around the struggles of Rim-Sin and Shamshi-Adad.

The more eminent of the two, Shamshi-Adad, was especially successful in the northern part of Mesopotamia. He might have been even more successful had it not been for the problems created by his sons Ishme-Dagan and Yasmah-Adad, who acted as governors and military commanders for their father. Judging from the accounts on the surviving Mari "bricks," Yasmah-Adad, the younger brother, was the least effective of the two. A number of letters from his exasperated father survive in which Shamshi-Adad attacks his son for spending too much time in the harem and not enough time tending to the busi-

ness of governing and conquering. A particularly biting letter, written after Yasmah-Adad had unnecessarily delayed a foreign ambassador at the border, asks the boy if he has lost the ability to make a simple decision because he spends all his time in the harem. "Have you lost your beard, or have the harem women pulled it out?" the father asks peevishly. (In ancient Mesopotamia, a beard was a sign of success and the mark of a man of affairs.) Somewhat later, Yasmah-Adad received from his brother an angry letter about Yasmah-Adad's hasty—and unwarranted—lighting of the warning beacons on the border and the resulting mobilization of the entire army to repel what was apparently a mere raid. Ishme-Dagan's sarcasm is unmistakable: "When the army arrives, try to beat the dozen or so invaders, and then send the army back, if you think you can spare it."

Shamshi-Adad died in 1780 B.C., and Ishme-Dagan succeeded him to the throne. Almost immediately, a subtle change appears on the Mari tablets. Hammurabi is progressively less willing to dispatch troops to the aid of Ishme-Dagan and more likely to act on his own. By 1764

B.C., Ishme-Dagan, tired of his southern subordinate dragging his feet when requests for troops were made, invaded Babylonian territory to teach Hammurabi a lesson. Although there is no surviving record of the details, it appears that it was actually Hammurabi who did the "teaching." The Babylonian army defeated not only the Assurian invaders but also Ishme-Dagan's allies from Elam and Eshnunna.

Although the records do not specifically say so, 1764 B.C. was a watershed year for Babylonia. The next year, Hammurabi's troops marched south and defeated an army under Larsa's Rim-Sin. This victory was apparently achieved through the use of a strategy Hammurabi had seen his father, Sin-muballit (1812–1793 B.C.), use in an earlier war against Rim-Sin: the Babylonian army advanced to a spot above Larsa, took control of the surrounding area, and then constructed a huge dam across the Euphrates. After the river had backed up behind this dam, the Babylonians broke it open, releasing a huge flood of water that tore out all of the irrigation works of Larsa. With Larsa's food-producing potential crippled, Hammurabi laid siege to the city itself. Rim-Sin died in this campaign from unknown causes, and by the end of the campaign season Hammurabi's troops were in control of Larsa. By 1762 B.C., the balance of power had definitely shifted, for by then Hammurabi's army was in the north attacking Ishme-Dagan's forces near Mari. Exactly what happened next and how the conflicts ensued is not covered in the clay records that survive, but when the fog lifts, we find Babylonian archivists in Mari, cataloging Ishme-Dagan's library. Strangely, although one supposes that the forces of Ishme-Dagan were defeated at this time, the king himself lived on until 1741, apparently as a puppet king in his own capital.

Finally, between 1757 and 1755 B.C., Hammurabi consolidated his hold over Mesopotamia by moving east and conquering the city of Eshnunna by repeating the strategy of drowning its fields in a sudden release of dammed-up water. With the defeat of Eshnunna, a new day dawned—and that sun rose with Hammurabi firmly in control of the region.

During Hammurabi's incredibly active reign, Babylon became dominant in Mesopotamia not only as a military center, but also as a cultural one. Hammurabi continued the tradition of learning and culture started by his father, and this tradition was in turn carried on by Hammurabi's son, Samsu-iluna (1749–1712 B.C.). This devotion to enhancing the arts and learning, which marks the Old Babylonian era as one of special creativity, continued to influence developments in Mesopotamia for the next millennium and a half.

The most famous event in Hammurabi's reign was his well-known law code being etched in stone. When French archaeologist Jacques de Morgan found the code inscribed on a seven-foot (2.25m) basalt column at Susa in 1900, scholars concluded that it was the earliest written law code in history. Subsequent investigation and discov-

The best surviving example of Akkadian bronze sculpture is this head of either Sargon of Akkad (2334–2279 B.C.) or his grandson Narram-Sin (2254–2218), Akkadian rulers who built empires in Mesopotamia and whose examples inspired later Mesopotamian conquerors.

The most famous artifact of ancient Mesopotamia is the famous Law Code of Hammurabi, recorded on columns of black basalt seven feet (2.25m) high, about 1790 B.C. The law code reveals that Hammurabi was not only a thorough administrator, but also a humane one who had the welfare of his subjects at heart. Long after Hammurabi's death, an Elamite king took the pillar home to Susa as a souvenir, where a French archaeological expedition discovered it in 1900. It is now in the Louvre, and the Museum of Natural History in New York has a full-size replica.

eries have shown that there were at least three earlier law codes issued by other Mesopotamian rulers, but this does not detract from Hammurabi's legal achievement. His code was an amazing and in many ways original document that demonstrates, as do many things in Hammurabi's reign, that he was a ruler whose concerns went far beyond winning personal glory to concern with issues focusing on the lives of his subjects.

The code represents a collection of legal reforms that Hammurabi made and then had copied and posted in the major temples of cities and towns throughout his kingdom for local priests to read to the *puhrum* (town council) when they met around the column. We are fortunate to have a complete copy (now at the Louvre Museum) that contains forty-two columns and covers 282 different laws divided into major categories such as property, land sales, trade and business, families, injuries, and labor. The law code is made up of specific conditionals: *if* somebody does something wrong, *then* a specific punishment will be assessed. If a person brings a charge of murder against another and cannot substantiate the charge, the accuser will die; if a man builds a house for another and the house subsequently collapses on the owner, then the builder dies; if a *mushkenum* (common man) strikes another mushkenum unjustly, he must pay a fine of ten shekels, but if he strikes an *awilum* (a man of higher station), he must pay sixty shekels. Punishment was often doled out in the form of death or mutilation. Death was the penalty for rape, kidnapping, incest, running away during a battle, burglary, highway robbery, dishonesty in public office, or producing bad beer—beer being the common drink for all Babylonians (they took their beer very seriously). Mutilation was a common penalty for other crimes: a son who struck his father lost his hand; a surgeon who botched an operation lost his fingers; and a nurse who knowingly substituted a sick infant for a healthy one lost her breasts.

Besides punishments, there are laws that govern the everyday acts of living. Wages are set for many professions, including stonemasons, carpenters, shepherds, cattle drovers, sailors, day laborers, and even surgeons. For successful cataract surgery on an awilum, for instance, a doctor could charge ten shekels. For the same surgery on a mushkenum, the fee was five shekels. A similar operation on a slave netted only two shekels. The code also es-

tablishes rules for inheritance. When a man died, his children, not his wife, were always the heirs to his fortune. On her husband's death, a wife was compensated by being given back her dowry and the equivalent value of her wedding gifts and by being guaranteed control of her house until she died.

Perhaps the most interesting law in the whole code was one that guaranteed a compensatory payment from the local treasury to a victim of a robbery if the thief was not apprehended and executed. What modern municipality, anywhere in the world, could be that certain of its law enforcement capabilities?

The law code does not cover all possible legal situations. For instance, it does not concern itself with an individual's relationship to the state or a province's to the empire. At most, it seems to be a guide that a local court might use to settle local matters. After years of learned debate about how the law code fitted into Babylonian society, historians have reached a rough consensus that it was a source for the puhrum which often sat as a local law court, to use in its deliberations in settling local matters. The harshness of the penalties does not at first strike a modern reader as reforming or designed for the welfare of the people, but the innovative quality of the law lay not in its punishments but in its being set down in a permanent form so that it could not be changed at the whim of a local magistrate.

How the local Babylonian courts that administered this law functioned has been a matter of some debate. The best guess is that the puhrum and its members, called *shibutumor*, or elders, met under the leadership of the *rabianum*, or mayor, to decide cases of local interest. Some evidence exists that during his reign Hammurabi created a specific class of judges who had special knowledge of the law. The puhrum met in the courtyard of the most important temple—probably the one honoring Marduk, the patron god of the city of Babylon—and there heard evidence and summoned and questioned witnesses. Juries were not part of the procedure. Generally, the court rendered judgment based on evidence, but in cases where there were no witnesses (how a shepherd had lost his sheep, for instance), they might require that the accused go to the temple and swear his or her innocence before the god. For three serious crimes—sorcery, adultery, and murder—where there were no witnesses to the

crime, the court might order trial by ordeal. In these cases, the accused was bound and thrown into a river. If the person sank, he or she was guilty, and the sentence of execution had conveniently been carried out (note that this is quite the reverse of a similar ordeal in medieval Europe, used mostly to try witches, in which a person was found guilty if he or she did not sink).

Although the code of Hammurabi may seem barbaric and incomplete, its promulgation was enough to establish the reputation of the king throughout ancient Mesopotamia.

This terra-cotta statue of a shepherd carrying a lamb dates from the time of Hammurabi and was found at Girsu, an ancient city about 112 miles (180km) southeast of Babylon.

After a scribe wrote a letter in cuneiform on a tablet (left), it was sealed and baked in a clay envelope (right) with the address written on the outside. When it reached its destination, the recipient simply cracked it like an egg. Although writing existed in some form from about 3200 B.C., formal letters did not become common until about 2400 B.C.

Writing, Early Literature, and the Religion of Babylonia

ammurabi's reputation, however, did not depend solely on his legal reforms. During his reign, Babylon became a center for learning and a collection point for the literature of the region. Before this time, a number of literary epics existed, but records of them were scattered and disorganized. Hammurabi's scribes systematized and organized them in much the same form as they exist today.

In ancient Babylonia, writing was a skill possessed by very few people. Most kings, judges, and priests were illiterate and depended entirely on a comparatively small number of trained scribes to conduct the business that their civilization required. The reason for this phenomenon is simple. Cuneiform, the written language of Babylonia, was incredibly difficult to learn. It had more than one thousand symbols with infinite variations to convey syntax, tense, and declension. Learning to write was an endeavor that took a lifetime to master. Perhaps to simplify their task scribes seemed to specialize in specific fields. We have evidence of military scribes, agricultural scribes, business scribes, and scribes called "name scribes," who appear to have specialized in making lists.

Writing seems to have been a Mesopotamian invention, and the idea spread east and west to influence both Egypt and China. Recently, scholars discovered where and how writing began. Since 4000 B.C., people in Mesopotamia kept records of "how much" and "what kind" by using small clay models of the item in question (ox, jar, bread, etc.) and specific symbols for the numbers 1, 10, and 60. To safeguard a business transaction, these symbols were often sealed inside a hollow clay ball that archaeologists call a *bulla*. To check the details of a transaction, it was necessary to crack open the bulla and check the contents. In time, it seems that some clever person, believing that cracking open the bulla was somewhat wasteful, suggested that the contents of the bulla could be more easily checked by making an impression of each clay marker in the wet clay's surface before sealing the markers inside the ball. Thereafter, one only had to check the surface to know what was inside. Eventually, people discarded the little clay objects and merely made suitable impressions on flat pieces of clay. Once the clay was dry, the "document" was permanent and the record was safeguarded. This complicated process may have taken eight hundred years to evolve, but by 3200 B.C., these kinds of documents were common in Sumer, the southern part of Mesopotamia. By then scribes were evolving signs to designate verbs and abstract objects, besides the more prosaic signs for objects, numbers, and animals.

At first, writing was used to keep records of livestock, grain production, and farming equipment. By 2900 B.C., however, the process of impressing messages on clay tablets in a standardized script was being used to record land sales. Three hundred years later, we find records of house sales, court records, letters, and even purely literary texts. By 2600 B.C., tablets were being used to record myths, stories, and accounts of royal expeditions, whether military, economic, or diplomatic, and the age of true literature had been born.

Nearly a thousand years later, Hammurabi's Babylon became the heir to this literary tradition. As noted earlier, Hammurabi's father, Sin-muballit, Hammurabi himself, and Hammurabi's son and successor, Samsu-iluna, seem to have been major supporters of literature. At Babylon and Nippur, Hammurabi established schools—called *edubba*, or tablet houses—where scribes undertook rigorous training to learn cuneiform. During the reigns of these three kings, Babylonian scribes spent a great deal of time collecting and cataloging older Sumerian myths and then combining these into new forms and legends. Archaeologists have discovered long lists of titles that show how much material has perished—in fact, surveying these lists, one realizes how tragically little of what they created and tried to preserve has survived.

Unfortunately, we do not know how widespread the devotion to literature was among the Babylonians. Nothing indicates that the great epics the scribes copied or created had a particularly wide appeal among the general population. There is no hint of a "bardic" tradition existing in Mesopotamia (such as that which would surround the *Iliad* or *Beowulf*, where wandering minstrels earned their supper by singing for the nobility). The literature that has come down to us could have been merely scribal "exercises." Perhaps Old Babylonian literature was created for only a small group of literati, a literary counterpart to the artistic endeavors of the Chinese scholars of the late Ming Dynasty, who between A.D. 1573 and

1644 created masterpieces of art and calligraphy that they shared only among themselves. Whatever the case, the Old Babylonians created a wide range of literature, from epigrams and poems to theology and epics.

The *Epic of Atrahasis* was one of the most popular myths of the Old Babylonian period, and although some elements may predate Hammurabi, it seems to have taken definite shape around his reign in the scribal *edubba* at either Babylon or Nippur. This story is unique because it pits one clever man against the gods, and the man wins. Mythologically speaking, that is a rare phenomenon.

The story goes that originally there were three chief gods in the Babylonian pantheon—Anu, Enlil, and Enki—who divided the world among themselves. Anu, the chief god, received the heavens as his portion of the world. Enlil, his chief advisor, received the earth. Enki, the third god, received the waters under the earth, and the sea. Enlil put the minor gods—Adad, We-e, Nintur, Nusku, Namtar, Ninlil, and some others—to work on

Although the archives at Ebla date from about 2400 B.C., considerably before the time of Hammurabi, the clay tablets found there are similar to Babylonian tablets from his time. Scribes carefully labeled and filed clay documents and stored them on wooden shelves. When the palace at Ebla was sacked, and burned, the fire in the archives created a giant kiln that baked the tablets hard and so preserved them for posterity.

Sacrifice of animals played an important part in Babylonian religious life throughout the long history of Mesopotamia. Here a group of Sumerian priests of the third millennium B.C. sacrifice a ram. People expected their rulers, like Hammurabi, to offici- ate at these sacrifices to ensure that the ceremonies pleased the gods. The large figure to the left of the sacrifice may represent such a ruler.

Earth, digging channels for the Tigris and Euphrates Rivers, but the work was hard and hot and the gods be- gan to complain. At first, the complaining took the form of grumbling, but then, after many days with no relief, the grumbling became louder. Finally We-e proposed an attack on Enlil, but Nintur, the birth goddess, went to Enlil to warn him of the attack. Strangely, Enlil was not angry but remorseful, and he offered to resign as chief god over the earth. Enki, whom many regarded as the wisest of the gods, proposed a compromise: why not get Nintur, as the birth goddess, to create men to do all the heavy work? Nintur agreed and she made careful plans. First she persuaded the other gods to kill the troublemaker, We-e. Then she scraped the flesh off his bones and drained his body of blood. She mixed the blood and the flesh with clay and made models of men. These she baked in an oven for nine months until they were ready.

The plan worked well, and the people worked hard for the gods for twelve hundred years. By that time, however, the humans had been so fruitful that their numbers had swelled beyond anything the gods could have imagined, because in this tale every time a woman and man had intercourse, the woman would become pregnant. Soon the world was filled with humans, and the noise from so many of them was so loud that the gods could not sleep. When the deities complained, Enlil gathered them all together to consider what could be done. After a short debate, the gods decided that the best solution was to kill all the people. So they asked Nimtar, the god of plagues, to send a disease to achieve this. When men and women began to sicken and die—a new experience, for mankind had never faced diseases before—the people turned to Atrahasis, the wisest of men, and asked him to help.

Atrahasis told them to transfer all their worship to Nimtar, to flatter him with prayers and burnt offerings, so that he would grow fat with their worship and come to depend on their adoration. The plan worked, and the population slowly began to reestablish itself.

In time, however, the human numbers again increased, and with them the noise level. The gods again gathered to discuss the situation. This time they decided to kill all the crops by withholding the rain. Adad, the rain god, locked up the heavens so that there was no rain for two years. The Tigris and Euphrates began to dry up, and people began to starve to death. When people became concerned, they again turned to Atrahasis, and he again suggested worship, but this time, he said, they should direct their efforts toward Adad. When Adad became satiated with human worship and sacrifice and feared to lose it, he reopened the skies; soon, the crops were growing and people were once more multiplying.

When the noise level yet again grew too loud, Enlil called the gods together a third time and demanded that they agree to collectively withhold everything that mankind needed. That way, the humans would be outwitted—they could not concentrate their worship on all the gods at once because there simply were not enough of them. Even if one god succumbed to concentrated flattery, the stinginess of the other gods would be enough to kill off mankind. The gods implemented their plan, and the crops stopped growing, the wild animals ran away, the cattle, sheep, and goats went barren, and the fish swam down the rivers to the sea. For six years, this situation continued, and people became so hungry that mothers turned daughters out of doors rather than share food.

The people once more turned to Atrahasis, who thought about the situation and realized that people could live on fish alone. If the people concentrated their worship on Enki, the god of the waters, he would bring back the fish. When the people did this, they were able to eke out an existence. By now Enlil was very angry, and he again demanded that Adad send the rains to drown mankind. But Enki, who had grown fond of Atrahasis, warned him, telling him to build a great boat and save himself and his family. There followed a great flood, the only survivors of which were the family of Atrahasis.

Atrahasis dutifully kept up the worship of Enki, and when the waters receded, the family emerged from their boat, built houses, and began to grow crops again. In time, the other gods became jealous, for Enki was the only god who received offerings and prayers. They realized that without worshipers it was really no fun being a god, and so they went to Enki and asked for advice. Enki in turn asked Atrahasis, who suggested a number of ways to limit the number of children women had. First, from this time on Nintur would not be as forthcoming with her blessings of fertility for women. Second, the gods created a female demon, Pashittu, whose joy was to kill and eat unattended babies. Third, the gods decreed that each city should maintain temples staffed by priestesses who were forbidden to engage in all sexual activity and who consequently bore no children. When these measures were adopted, they kept the human population from growing so large as to be unmanageable, but large enough to satisfy the gods' lust for worshipers.

The *Epic of Atrahasis* may have been popular among the literati in Old Babylon, but it is hardly known at all today. Conversely, one of the least popular (to judge from surviving copies) epics of that time, *Gilgamesh*, is today the best-known piece of Old Babylonian literature.

Parts of the *Epic of Gilgamesh* existed long before Hammurabi's Babylon; individual episodes from this epic can be found on clay tablets from the Third Dynasty of Ur (2132–2004 B.C.). It was, however, an Old Babylonian scribe (or scribes) who collected those fragments and combined them into a more or less complete epic that follows Gilgamesh from his birth through his unsuccessful quest for eternal life and his return to Uruk. Gilgamesh, the hero of the epic, was an historic king of Uruk, a city in southern Iraq about 19 miles (30km) northeast of Ur on the Euphrates, who lived sometime between 2700 and 2600 B.C. Unfortunately, there are no independent historic episodes about his life—everything we know about him comes from the legend.

The *Epic of Gilgamesh* is a wonderful piece of literature that combines not only dynamic battle scenes between Gilgamesh and various monsters and men but also episodes that treat themes of jealousy, pride, the evils of city life, women spurned, and the quest for immortality. As put together by the Old Babylonian scribes, the epic begins with a description of the deeds of King Gilgamesh of Uruk. Apparently, he has been making a reputation for himself at the expense of his people, forcing himself on

This scene from a relief at Tell Halaf (ancient Guzana) dating to the ninth century B.C. may record a variant of the Gilgamesh legend where the hero and his friend Enkidu drive the Imdugud bird from the branches of the huluppu tree, sacred to Ishtar, the goddess of love.

the women and demanding too much work from the men. The people, in their frustration, address prayers to Anu, the god of Uruk, for help. Anu in turn demands that the goddess of creation, Aruru, create a creature that is the equal of Gilgamesh to defeat him. Using clay and water, Aruru creates a massive and primitive human called Enkidu who is happy roaming the lands with the wild animals. This creature is innocent of mankind and of the city, and by avoiding the corruption of the city, he gains enormous strength and power. When he begins to take the side of the wild animals against the hunters of Uruk, reducing their kills, they ask Gilgamesh for help. Before challenging Enkidu to battle, Gilgamesh decides to weaken him by introducing the wild man to sex.

Gilgamesh sends a prostitute from the Temple of Ishtar to seduce Enkidu. Once the prostitute seduces Enkidu, not only are his powers diminished, but his friends, the animals, shun him. When he and Gilgamesh finally fight, it is on equal terms—having lost his innocence, Enkidu has lost his strength. Still, Enkidu is very strong, and the battle between the two champions lasts all day. At the end of the day, both men are exhausted, and they concede that there can be no victor. Rather than continue the futile contest, the two decide to become friends.

Gilgamesh and Enkidu then undertake a great adventure. They travel north to the Mountains of Cedar and kill the giant Humbaba, who makes the earth tremble and emits fire from his mouth. Some authorities speculate that

Humbaba is a pale literary reflection of a volcano. After wandering through a forest ten leagues wide, the two heroes find Humbaba and engage him in battle. As Enkidu prepares to deliver the death blow, Humbaba makes a plea for mercy. Gilgamesh is inclined to grant it, but Enkidu will not agree and slices off the giant's head. The two take the head to Enlil, the god of earth, air, and wind, who curses them for killing Humbaba. In their arrogance and pride, they had forgotten that Humbaba was the guardian of the Cedar forest, appointed by Enlil to guard the great trees. The two have made a powerful enemy.

When Enkidu and Gilgamesh return to Uruk, Gilgamesh receives a message from the goddess Ishtar telling him to come see her. She is impressed with the prowess of the hero and wants to seduce him. Ishtar offers herself to Gilgamesh, but the hero, remembering that Ishtar is notorious for her fickleness, refuses her. He even goes so far as to insult her, reminding her of her many lovers, including not only men but the lion and the stallion. He points out how each of her lovers not only has been jilted, but often punished and transformed. Ishullana, for instance, the gardener of the gods, was turned into a mole after Ishtar had tired of him.

When Gilgamesh rejects her, Ishtar goes to her father Anu, the king of the gods, and demands that he send the great Bull of Heaven to kill the king of Uruk. Anu dispatches the bull to kill the hero, but Gilgamesh and Enkidu kill the beast. This makes Anu angry, and he decrees death for Enkidu as a punishment. Enkidu has a dream foreshadowing his death; this dream also shows him the dreadful world of the dead ruled by the awful queen of hell, Ereshkigal. This hell is a gloomy place where the dead sit in darkness eating clay seasoned with dust. When he tells Gilgamesh about his dream, the hero is doubly distressed, not only for the death of his friend but also because of the terrors of the afterlife. Enkidu dies shortly after, and Gilgamesh refuses to let him be buried until Enkidu's body begins to rot.

From this point on, the Gilgamesh epic becomes a philosophical consideration of the finality of death. The Babylonian afterlife is a gloomy, joyless place. Death, with no promise of reward, is to be feared. Gilgamesh broods over this, realizing that soon he, like Enkidu, will be facing the same dismal eternity. It seems unfair that a glorious life filled with fame should end so badly.

But Gilgamesh sees a way out. He remembers hearing of Utnapishtim, a man who survived the great flood that killed mankind and who lives eternally on the island of Dilmun. That island (which most historians assume to be the modern state of Bahrain) lies far to the east across the poisoned sea, and Gilgamesh, believing he can overcome any difficulty, sets off to find Utnapishtim. The king of Uruk journeys first to the gates of Mashu—two high peaks from whence the sun rises. These gates are guarded by fierce, half-scorpion, half-man monsters. Gilgamesh speaks to these guardians, and they let him pass, no doubt certain that the journey to Dilmun will kill him. Gilgamesh easily overcomes twelve leagues of utter darkness and finally reaches the Garden of the Gods on the shore of the poisoned sea.

The gentle goddess Siduri, who protects brewers and wine makers, waits for him by the poisoned sea, concerned with protecting the well-being of mankind. When Gilgamesh tells her about the goal of his trip, she tries to dissuade him. She tells him this life is all that mankind can hope for and that he should "fill his belly with wine, eat, drink, and be merry, cherish his children and the embraces of his wife, for these are the proper concerns of mankind, not the gloom of afterlife."

When it becomes clear that Gilgamesh will not change his mind, Siduri directs him to Urshanabi, the man who ferries Utnapishtim back and forth to Dilmun. If the hero can persuade Urshanabi to take him, then perhaps he can find Utnapishtim and gain eternal life. On his way to find Urshanabi, Gilgamesh loses his way, becomes frustrated, and in a rage destroys the sails of a boat drawn up on the shore. Settling down and regaining his composure, he goes on to find Urshanabi, only to discover that

This sculpture may be a representation of Utnapishtim and his wife. Utnapishtim was the Babylonian Noah who at the command of Ea, the god of wisdom, and the creator of mankind, built an ark to escape the flood that the gods Ishtar and Enlil had sent to destroy mankind.

A clay tablet with cuneiform script surrounding a portrait of the ruler, perhaps Zimri-Lim, ruler of Mari about 1782–1759 B.C. Hammurabi later deposed him and tore down the walls of Mari.

the sails he has just destroyed are the propulsion that allows the boat to cross the poisoned sea. Still, Gilgamesh is so insistent that Urshanabi tells the king that if he gathers 120 poles, each 60 cubits long, and covers each with bitumen (asphalt), he may be able to help Gilgamesh reach Dilmun. Obediently Gilgamesh cuts the poles and paints them with bitumen. The poles are used to propel the boat by being thrust into the bottom of the sea. One hundred twenty poles are needed because of the poisonous nature of the water—no human hand should touch a pole once it has been immersed. Gilgamesh uses all the poles and still has not reached Dilmun; to travel the rest of the way, he creates a sail by holding his clothes between his outstretched arms.

Once ashore on the island, Gilgamesh meets Utnapishtim and tells the immortal of his quest for eternal life. Utnapishtim explains that his immortality was a gift from Enlil after the great flood that killed all the other humans. Apparently, Enlil had suffered remorse for sending the flood and gave Utnapishtim eternal life as compensation for his suffering. Utnapishtim further explains that eternal life can be gained simply by staying awake for six days and seven nights. In doing so, a human can demonstrate that he has godlike powers, and the gods,

Utnapishtim says, reward those who are like them. Unfortunately, Gilgamesh, who is tired from the exertions of poling the boat, falls asleep almost immediately and does not wake up for six days. Feeling sorry for the king, Utnapishtim tells him that he still has one chance to gain immortality.

Utnapishtim tells the king of a prickly plant that grows at the bottom of a nearby pool. He tells Gilgamesh that if he swims down to this plant and eats it, he will regain his youth. This will not give him true immortality, for he cannot repeat the process indefinitely, but eating the plant will give Gilgamesh an extended life span. Gilgamesh finds the pool and swims down to the plant and plucks it, but, inexplicably, he does not eat it. Instead, he lays it by the side of the pool and washes himself. As he does this, a snake swims up from the bottom of the pool and eats the magical plant. Immediately, the reptile sloughs its skin and, rejuvenated, dives back into the water, leaving poor Gilgamesh a failure once again.

Dejected, the hero returns to Uruk. As the epic nears its end, Gilgamesh looks at the great walls of Uruk—the walls he built—and contemplates the great size of the city. He realizes that his life has counted for something, and he decides to inscribe his adventures on a stone so that later generations can marvel at his deeds.

In the final chapter of the epic, the writer explains that Gilgamesh returned from his quest a changed man. Realizing the importance of this world and the futility of his quest for eternal life, the king determines to rule wisely and well, hoping that his subjects will remember him with affection. When he dies, the people of Uruk grieve along with his wife, his son, and his mistress, and they praise him for his great deeds and benevolent rule.

These two epics notwithstanding, not all Old Babylonian literature was religious or epic in nature. The Old Babylonians also had an art called Dialogue Literature, so called because it consisted of debates about the relative value of two different entities: a pickax and a plow, a bow and an arrow, winter and summer, a shepherd and a farmer, or a goat and an ox. This genre, which consisted of writing about commonplace things, was tedious, pedantic, and had a standardized format. Each debate was preceded by an introduction. In the meat of each tale, two friends meet by chance in the city and fall into conversation. Each participant does his best to point out with clever arguments the different merits of a particular topic. From the wording, the tone, and the play on words, it is clear that these debates were scribal exercises designed to entertain a small group of literati who were proud of their special skill in writing. Apparently, a similar motive lies behind the large number of epigrams and proverbs that have survived from Old Babylonian libraries: "Where there are beauticians, there is gossip." "There are no friends in business." Or, "The gods reward the faithful."

The major impression with all literature of the Babylonian era is that though some of it is excellent, with real artistic merit, and some offers profound insights into human behavior, it was part of a craft practiced by an elite few. There is no evidence to suggest that the scribes ever shared any of their written products with the general population. The survival of Old Babylonian literature was in fact the result of the scholarly and antiquarian tastes of Assyrian kings of the late eighth and early seventh centuries B.C. who collected vast libraries of these writings because they admired the old stories.

Architecture and Art

Although the general populace of Babylonia was not familiar with literature, they certainly were aware of the architectural developments initiated by Hammurabi. Surviving written records indicate that not only Hammurabi but every king of his dynasty built on a grand scale. Unfortunately, little remains of this aspect of Babylonian culture. There are probably two reasons for this: first, most of the buildings that Hammurabi himself commissioned at Babylon now lie beneath the water table at that site, which makes them inaccessible to normal archaeological techniques, and second, the Kassites, the people who succeeded the Babylonians and ruled the area from about 1570 to about 1155 B.C., almost always built their temples and palaces directly on the foundations of the older Babylonian sites. This homage to the Babylonians, whose culture the Kassites revered, has made it particularly difficult to appreciate Babylonian architecture.

Luckily, at Tell al Riman, near modern-day Mosul, Iraq, there is one outstanding example of Old Babylonian architecture that has survived. In Babylonian times, this was the site of the capital of the small kingdom of Karana. Around 1790 B.C., Karana enjoyed a brief period of

Life-size sculptures of lions were frequently found at temple entrances throughout Babylon and are practically the only free-standing statues associated with this era.

Below: This ziggurat at Choga Zanbil in western Iran was built as a temple to the god Inshush-inak. As no ziggurats from the time of Hammurabi survive, we must be content with ones from later periods.

prosperity, which its inhabitants celebrated by importing Babylonian architects to construct a ziggurat. The building had a complicated facade with 270 half-columns, whose brickwork simulated the trunks of palm trees built into the outside wall. The architect who designed this temple must have had an affinity for arches and vaults because he used them again and again, not only for major entrances and ceilings, but for minor passageways and doors as well. The building owes its survival to the fact that soon after the construction was completed, the kingdom of Karana fell onto hard times and was never rich enough to alter the temple. For six hundred years, until the site was abandoned, the most Karanan builders could do was carefully repair what was there.

A terra-cotta plaque 19 inches (50cm) high showing the Babylonian demon goddess Lilith, who supposedly haunted abandoned places and ruins. She is usually associated with lions and owls. Lilith is also mentioned in Isaiah 34:14.

Records indicate that when Hammurabi rebuilt Babylon, he built a great temple to the god Marduk in the center of the city. Whatever remains of that temple now lies beneath the temple to the same god that the New Babylonians built a millennium later; however, the temple at Rimah gives a taste of what the earlier building must have been like.

Like the architecture, only fragments of sculpture have survived to demonstrate what Hammurabi's artists might have created. One of the most famous surviving examples is the relief portrait 25 inches (65cm) high, 21 inches (55cm) wide atop Hammurabi's stele that portrays the king receiving the famous laws from Samash, god of the sun and wisdom. Carved out of black basalt, the scene shows Hammurabi holding his left hand in front of his face—a traditional sign of submission—while Samash holds out a staff of justice toward him. Rays of sunlight emanate from the god's shoulders, signifying his divinity. This is a beautiful and effective piece of sculpture.

Other small pieces have also survived. A rare piece of terra-cotta relief sculpture—a frontal relief sculpture 19 inches (50cm) high, 12 inches (30cm) wide of the bird-footed demon Lilith standing on a crouching lion—illustrates the type of work that must have been common during the Old Babylonian period. From various documents and investigations, we know that it was common practice for temple worshipers to buy small plaques featuring representations of various divinities and religious figures. In this sculpture, Lilith is nude; she is flanked by two owls—the Babylonian symbol for death—and she holds the symbols for justice in her hands. In Babylonian mythology, Lilith was a vampiric demon whose specialty was sucking babies dry of their blood. She later found her way into Jewish mythology as the night hag mentioned in Isaiah 34:14–15. She is also mentioned in the Talmud, a book of Jewish law, as the first wife of Adam.

This period in Mesopotamian history may be the first to have seen freestanding monumental sculpture. Most Old Babylonian temples appear to have had figures of lions standing guard at their entrances. Again, surviving examples are rare, but there are two surviving life-size examples of terra-cotta lions that once stood outside temples at Shaduppum and Isin. Both examples sit on their haunches, open-mouthed, showing prominent fangs, in a stance befitting a temple guardian.

Babylonian Society

lthough examples of formal architecture and sculpture from Hammurabi's day have survived only rarely, an abundance of other material remains to show how the common man lived. Nothing of the sort remains from the site of Babylon, but at the site of Ur, Sir Leonard Woolley, dean of Mesopotamian archaeologists, excavated a "middle class" neighborhood in the 1950s that was built during the reign of Samsu-iluna, Hammurabi's son. These small houses from the Old Babylonian period measured about 358 square feet (400sq m). This is considerably smaller than the small houses from earlier eras, and archaeologists cannot explain this reduction. Because space was abundant within the city walls, one could speculate that these smaller houses reflected a change in the then-traditional family structure.

Houses were cheap to build. The bottom ten or twelve layers consisted of fired bricks to protect the foundation against dampness; the remaining levels of bricks were simply dried. The floors were also of fired brick; the walls were plastered, and the roofs were made of mud applied to an interlaced poplar base. The only expensive parts of a house were the wooden roof beams, the doors, and the doorposts. Because large trees do not grow in southern Mesopotamia, wood for building had to be imported. Some houses consisted of only a few rooms, whereas others rose two stories and enclosed an internal courtyard. Many houses included a private shrine with an altar in one corner that was dedicated to the family god. A brick ledge for offerings to the god ran along one wall of this shrine. The dead traditionally rested under the floor of this shrine, and it was the duty of the eldest son to maintain the house as a memorial to his parents. It was for this reason that the eldest son alone inherited the family house; his male siblings received other property as their portion of the father's legacy.

Archaeological excavations and surviving legal documents give us a reasonably complete picture of the ancient Babylonian family. Families were patrilineal and patrilocal, and there is no evidence of extended families living together. We know from surviving wills that although the family house became the property of the

eldest son upon the father's death, the other sons collectively inherited the family farmland. The Babylonians, it seemed, were well aware of the danger of subdividing farmland into plots too small to support a family.

From records of marriage contracts and divorce proceedings, we can establish a fairly clear picture of the life of women during the days of Old Babylonia. Like the situation of most women in the ancient world, it was restrictive. Marriages were contractual arrangements in which one family promised to supply a wife and another family a husband. The contracts do not appear to have had any particular son or daughter in mind, as long as an exchange occurred between the families. Marriages had four formal stages. First, the engagement spelled out the terms of the arrangement. Second, the groom's family put down "earnest money," in the form of a specific amount of sheep, loaves of bread, barley flour, and beer—usually beer of a designated quality, often described as "second class." Next, the bride's family made a similar down payment of the same items. These payments were guarantees, and these deposits were repaid once the marriage

The wall of an average Babylonian house lies in front of the much grander restored ziggurat at Ur. Sir Leonard Woolley, the great English archaeologist, excavated this house. About 1740 B.C. Hammurabi's successor, Samsu-iluna, destroyed the city of Ur, but, happily for historians, the destruction involved a violent fire that literally baked much of this ancient city so that it was preserved.

This door plaque from Kahfajah on the Diyala River in Syria preserves scenes from a dinner party. Although this plaque dates to about 2500 B.C. there were many similar ones made at the time of Hammurabi. Over time, the wooden door jambs to which the plaques were attached have rotted away, leaving only these small clay scenes to mark entrances.

took place. Third, the girl took up residence in the house of her future father-in-law, where she lived until the actual marriage. Once the marriage ceremony took place, the woman and her husband moved to their own house. On the date of the marriage, the bride's family delivered a substantial dowry to the groom's family.

A number of legal cases survive that deal with potential daughters-in-law who were seduced by their prospective fathers-in-law while awaiting marriage. The law was quite clear in these cases—the marriage contract was void, the down payment had to be returned, and the father-in-law paid a fine in silver. Should the violation take place after the marriage ceremony, the offending male was drowned.

As in many ancient (or not so ancient) societies, virginity was an important matter in Old Babylonia. Any doubt about a potential bride's virginity was settled in court: a number of older women would perform an examination and give testimony. Nonvirgin status was grounds for voiding a marriage contract. Once virginity was established, but before the actual marriage, the Babylonians pursued a unique custom. The bride-to-be had to visit the local temple of Ishtar, where the law required her to "take" the first man who came to her and paid a small fee. The Greek historian Herodotus reports this strange custom in the fifth century B.C., and cuneiform records of a much earlier date confirm it. Herodotus attests that after this one act of legally sanctioned infidelity Babylonian women were as virtuous and faithful as Greek women.

Although Herodotus states that Babylonian women were among the most virtuous in the world, infidelity did occur, and punishment for a woman found guilty of this crime was much more severe than that for a man. Unfaithfulness on the man's part was punished by a fine, but the same crime on the part of the woman was punished by drowning, being thrown down from a high tower, or being sold into slavery.

Divorce was possible in Old Babylonia. The most common reason, according to surviving court records, was infertility on the wife's part—and failure to have a child was always assumed to be the wife's fault. When a couple could not have a child, the marriage did not necessarily have to end—the couple could agree to let a slave girl stand in for the wife, and if the slave conceived and bore a child, it was adopted into the family. If infertility did bring the marriage to an end, the dowry was returned. If a man determined to end his marriage for some other reason, it was accomplished by the payment of a fine and the return of the wife's dowry to her family. Should a woman determine to divorce her husband, however, she could be drowned.

Besides giving us an unusually clear picture of family life in Hammurabi's Babylon, the thousands of surviving cuneiform tablets "speak" clearly about the central organ of the Babylonian city—the temple. Each city had several temples dedicated to the chief god of the city, as well as others dedicated to lesser deities. In Babylon itself, there was a main temple to Marduk and other temples to Ishtar, Gula, Adad, and Shamash. By the time of Hammurabi, most of these temples also had a sacred precinct area and a ziggurat. These later temples usually stood over the site of earlier temples to the same deity. When archaeologists excavated the main temple mound at Eridu, they discovered sixteen different temples below the most recent one. Over the millennia, the typical temple grew from a simple hut (built about 5000 B.C.) to an impressive multistory ziggurat with a temple at the top. Temples throughout Mesopotamia had two small rooms:

one served as a vestibule, and the other contained a square altar on which a sculpture of the temple god stood. The figure of the god was probably made with a wooden core and covered with beaten gold or silver. Temple priests made two daily offerings of bread, fish cakes, emmur wheat, barley flour, wine, and beer to the local god. The priests placed the food in bowls on the altar and poured the liquid offerings down pipes that emptied into pits under the temple.

Throughout the year, the city celebrated festivals at the temples. Besides festivals particular to each god, there were three monthly festivals held on the first, seventh, and fifteenth of each month. Periodically, the gods were taken on tours. The priests removed the temple statues and carried them from Babylon to outlying towns to "visit" temple lands or occasionally to make a "social call" on another god or goddess.

The cuneiform records preserve a great deal of information about who staffed the temples. With a few well-known exceptions, a professional priest class did not seem to live permanently at the temple. Instead, townsmen owned the various official positions at each temple. A temple priesthood or other office carried with it a regular stipend paid from the temple's agricultural lands or factories and could be willed from father to eldest son. Sometimes a position was filled by several men who took turns fulfilling the duties on different days of the month. Wills from the Old Babylonian period make it clear that a temple priest could even hold positions at several temples. This situation is an almost exact parallel to medieval Europe—a situation that the medieval Catholic Church periodically attempted to reform, without success, and that the Protestants in the sixteenth century A.D. found especially odious. Ancient Babylonians would have wondered at this fuss; they were a business-minded people, and the temple was a place of constant business.

Besides priests, there was a small permanent staff of specialists that was responsible for conducting the extraneous business at each temple. In addition to the scribes who kept careful records of the assets of the temple, there were fortune-tellers, snake charmers, musicians, lamentation priests, and priestesses called *naditum*.

Reading the future was one of the most important activities of each temple. An experienced fortune-teller, called a *barum*, made a comfortable living predicting the future. Rarely did a Babylonian make an important decision without recourse to the *barum*, and each Babylonian army had a soothsayer on staff. The most popular method of divination was reading a sheep's liver. Archaeologists have found a number of clay liver models marked off in sections, with each section identified as to what it reveals about the petitioner's future. These tools are somewhat similar to the mapped models of human heads used by nineteenth-century A.D. phrenologists to define the character and traits of a human personality.

Although this pot shard from Ashnunak is not strictly from the period of Hammurabi, the figure displays a resemblance to depictions of harps and harpers from Hammurabi's time. Music was a regular part of Babylonian religious and social life.

The most important part of the liver for prediction purposes was the neck, the part that attaches the organ to the bile duct. If the neck was whitish in color, a business venture was sure to fail. If there were bumps on it, it was a sure sign to an expectant mother that her child would have some blemish. The degree of elongation from the neck of the liver to the bottom of the organ was a sure way to estimate the success of the king's latest venture, be it diplomatic or military, and woe to the king whose diviner found a sheep's liver with a right lobe shaped like a purse—it was a sure sign of impending disaster. One of the main contributions of the Old Babylonian period to later ancient civilizations, in the opinion of those civilizations, was the production of standardized divination books on interpreting sheep guts.

Lamentation priests—probably individuals who assisted mourners—were most likely eunuchs who had been presented to the temple as children. Additional evidence suggests that they were homosexual. These priests were required to be completely hairless, so a barber was also a regular feature of each temple.

The most famous permanent resident of a Babylonian temple was the *naditum*. Almost every Mesopotamian temple had one of these women living in a semi-cloistered state, carrying on a tradition that predated the Babylonians by a millennium. The *naditum* were always virgins. This fact is supported not only by the name *naditum* itself—which means "unplanted"—but also by several surviving cuneiform tablets that state that a *naditum* could marry but not consummate her marriage. A *naditum* could adopt children, however, and could will her office to an adopted daughter. Within the temple, the *naditum* accumulated large fortunes, perhaps as bankers. We know that the temples made loans at steep rates of interest: 30

Although this relief comes from a period almost seven hundred years after Hammurabi, it does preserve a characteristic of religious art from his time. The human (the figure on the right) is the governor of Mari, Shamash-resha-usur; he is worshiping two gods, Adad, who holds bolts of lightning, and Ishtar, armed with a bow. Shamash-resha-usur is using the traditional sign of supplication by holding his hand in front of his face. Gods were generally shown much larger than their human worshipers.

percent for loans made in barley and 20 percent for loans made in silver. The most famous *naditum* was Enheduana, the daughter of Sargon of Akkad, whose temple hymns, written about 2290 B.C., are the first pieces of literature by a known author.

Hammurabi's Babylon was not just temples and ziggurats, however. The wealth of the empire was based on business. Any Babylonian in the street would have grasped the significance of President Calvin Coolidge's famous statement, "The business of America is business," for certainly the business of Babylon was business. There was an established class of merchants called *tamkarum*. These men appear to have been licensed traders who acted as agents of the temple and disposed of the surpluses in taxes collected by the royal government. Because Old Babylonia was a nation without coinage, these taxes were in the form of perishable goods. After the palace had deducted the amount of foodstuffs and commodities it needed to live on, the *tamkarum* paid for the surplus with copper, silver, or tin ingots and then sold or traded these commodities throughout the kingdom.

The *tamkarum* had wide-ranging connections. Through them, Babylonia acquired copper from Oman (then called Magan); carnelian stone from the Indus Valley (Meluhha); tin, gold, and silver from the Anatolian plateau; and lapis lazuli from the area of modern Afghanistan. The most active trading station was Dilmun (modern Bahrain). Babylonian merchants did not travel beyond that point—no doubt because the natives of the region did not want to share the rich routes to Oman—but they did make yearly treks down the Euphrates and across the Persian Gulf to this fabled isle, returning with rich profits.

Back home in Babylonia, local trade seems to have resided in the hands of a *sabitum* (which means "ale wife"). Besides manufacturing beer and running a tavern, the *sabitum* dealt in the basic necessities of life. Babylonian society was based on a barter economy, and a householder would need to take whatever surplus wages in kind he had received to buy the necessities of his table.

The most common foods were dried fish, yogurt, barley baked into a flat unleavened bread, and lentils, punctuated with an occasional feast of meat. The Babylonians did not consume milk with their meals, but they did use it as a medical ingredient. As is true today in the region,

Though this small (13.5 inches [33.8cm] tall) statue of the goddess Ishtar is actually a much earlier (c. 2500 B.C.) Sumerian representation from Mari, she was one of the most popular goddesses of the Babylonians. In Babylonian mythology Ishtar combined the seemingly contradictory facets of being the goddess of love and war. She became a bitter enemy of Gilgamesh when he refused her advances.

pork was not a popular food, although pig fat was a widely used lubricant. For fruits and vegetables, the Babylonian housewife had cucumbers, lettuces, apples, figs, grapes, pomegranates, lemons, onions, garlic, and sesame oil. It was not a particularly interesting diet, but it was healthy, and in Greek times, Herodotus stated that the Babylonians were so healthy that they did not have doctors at all.

There was a dark side to this commerce—debt. In sparse years, when crops failed, people had to borrow to survive, and although there are heartwarming accounts of

This astrological table from Uruk (third millennium) was probably a representation of the Table of Destiny by which the god Enlil had foreknowledge of the fate of both men and gods. Under the Babylonians, however, Enlil's knowledge was usurped by Marduk, the protector deity of Hammurabi's Babylon.

temples giving interest-free loans to farmers during times of drought, that seems to have been the exception rather than the rule. A loan was generally secured with a child or a wife, and if there was a default, the "security" became a slave. The Babylonians did not especially like this system, but "business was business." Periodically, Babylonian kings would issue a decree that forgave such debts, and then the "security" was free to return home. But such acts of clemency were granted only to people who had borrowed in time of need, and the wives and children who had been pledged as security against the default of a loan made purely for business purposes were exempted from this royal benevolence.

Medicine, Science, and Mathematics

Despite Herodotus's assertion that the Babylonians had no doctors because they were the healthiest people in the world, we have thousands of cuneiform tablets that recount their illnesses and describe both the cures and the fees of their doctors. In Babylonia, there were two different types of doctors: the *asu*, who practiced medicine (*asutu*), and the *ashipu*, or magician, who practiced magic (*ashiputu*). Strangely, the two professions were not exclusive of one another, and there were plenty of instances in which both treated a case as a team.

The *asu* had medical texts that correctly describe hepatitis, indigestion, lung ailments, eye diseases—especially common in a desert environment—weak hearts, and intestinal disorders. These same texts prescribe cures made from willow, pine, or date tree bark or from medicinal plants like thyme and sassafras. They also discuss the significance in diagnosis of the pulse, temperature, consistency of the stool, and color of urine. Although there is little evidence of surgery in general, there are descriptions of cataract operations. The excellent reputation of Babylonian physicians was well known, and foreign rulers often requested that a Babylonian doctor be sent to their courts when their own medical practitioners had failed. Also of note for such an early society—one that was sexist in many other respects—is the fact that an *asu* could be a man or a woman.

The *ashipu* approached disease from an entirely different perspective. From his standpoint, all disease was caused by demonic possession, which was the result of some sin the patient had committed. The cure, therefore, was to rid the patient of the resident demon either by scaring it out of the patient or by sickening the demon so that it wanted to leave. To begin the treatment, the *ashipu* chanted and threatened the resident demon. He might invoke the name of a mighty god to help him, even to the extent of wearing a costume to gain the god's favor. For instance, invoking the god Ea, the water god, required wearing a fish costume during the healing ceremony. If these mild measures did not work, the *ashipu* proceeded to the next phase and tried to make the demon sick by forcing the patient to eat such things as rotten meat, crushed bone, dirt, and animal urine. Radical treatments like these must have worked, for the *ashipu* appear to have been more popular that the *asu*.

The Old Babylonians excelled in mathematics. Their use of mathematics was mostly confined to the practical arts of measuring fields and calculating volumes, but archaeologists have also found theoretical works. Most of the surviving mathematical texts, be they theoretical or practical, seem to date from the period around the reign

of Hammurabi. Many of them are tables for multiplication and division, as well as other tables necessary for calculating volumes. There are also large numbers of tablets that record problems on estimating the amount of dirt to be removed from a canal, or how much dirt was needed to build a canal; and tables calculating weights and measurements, as well as compound interest. However, there were also purely theoretical tablets, and one of them clearly presents what came to be known as the Pythagorean Theorem—long before Pythagoras thought of it.

Like many ancient mathematicians, the Old Babylonians counted on their fingers for the first 10 of anything. Their next unit of calculation was not 100, however, but 60. Their reliance on this sexagesimal system led them to divide the circle into 360 degrees, with each degree being further divided into 60 minutes, and each minute divided into 60 seconds—the same system we use today. They adapted this system to their concept of the day, which they divided into two 12-hour periods that were further divided into 60-minute segments.

Although they worked wonders with mathematics and measuring the length of a day, they had problems with calculating the length of the year. Their calendar had 6 months of 30 days and 6 months of 29 days, which added up to 354 days, 11 days short of the actual length. Because an accurate calendar was necessary to know when to begin planting crops, this calendar was problematic—every 3 years the planting month on the official calendar did not correspond to the actual time to plant. The only solution the Babylonians could come up with was to insert an extra month every now and then to bring the calendar back into alignment with reality. From a surviving edict, we know that Hammurabi ordered this additional month added to the calendar.

Despite a reputation as gifted astronomers, the Babylonians were no more accurate with astronomy than they were with the calendar. In fact, it seems that the Babylonians were wildly inaccurate in predicting eclipses and even had difficulty determining solstices and equinoxes with any certainty. The legend of their "advanced" astronomical abilities apparently comes from an apocryphal story first mentioned in the seventh century A.D. According to this tale, in 326 B.C., while visiting Babylonia with Alexander the Great's army, Callisthenes,

Aristotle's nephew, sent his famous uncle a list of all the eclipses the Babylonians had observed and predicted for the last two thousand years. Although the story sounds impressive, the list has not survived, and there is no other evidence to back it up. The only ability we can be sure the Babylonians had with regard to eclipses was simply keeping records of their appearances. The contemporary Egyptians, far to the west, were much more skilled in these matters.

A cuneiform mathematical text from Hammurabi's time. Most mathematical texts come from a site at Tell Harmel in modern Iraq and are primarily school assignments used to instruct students. Many are tables for multiplication, division, finding cubic measurements, or calculating weights. The Babylonian number system used the number sixty as a base.

Chapter Two

The New Kingdom in Egypt

The Golden Age on the Nile, 1479–1224 B.C.

When the King Tut exhibition toured the United States in 1977, more people turned out to see the fabulous treasures of this boy king than had attended any other museum show in history. Egypt fascinates modern people like no other ancient civilization. This may be because of the material richness, preserved so well in the arid, hot climate of the desert, or possibly because of the overwhelming impression made by the huge, immutable pyramids, or just possibly because their burial practices are so ghoulishly fascinating.

Opposite: Pharaohs of the New Kingdom often built statues of themselves to decorate the temples they built to honor their gods. A massive representation of Ramses II stands at the temple complex at Karnak. A far smaller sculpture of one of his queens stands at his feet.

During the New Kingdom period, the Temple of Amon at Karnak, the ruins of which are pictured here, became the most important temple complex in Egypt. Every pharaoh from Ahmose I (1550–1525 B.C.) to the Nubian Pharaoh Taharqo (690–664 B.C.) felt duty bound to add to the structure. At the left-hand side of the photo is the Obelisk of Hatshepsut, the female Pharaoh of Egypt (1479–1457 B.C.).

Ancient Egypt was certainly a less stressful place to live than ancient Mesopotamia, where warfare was continual, crops chancy, and natural resources scarce. By contrast, the regular flooding of the Nile made food production dependable, geography made warfare comparatively rare, and the land readily yielded available building stone. Even foreign invasion was rarely a problem because of the natural barriers of the desert to the east and the west.

From very early times, Egypt was more unified than Mesopotamia. Whereas in the Tigris and Euphrates river valleys the open and featureless geography encouraged cities to fight against one another, Egypt was centered around the Nile and contained within the high cliffs of the narrow Nile River Valley, which is rarely more than seven miles wide. Although armies of one city or another might fight in this constricted area, neither could easily maneuver around the other or make surprise attacks.

Because of this, it was easier to solve disputes and cooperate than to engage in war. During the period when Mesopotamia was fragmented and its cities continually at war, Egypt had already been a united country for a thousand years.

Whereas Mesopotamia had the Tigris and Euphrates rivers, Egypt had the Nile—the most dependable of rivers. Until 1960, when the Aswan Dam was completed, the Nile had for millennia regularly overflowed its banks around the time of the summer solstice, sending a flood of water over the land that lasted for nearly three months before beginning to recede around September 1. These floodwaters brought rich soil, renewing the land each time. The waters receded just in time for the new planting season, and crops were ready to harvest in May, just before the next flood. It was (and is) a perfect and comfortable system—one conducive to order, harmony, and good planning.

True, there were times when the Nile did not flood high enough to irrigate and fertilize adequately, and sometimes the waters came too soon or rose too high, destroying the last crop before it could be harvested. The result in either case was famine—unless there was a strong, centralized authority who had made provisions for the lean times.

The History of Egypt and the Rise of the New Kingdom

That type of strong leadership was seen in Egypt from earliest times, when a king named Menes assumed the title of pharaoh ("the great one") and united Lower Egypt—the area of the Nile Delta, where the great river flows into the Mediterranean—with Upper Egypt, the Nile Valley to the south of that delta. His successors, divided into two dynasties or families, ruled Egypt during a period called the Archaic, which lasted from 3168 to 2705 B.C. During this period, the Egyptians built the first pyramids to house the remains of Menes and his successors, developed the form of writing called hieroglyphics, and built the first towns out of brick instead of reeds and wood.

From 2686 to 2160 B.C., Egypt was ruled by a group of kings divided into four dynasties in a period called the Old Kingdom by historians. This was the classic age of the pyramids, when the entire resources of both Upper and Lower Egypt were diverted into building ever bigger pyramids to house the bodies of the pharaohs who had passed into the next life. Herodotus, that great Greek gossip and historian, whose books are full of the "dirt" of the ancient world, claims that three pharaohs of the Fourth Dynasty—Khufu, Khafra, and Menkaura—spent so much building their pyramids that they bankrupted the kingdom and were cordially hated by their subjects. Khufu, he claims, even forced his own daughter into prostitution to help him pay for his pyramid. The enterprising young woman reportedly levied a surcharge on each customer, combining her monies to build her own smaller pyramid.

Ancient Egypt centered around the Nile River, which provided Egyptians with water for their crops and transportation for their goods.

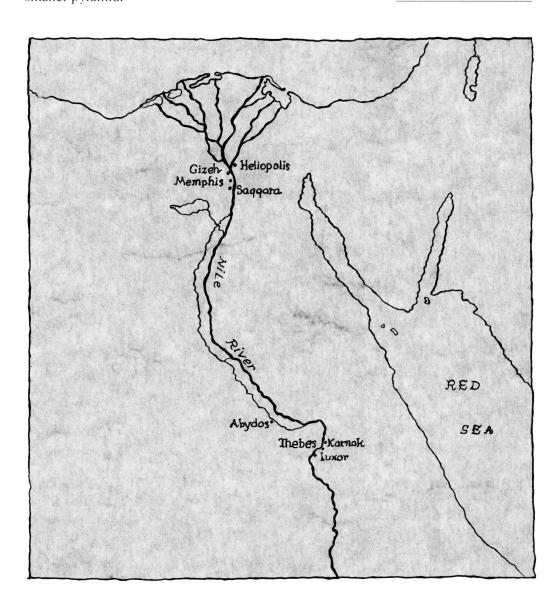

Opposite above: The New Kingdom conquered territory far beyond the traditional borders of Egypt and brought home diverse peoples as slaves. Here, painted on leather intended for sandals, are pictures of bound captives from Asia (left), and Nubia (right). It was common to wear sandals with the pictures of conquered enemies on the soles—it was symbolic of having trod on them.

Below: The famous pyramids of Egypt were all built long before the time of the New Kingdom, in the period called the Old Kingdom (2686–2160 B.C.) The pyramids were surrounded by smaller pyramids and other tombs in which favored court officials hoped to share in the eternal life of the pharaoh. The three pyramids in this picture are those of the pharaohs Khufu, Khafra, and Menkaura.

For whatever reason, the Old Kingdom ended in a period of political chaos—the First Intermediate Period (2160–2040 B.C.)—when the central government collapsed and a few powerful nobles took over the function of pharaoh. This period of disorder ended when a noble named Nebhepetra Mentuhotpe assumed the title of pharaoh and founded the Middle Kingdom, which lasted from 2040 to 1640 B.C. This was not a very vigorous era in Egyptian history, and there is evidence of repeated famine and revolt. One factor contributing to these problems may have been the outside pressure of the Hyksos, a group of "barbarians" from Palestine. The Hyksos had entered Egypt as mercenary soldiers, bringing with them marvelous and revolutionary new weapons—chariots, scale body armor, slashing swords, and composite bows. These tools of war put the lightly armed and unarmored Egyptians at a distinct disadvantage. It did not take the Hyksos long to become aware of their military superiority, and around 1640 B.C. one of their leaders, Salatis, seized power in Lower Egypt, declared himself pharaoh, and built a new capital city at Avaris, abandoning the old Egyptian capital at Memphis.

The Hyksos did not, however, overrun all of Egypt. In the south, centered around the city of Thebes, a native Egyptian dynasty continued to rule. Egypt remained divided for about ninety years, until around 1550 B.C., when a Hyksos king named Apophis decided to take over all of Egypt. Not wanting to appear a total barbarian, he did not simply attack Upper Egypt unprovoked. He first complained to Seqenenra, the pharaoh ruling in Thebes, that he could not sleep for the bellowing of the royal hippopotami in the palace pools at Thebes—350 miles (560 km) south of Avaris! Surviving records do not recount the outcome of this ridiculous diplomatic exchange, except to note that Apophis soon led his army south. To his surprise, he did not win. The Egyptians at Thebes had learned from the Hyksos' original victory and had adopted their new weapons. Now chariot and bow faced chariot and bow. We can assume that Pharaoh Seqenenra died sometime during the war because archaeologists have found his mummy with the left side of the skull bashed in, but we can also assume that the native Egyptians must have won the battle because they recovered the body for burial.

Egyptian preoccupation with the Hyksos and invaded Egyptian territory. Determining that a buffer in the south was just as important as the one they were creating in the east, Ahmose initiated war with the Nubians, and his successors, Amenhotep (reigned 1525–1504 B.C.) and Thutmose I (r. 1504–1492 B.C.), continued this conflict. Thutmose I finally succeeded in pushing the Egyptian frontier to the Nile's fourth cataract, some 744 miles (1200 km) south of Thebes. He slaughtered the Nubians, burned their villages, and returned home with gold, prisoners, and the bodies of Nubian leaders hanging head down from the prow of his flagship. Some Nubians continued to engage in raids along the Egyptian borders whenever the power of the New Kingdom weakened, but others saw the advantages of Egyptian civilization and served in the Egyptian army. A great many became prominent commanders and officials in the Empire.

The successors of Ahmose also continued the Egyptian advance to the northeast. Thutmose I advanced all the way to Carchemish on the upper Euphrates, where the Egyptians found a collection of small, independent states. The Assyrians were beginning to become a power in northern Syria, as were the Mitanni east of them. To the north, in Anatolia, the Hittites were becoming a force to be reckoned with, and the Kassites had taken over the ancient territory of Babylonia.

The Egyptians soon learned that controlling these northern regions was more difficult than keeping Nubia contained. These kingdoms, which were based in fortified cities with interlocking systems of alliances and whose armies were as technologically advanced as that of Egypt, could be formidable foes. There were constant attacks against Egyptian garrisons and border posts. Still, as long as the Egyptians maintained adequate troops in the region, most of their Asian subjects paid their annual tributes. To cement their relationship, the pharaohs entered into marriage alliances with some Asian kings, and some New Kingdom leaders actually condescended to take a bride from among them. However, this arrangement tended to be one-sided—when a Kassite king petitioned Thutmose III for an Egyptian princess, he was firmly and none-too-politely refused.

Below: The third pharaoh of the New Kingdom's Eighteenth Dynasty, Thutmose I (1508–1493 B.C.), portrayed by this statue, extended the borders of Egypt south of Nubia and east into Palestine. This expansion brought abundant wealth into Egypt to finance the New Kingdom's aggressive building program.

A new Theban pharaoh, Kemose, took command and continued the war until he died. He was succeeded by his brother Ahmose, the first ruler of the New Kingdom (also known as the Empire). He adopted a new tactic in an effort to defeat the Hyksos once and for all—instead of simply defending Thebes, he led the Egyptians in an attack on Avaris. The first step was to isolate the Hyksos capital by seizing control of the Nile and the nearby canals. Once the city had been weakened by siege, it fell to a direct assault, and the Hyksos retreated to the east, back to their homeland in Palestine. The Egyptians, their bloodlust up, followed them, and for the first time in Egyptian history, an Egyptian army marched out of the Nile Valley bent on foreign conquest. Their intention was to build a buffer in Palestine so that Egypt would never again be threatened from that direction.

This impetus toward expansion was not, however, confined to the east. In the south, past the first cataract of the Nile, the Nubian tribes had taken advantage of the

Back in Egypt, the pharaohs of the New Kingdom were working to consolidate control over the homeland. Many of the Egyptian nobles had refused to help Kemose and Ahmose in their fight against the Hyksos, preferring to wait it out and support the winner. After the war, Ahmose and, later, Amenhotep deposed these nobles, confiscated their lands, and put loyal commoners in their place. These "new men" were lent the land of the nobles to use as their own for the extent of their good service— as long as they worked hard and were supportive of the pharaoh. A fundamental change had taken place in Egypt. Whereas before there had been the pharaoh's land and the nobles' land, now all land belonged to the pharaoh. Even the land controlled by the temples became the property of the pharaoh, and the priests, who from time forgotten had been nobles, were replaced with professional priests who stood in for the pharaoh, the chief priest of every temple in Egypt. With these changes, the land of the Nile became an absolute monarchy.

Architecture and Art

The changes in Egypt were not, however, solely political; economics also came into play. With the foreign tribute from Asia and Nubia, Egypt became a land of immense wealth, making the greatness of the New Kingdom possible. The gold and silver gained by foreign conquests was used to pay for architectural and artistic marvels. The temples were a major focus of royal largesse, for the temples glorified the gods and the pharaoh as the earthly embodiment of the sun god Amon, and the pharaohs understood that the temples provided them with additional control of the citizenry. There were plenty of funds left over for harbors, canals, palaces, and fortresses.

The most visible example of these changes was the architectural marvels of the New Kingdom. Hundreds of monuments from this period dot the landscape of Egypt.

The Amon temple at Karnak is one of the most artistically balanced and harmonious structures of ancient Egypt. When Rameses II added the court pictured here, his architects preserved the proportions and style of Amenhotep's work.

Most are immense, and even in their ruined state, they inspire awe in anyone who sees them. The best known of these are the temples at Karnak and Luxor, the mortuary temple of Hatshepsut, and the great temple at Abu Simbel. These great monuments contain on their inner walls the remains of stone reliefs that commemorate the deeds of the New Kingdom pharaohs. At first glance, the reliefs repel modern observers with their stiff formality—their dominant style is not at all the kind of free and unrestrained art that the modern world values. But they were not designed to please the eye so much as to awe the heart and, by their sheer size and forceful presentation of the pharaohs, to impress an ancient viewer with the power of the god-king.

At Karnak, pharaohs from Thutmose I to Rameses II spent much of their plunder building the huge temple complex to Amon, the Egyptian god of the sun and the major deity of their pantheon. The statistics of this temple, which is the largest building of its kind ever constructed, boggle the imagination but, at the same time, help one realize the grandeur of the Empire. The temple compound covers 1 square mile (2.6sq km) and includes seven major temples; the main one measures 341 by 171 feet (103 by 52m). The entrance to the compound leads between two massive, 79-foot (24m) pylons (rectangular, truncated pyramids), which were once covered with reliefs accented with beaten gold and precious gems recounting the major events of the reign of Amenhotep III. This doorway was further flanked by two 70-foot (21.3m) obelisks covered with electrum, an alloy of 75 percent gold, 22 percent silver, and 3 percent copper. (In 663 B.C., when the Assyrian king Assurbanipal looted the temple, he melted down the two obelisks and found that they contained the Assyrian equivalent of 83 tons [75,591kg] of gold.) Immediately inside the pylon wall, an open courtyard gives way to a hypostyle hall in which dozens of pillars support the roof, which is made up of massive stone beams that weigh 7 1/2 tons (6,750kg) each. The twelve pillars in the center of this hall are 69 feet (21m) high and measure 22 feet (6.7m) across at the top; each is wide enough for a hundred men to stand on. Surrounding these twelve center pillars are 134 others in nine rows; each pillar is 43 feet (13m) high and 27 1/2 feet (8.38m) in circumference. At one time, every pillar was covered with carved relief scenes of Rameses II worshiping Amon.

Throughout the rest of the temple were six acres of brightly painted relief sculptures recounting the deeds of the various pharaohs who contributed to Karnak.

The most aesthetically pleasing of all Egyptian temples is the temple that Amenhotep III built to Amon 1 1/2 miles (2.5km) south of Karnak at Luxor. This temple is smaller than its sister building at Karnak, but its elements are more integrated. Although dozens of pharaohs contributed bits and pieces to Karnak over the course of two millennia, Amenhotep's temple at Luxor was almost exclusively the work of one man, Amenhotep's architect, Bakrenef. The basic style is the same as at Karnak—an imposing pylon entrance stands in front of the same type of courtyard and hypostyle hall that leads to a small sanctuary—but Luxor's details are unique: the capitals of the

Rameses II's statue stands at his temple at Luxor, with one of his queens between his legs. It was usual for individuals pictured or sculptured with pharaohs to be smaller.

an obelisk covered in gold, silver, and 1,200 pounds (544kg) of malachite brought up the Nile from quarries near present-day Cairo.

Almost directly across the Nile from Karnak is the great mortuary temple of Hatshepsut. Hatshepsut, the wife and half-sister of Thutmose II, was a strong-willed woman who was brilliant at forcing a bad situation to fit her needs when events did not go her way. During an eighteen-year reign, the two produced only two daughters, so when the pharaoh died, the throne went to a son whom Thutmose II had conceived with a harem girl named Isis. This boy, ten years old when he became pharaoh, was also named Thutmose and so became the third pharaoh of that name. He was quickly pushed aside by his stepmother. The power-hungry Hatshepsut did the unthinkable: she had herself declared a man, took to wearing a beard, and assumed the throne as the co-ruler with her stepson-nephew, whom she subsequently married. They ruled together for fourteen years until the forceful queen died in 1458, and Thutmose III was left sole ruler of Egypt. In a startling transformation, the previously hen-pecked son-nephew-husband became the greatest ruler of the Empire, reforming the government, expanding the borders of the Empire, and building on a vast scale—not to mention chipping Hatshepsut's name off every monument she had built in Egypt.

Before her death, however, Hatshepsut had built a vast mortuary temple to her honor and memory. By this time, Egypt's rulers had stopped building pyramids, because they realized that the giant structures served as "beacons" for grave robbers. From Thutmose I on, the Egyptian ruling class memorialized themselves in mortuary temples, built to receive the prayers of the faithful though the bodies lay in secret underground tombs several miles away in the Valley of the Kings. Members of the royal family and favored officials found resting places farther south in the so-called Valley of the Queens.

Hatshepsut's temple at Deir el-Bahari lies surrounded by mortuary temples of Thutmose III, Seti I, and Amenhotep I through III. It is positioned against a high desert cliff face and consists of three broad terraces, connected by broad ramps, that descend to the banks of the Nile. A sanctuary cut deep into the cliff face sits on the topmost terrace; here, priests could offer worship to the great man-queen of Egypt.

Top: The temple of Amon at Karnak with the Obelisk of Hatshepsut.

Bottom: The mortuary temple of Queen Hatshepsut.

columns are renderings of palm fronds, and the painted reliefs on the columns extol the great deeds of the king. It is with this building that Amenhotep III's architect perfected the pylon and hypostyle temple design that dominated Egyptian architecture for the next millennium. Amenhotep built a parkway lined with ram-headed lions, trees, and shrubs that connected his temple at Luxor with Karnak. The king also built the pylon of the temple at Luxor, and on each side of the pylon he added

At the back of each terrace is a portico supported by columns whose designs vary from square to sixteen-sided. The walls of these porticoes are covered with painted stone reliefs portraying the great events of Hatshepsut's reign, the most famous of which is the voyage to Punt. To an Egyptian, Punt—which probably lay somewhere on the north coast of Somalia—represented the absolute ends of the earth. For a pharaoh to send an expedition to Punt was the fifteenth century B.C.'s equivalent of a modern trip to the moon. The reliefs record for posterity the 1473 B.C. voyage of five Egyptian ships that sailed up the Nile to delta, through a canal that connected that river to the Bitter Lakes at the head of the western arm of the Red Sea, and then south to Punt. Next the murals show the unnamed Egyptian admiral addressing the extremely tall king of Punt, Pe-re-hu, and his dwarfish and grossly obese wife, Ety, as they haggle over the price of myrrh trees, the resin of which was the basis for perfumes. The Egyptian artists dwell on and perhaps exaggerate the deformity of the woman—Egyptian artists rarely dwelt on the blemishes of Egyptians, but any shortcomings of foreigners were fair game. Egyptians tended to be fascinated with dwarfs: they found them extremely amusing and paid high prices for them.

The voyage must have been successful, for the terraces of Deir el-Bahari were later covered with myrrh trees set amid other plants and small trees. The visual effect of the glistening white temple of Hatshepsut with deep green, plant-covered terraces set against the imposing red sandstone cliffs must have been an impressive and startling sight in the ancient world. The Egyptians obviously thought so—the young pharaoh Tutankhamen (r. 1336–1327 B.C.) had scenes of Hatshepsut's temple carved on the walls of the Temple of Amon at Luxor.

For people today, the most famous Egyptian monument, after the Great Pyramid, is the Great Temple at Abu Simbel, which Rameses II built in Nubia, 217 miles (350km) down the Nile from Hatshepsut's monument. Surviving to this day, this amazing piece of architecture is so admired that some thirty-two hundred years after it was built, when the waters of Lake Nasser, created by the Aswan Dam, threatened to drown this mighty work, an international appeal for funds netted $40 million, which enabled Abu Simbel to be raised 215 feet (65.6m) out of harm's way.

Rameses II ruled for sixty-six years, from 1279 to 1213 B.C. His reign marks the last vestige of the golden age that was the Egyptian Empire. Much of Rameses II's building was gross, overbearing, and not particularly well done; his portion of the great temple at Karnak, for instance, is overwhelming, but the workmanship is poor. In fact, examples of substandard workmanship exist on many of Rameses's temples. One of the most obvious, though, is at Abu Simbel, where one of the great figures on the facade of the temple was cut on a fault in the rock face and split away soon after it was built. Many of the monuments he built reflect the grand appearance without substance that characterized his reign.

At Abu Simbel, we see Rameses at his most colossal. His father, Seti I (r. 1294–1279 B.C.), had begun hacking a temple out of the rock here; Rameses completed it on his characteristic massive scale. The temple is built into a red

A wall relief at Rameses II's mortuary temple at Thebes, just one of the many temples and monuments to Rameses. He also built the great hypostyle hall at Karnak, two impressive temples at Abu Simbel, a temple at Abydos, two temples at Tanis, another near Ptah at Memphis, and a palace at Kantir. In addition he perpetuated his name by ordering his architects to usurp the temples of earlier pharaohs and carve his reliefs over theirs.

sandstone cliff face with a great hall, anteroom, side chapels, and a sanctuary dug nearly 200 feet (61m) into the cliff. It was designed so that twice a year the rays of the rising sun penetrate to the innermost recesses of the temple to illuminate the statues there.

Along the walls of the great hall, Rameses recorded in hieroglyphics and painted relief sculpture the story of his great victory over the Hittites at Kadesh in 1288 B.C., before his reign began. Typical of Rameses, he made the victory at Kadesh appear much bigger than it actually was. In fact, the Battle of Kadesh, although a tactical victory for Rameses, was a strategic defeat for his invasion of Syria, and Rameses was forced to retreat after the battle—a fact that is conveniently missing from the account on the walls at Abu Simbel. Furthermore, this battle, as pieced together from the accounts of other participants, almost ended with the annihilation of the Egyptian army. When Rameses advanced too rapidly on the city of Kadesh and allowed his army to be strung out in three sections, Mutallu, the Hittite commander, attacked the middle section with his entire army, destroyed it, and then turned on the segment that Rameses had under his immediate command. It was only the personal courage of the pharaoh (stressed heavily in the reliefs at Abu

Two of the four huge statues of Rameses at his great temple at Abu Simbel. This temple is in keeping with the colossal ego of Rameses. It is dedicated not only to the pharaoh, but also to the gods Amon, Ptah, and Ra-Harakhty. Rameses saw no difficulty in comparing himself to these three great Egyptian deities. He did everything in a big way. History has preserved the names of seven of his queens, seventy-nine sons, and thirty-one daughters. He had at least thirty more children whose names did not survive the ages.

Simbel), combined with the timely arrival of the third section of the Egyptian army (barely mentioned in the reliefs) and the technical superiority of the Egyptian chariots and bows over those of the Hittites (totally ignored), that prevented total defeat. Rameses had to retreat from the area and repeat the campaign the next year.

The interior reliefs are not, however, the only impressive aspect of this temple. Equally impressive—if not more so—are the four colossi of Rameses that are attached to the outside front of the temple. Each is 65 feet (20m) tall and was originally painted in flesh hues, with the pharaoh's huge crown colored red. Scattered among the legs of these statues of Rameses are smaller statues of his mother, his favorite wife, and eight of his 140 children. There is also a statue of the god Ra-Harakhty in the center of the facade, but this sculpture is only half the size of the pharaoh's statues—another indication of the character of Rameses.

Rameses ruled another forty-five years after construction was completed at Abu Simbel. He lived an opulent life, ate and drank without restraint, maintained a huge harem, and fathered so many children that they and their descendants became a separate group of nobility. He found four of his daughters so attractive that he married them and conceived children with them, apparently without any genetic ill effects.

In the last five years of his reign, Rameses II became obese and senile, and he let the affairs of the empire decay. Pirates from Sicily, Sardinia, Etruria, and Mycenae began to raid the coast of Egypt. Libyans conquered a section of the Nile Delta, and various dissident elements within Egypt itself began to complain about the hard conditions of their lives. Under his feeble rule, the Empire was crumbling. Fortunately for the country, Rameses died in 1213 B.C., and his aggressive son Merneptah became pharaoh just in time to restore the fortunes of Egypt. Merneptah defeated the pirates and persuaded many of them to enlist in the army. He also inflicted a crushing defeat on the Libyans in 1207 B.C., driving them out of Egypt. Finally, he expelled the dissidents and sent them packing to the east under their leader, Moses.

Grand temples that overawe an observer are only one aspect of the genius of Egyptian artistic skill. The minor arts of sculpture, painting, and jewelry-making also show the Empire as a period of unprecedented achievement. A

great deal of painting, more than that of any other ancient civilization, has survived on the walls of tombs. During the Empire period, more and more middle-class officials, who ran the day-to-day affairs of the Empire, built their own tombs. Egyptian religion had come a long way from the days of the Old Kingdom, when only the pharaoh was "eligible" for life after death. Eternity and the gods had been "democratized" so that anyone who could afford to build a tomb and to pay for mummification could aspire to reach the underworld and plead his or her case before Osiris, the Judge of the Dead.

The tombs of these aspirants were equipped similarly to those of the pharaoh but on a much smaller scale. The walls were covered with elaborate paintings, some of which were religious, but many of which present scenes from the everyday life of the deceased. The tomb of Menena, a scribe to the pharaoh Thutmose IV (r. 1400–1390 B.C.), has wonderful and revealing portraits of Egyptian family life. One famous painting shows Menena and his family on a pleasant outing on the Nile. The members of the family are standing on the deck of their papyrus boat, hunting ducks and admiring the natural world around them. Menena is in the act of hurling a throwing stick at a group of ducks just rising from among a group of nearby papyrus plants. In his other hand, he holds two ducks that he has already killed. Menena's young son is standing in the prow holding some ducks

Wall paintings in the tomb of Menena, a scribe who served Thutmose IV. Besides the naturalistic portrayals of Menena and his family, there are depictions of Egyptian food. These images of food were intended as an illustrated larder for use by the deceased.

Below: The famous life-size limestone bust of Nefertiti. The bust, which was made at Akhenaten's new capital of Amarna, is indicative of the new natural style of art that he encouraged.

and gesturing ahead to his father—perhaps in the act of pointing out more game. His wife and one daughter stand at the back of the boat, their arms full of lotus flowers that they have plucked from the water, and another daughter, young enough so that she did not have to be troubled with clothing, crouches on the deck of the boat plucking more lotus flowers from the water. In another scene, Menena is spearfishing. He draws in a speared carp. His wife stands behind him with one arm around him as if she is holding him back, perhaps fearing he may fall out of the boat in his fishing zeal. Their little daughter kneels beside her father's feet holding onto one of his legs, and the same small son stands in the front of the boat looking intently at what his father is doing.

Although the human figures are stiffly posed in that frozen stance everyone associates with Egyptian painting, the water and air around the boat teem with animal life that is very natural. The fish are painted with such detail that ichthyologists have been able to identify the species being depicted. A small crocodile lurks in the water near the hand of the daughter picking lotus, and the ducks rise from the papyrus rushes flapping their wings. The colors are still brilliant after nearly thirty-four hundred years.

The tomb paintings of Menena and his family reflect the classically formal art style of the Empire period. This style, however, was not the only one to emerge from that period. Between 1352 and 1336 B.C., Egypt was the domain of Akhenaten, who was originally known as Amenhotep IV. Not everyone agrees about

Akhenaten. Some see him as a visionary religious reformer, others as a political reformer whose goal was to take power away from the priests and to restore the pharaoh to the heights of power that the ruler had known in the Old Kingdom. There is no disagreement, however, over his method. Priests had become inordinately powerful by this time, and Akhenaten chose to destroy the priesthood by destroying the gods they served—he wiped out polytheism. He abandoned the temple-dominant environment of Thebes and moved the capital to Amarna, 186 miles (300k) down the Nile. Here he built a new city called Akhetaten (City of the Rising Sun), where he tolerated no worship except that of Aten (formerly called Amon), the sun god in his purest and most supreme form. He even changed his name from Amenhotep ("Amon is content") to Akhenaten ("of service to Aten").

From this new capital, he ordered the name Amon removed from temples throughout the Empire, along with any inscription that made reference to "the gods." In less than ten years, his attempts at reform ended in failure. He died, apparently of natural causes, after a reign of sixteen years, and the priests of Amon swept away his name,

class Egyptians appeared with loving attention to moles, misshapen heads, and large stomachs. In one instance, this naturalism was fortunate, for the natural sculptures and pictures of Akhenaten's wife Nefertiti (which means "beauty that has come among us") present an image of a woman so beautiful and graceful that she is still a physical ideal (her portrait bust is one of the most reproduced statues in the world).

The artistic revolution outlasted not only the pharaoh's political-religious reforms but also the pharaoh himself. Egypt returned to its old gods after Akhenaten died, but Egyptian artists never completely abandoned the new naturalism. The Amarna style, as it was called, is evident, for instance, in much of the art found in the tombs of Akhenaten's successor, Tutankhamen (r. 1336–1327 B.C.), where representations of Tut and his queen, Ankhesenamon, show the same realism (and affection) that was found earlier in reliefs of Akhenaten and Nefertiti.

The best examples of Empire craft art come from the tomb of Tutankhamen. In this tomb—the only one to have escaped the worst depredations of the tomb robbers—there stood examples of wondrous alabaster jars; each of these jars was made from a single stone, the sides of which were ground to a thin opaqueness. The same tomb yielded breathtaking examples of Empire glazing work on jewelry, tiles, beads, and scarabs. Also found were glass vessels made not by blowing, but by spreading the molten glass over a pottery form that could later be broken apart inside the jar and removed.

The most memorable Egyptian examples of gold work also come from the tomb of Tutankhamen; in fact, these pieces are probably some of the best from the Empire period. They range from tiny statues of minor deities such as Serket, the scorpion goddess, to decorations on a royal fly whisk. The finest representation of classic Egyptian gold work is the mummy case of the pharaoh, made of one ton (1,016kg) of pure gold.

Tutankhamen, however, was a minor king who was, in all likelihood, murdered by his successor; he was hastily buried in a borrowed tomb with comparatively few tomb furnishings. One can only imagine what the tombs of the great pharaohs—Thutmose III, Amenhotep III, and Rameses II, for instance—must have held before grave robbers raided them.

Opposite above: A stone relief of Nefertiti, wife of the pharaoh Akhenaten, worshiping the sun god Aten as a devotee of her husband's new religion. In the end, however, she abandoned her husband's religion and returned to the old worship of Amon.

Left: Tutankhamen, whose gold funeral mask is pictured here, was most likely the son of Akhenaten and a second wife Kiya, not Nefertiti. He probably served only as a figurehead, controlled by Horemheb, the commander of the army. Had he not had the fortune to be buried in a tomb that was found relatively intact instead of stripped clean by grave robbers, he would probably not be remembered at all.

monuments, and city. The priests would have eliminated any reference to him at all, but custom required that calendar years be named for the pharaoh: "the first year of Akhenaten," "the second year of Akhenaten," and so on. To make clear the disfavor in which he was now to be viewed, the priests decided to make this formula "the second year of the Criminal Akhenaten."

During his reign, Akhenaten had encouraged a revolt in art to match the revolt against the established religion, and this artistic revolt in fact outlasted the religious-political one. The sculpture, paintings, and reliefs that he ordered for his new capital can only be described as a revolt against the stiff formality of the old work and a glorification of reality and nature. Sculpture and painting of this period attempted to reconstruct the way things and people actually looked. Portraits of the pharaoh, for instance, were no longer generic idealizations in which the pharaoh was presented with a physically perfect body and a face that was a generalized conception of power. Now the pharaoh appeared as a skinny, pot-bellied fellow with a narrow head and spindly arms. Depictions of other subjects soon followed this new style, and portraits of upper-

Literature and Medical Treatises

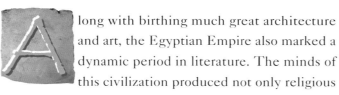

Along with birthing much great architecture and art, the Egyptian Empire also marked a dynamic period in literature. The minds of this civilization produced not only religious literature such as the hymns of Akhenaten but also grand epics extolling the deeds of various kings. Scholars have found poems, songs, novels, satires, folk tales, and myths dating to this time. The New Kingdom also produced some profound scientific works, especially in the field of medicine.

The New Kingdom was in fact the great age of Egyptian medicine. Most of the surviving papyri that describe Egyptian medical practices come from this period. Egyptian medical literature certainly has its share of magical cures and superstitious explanations for the causes of disease, but for the first time in history, we have evidence of a prodigious amount of purely scientific study devoted to illness and injury. Two of the most important representatives of these kinds of treatises are the Edwin Smith

Surgical Papyrus and the Ebers Papyrus. The Smith Papyrus is named after the American diplomatic resident at Luxor who acquired it in 1862. This papyrus is purely scientific; magic and spells have no place in its cures. It identifies forty-eight specific medical problems, starting with those of the head and working down the body to the feet. Each section has a specific title, such as "How to Treat a Deep Wound in the Head that Has Split Open the Skull" or "How to Treat a Deep Gash in the Face." In the latter case, the treatment was to cover the wound with a piece of raw meat, replacing it every day until the swelling decreases. Once the swelling subsided, daily applications of honey were recommended. Other sections deal with sutures for wounds, splinting broken bones, and reducing swellings.

The Ebers Papyrus, named for Georg Ebers, a German professor of Egyptology who published it in 1873, has some appeals to magic, but a good portion of its contents are scientific. It has sections that describe the structure of the heart and the blood vessels leading to and from it. Other sections describe the various vessels leading from the liver, testicles, and bladder, as well as the

and watering eyes, trachoma, bleeding eyes, and inflammation of the eyes. Egyptians were renowned throughout the ancient world for their skill with diseases of the eyes. This may have been because the harsh desert sunlight and/or the blowing sand of the Egyptian desert resulted in a high incidence of eye problems, and the clever Egyptian doctors had been forced to address these problems more than the physicians of other civilizations. Herodotus, always ready with an anecdote, records that when the Persian king Cambyses wanted an eye doctor, his own physician recommended that the king send to Egypt for one.

Much of the literature of the Empire was less practical than these medical papyri. A considerable amount of written work involved stories of magic, deception, and adventure, either among the gods or humans. Many of these tales have too much magic in them for the average modern reader, for today we have come to expect realism in our entertainment; in many of these tales, just when all is lost, the gods intervene and make everything right. This kind of plot manipulation was accepted (if not expected) by the Egyptians, as *The Tale of the Two Brothers* demonstrates.

As the title suggests, this story revolves around two siblings: Anubis, the older brother, and Bata, the younger. Their parents had died years before, and Anubis had raised Bata almost like a son. When Anubis got married, he brought Bata to his home. Unfortunately, Anubis's new wife was a lustful woman, and she had eyes for every man in the neighborhood. Anubis, however, was too taken with her to notice—she was exceptionally beautiful—and he never questioned her mysterious comings and goings, nor did he observe the longing glances she exchanged with the other men in the village. In time, Anubis gained a reputation for being a complete fool. Bata, of course, heard the rumors, but he loved his brother too much to tell him why people were snickering.

The years rolled by, and for a long time, the wife took no notice of her brother-in-law. One day, however, she saw Bata lifting heavy roof beams into place. She watched in admiration as the young man lifted beam after beam above his head and held it in place until Anubis secured it. She felt herself grow excited as Bata's young muscles formed into tight knots. The next day, when Anubis was in the fields, she said to Bata, "Stay with me awhile and I

major blood vessels of the arms and legs. It is clear that the author had some knowledge of anatomy, but there is no hint of how he got it. It is tempting to suppose that he got it from the embalmers, although there is no evidence of this. Egyptian embalmers had a precise knowledge of the major aspects of human anatomy, for they regularly and very efficiently removed the viscera during the embalming process.

The Ebers physician included in his treatise sections on surgical practices, drugs, and contraception. This papyrus gives the first description of migraine headaches and recommends as a cure the frying of a catfish head in oil and the application of the resulting liquid to the head. It recommends a contraception compound for women—a paste made of ground acacia leaves, carob, dates, and honey. The patient was to apply this mixture on a wad of lint and place the lint at the mouth of the uterus. The writer also identifies castor oil as a laxative and recommends treating crocodile bite with regular applications of raw meat. The writer of the papyrus was apparently a specialist in diseases of the eyes, for he included an impressive section detailing cures for growths in the eyes, cloudy

and when I refused, he threw me on the ground and raped me. I did not want to tell you because I wanted to spare you this humiliation." Of course, Anubis believed her without question, just as he had always believed her lies about her mysterious comings and goings. He picked up a knife and ran out of the house to kill his brother.

Meanwhile, Bata was out in the barn, feeding the cattle. The cows, whose big ears picked up everything, heard the wife's lies and quickly warned Bata. "Your brother is coming to kill you," said one cow. Bata ignored the animal. "Cows are very silly animals," thought Bata. "Their opinions are not to be trusted." But then he heard the same warning from another cow, then from another, and another, and another. Bata heard his brother approaching and decided to be cautious, thinking that just maybe the cows were right. He ran out the back of the barn as his brother ran in the front door. The older brother gave chase, and the two raced across the barnyard with Anubis gaining on the terrified Bata. Knowing he would be caught, Bata addressed a prayer to the god Re, who responded by suddenly creating in the middle of the barnyard, between the two brothers, a deep river filled with crocodiles and carp. Anubis danced up and down with rage, but Bata took the opportunity to ask the cause of his anger.

When Anubis told him, Bata denied the tale, but that only angered Anubis more. "Will you add lying to rape, dog?" Desperate to save himself, Bata decided on a dramatic gesture. He pulled out his knife, lifted up his kilt, and sliced off his penis. Defiantly, he threw it into the water that separated him from his brother, and a giant carp came up and ate it. Impressed with this dramatic act, Anubis realized that his brother was telling the truth. Anubis, seized with remorse, begged his brother's forgiveness. Bata gave it, but told his older brother, "I can no longer stay here. I am going to a far land, Lebanon, where the giant cedar trees grow." Then the story takes an unexpected turn. Bata tells his brother that he is going to put his heart in the topmost branches of one of the cedars to keep it safe. However, he says, the day might come when somebody will cut down the tree, letting the heart fall to the ground and causing Bata great pain. "If that happens, dear brother, you must remember what has happened here this day, and come help me. You will know to come when a pot of your best beer goes bad."

will show you the way of men and women." Bata became enraged and pushed her rudely aside. "You are my brother's wife, and I will have nothing to do with you," he said, and he stalked off into the field.

That night, when Anubis returned home, he found his wife crying in a corner. He tried to get her to explain the problem, but she refused again and again to tell him. Finally, he threatened to beat her if she did not explain herself. "Oh, Anubis, I wanted only to shield you. Your wicked brother asked me to lie with him this morning,

The two brothers then go their separate ways. Anubis returns to his house in tears, kills his wife, and dumps her body on the rubbish heap. In the meantime, Bata makes his way to the coast and sails to Lebanon. Once there, he finds a tall cedar tree, puts his heart in the top, and settles down. No explanation is given about how he removes his own heart, nor is there any description of how the gods, who are impressed with this young man, restore his penis. Apparently, these details made no difference to an Egyptian reader.

Next the gods create a girl for Bata, who has the odd characteristic of always exuding a strong perfume. The two young people settle into wedded bliss for a time, and Bata, a trusting man, tells his bride about his heart in the cedar tree. She is impressed, and a little fearful of this man with no heart, but he is loving and kind, and she soon forgets about it.

Meanwhile, the local sea god has noticed the girl and her strange perfume. He waits for her, and one day as she is walking on the beach, he suddenly appears before her and grabs for her. The girl is too quick, however, and runs away, leaving the god with only a handful of sweet-smelling hair. The god tucks the lock of hair away. Later, when he is in Egypt, he tells the pharaoh of this wondrous girl, and the pharaoh decides that anyone who smells that sweet must be his. He sends messengers to Lebanon to demand that the woman come to him, but she refuses to go. When the messenger returns, the pharaoh decides to appeal to the woman's vanity. He sends his chief wife loaded down with jewelry of gold, silver, and electrum, with settings of lapis lazuli, carnelian, jasper, feldspar, and turquoise. When the girl sees this jewelry and hears the chief wife's stories about life in the harem, she forgets about poor Bata and gladly agrees to go to Egypt. No explanation is given about the motives of the chief wife, who is inexplicably doing everything she can to ensure that she has a rival. She even finds the tree where Bata's heart is and cuts it down, allowing the organ to fall on the ground, killing Bata, and thus ensuring that Bata will not follow his wife back to Egypt and make trouble.

No sooner does the heart hit the ground than Anubis notices that his best beer has gone bad. He remembers his pledge to his departed brother, jumps up, grabs some food and weapons, and sets off for Lebanon. Once there, he finds his poor dead brother and the fallen heart. He re-stores the heart to his brother's chest and so brings his brother back to life.

From here, the story continues to take a number of fantastic turns. In quick succession, Bata determines to go to Egypt and gain revenge on his faithless wife. Once at the pharaoh's court, he disguises himself as a sacred bull, but the girl sees through the subterfuge and gets the pharaoh to sacrifice the bull. Just before the sacrifice, however, Bata shifts into the shape of two trees. Again the girl recognizes her first husband in his new shape, and she asks the pharaoh to cut them down. As one tree falls to the ground, the girl looks up and a berry falls off the tree and into her mouth. Of course, the berry is again Bata in disguise, and the girl becomes pregnant—with Bata himself. When the child is born, the pharaoh believes it is his own child. Eventually, Bata succeeds as pharaoh, and his first act is to arrange for the public condemnation and execution of his wife-mother. All this time, however, he has not forgotten his faithful brother Anubis, and the story ends with Bata's appointing Anubis his vizier, so that the two can rule Egypt together.

The New Kingdom also produced a good amount of love poetry. At first, these works strike the modern reader as somewhat risqué, because much of it is addressed to a sister or brother, and images of incestuous marriages spring immediately to mind. In fact, brother-sister marriage was extremely rare in ancient Egypt and was confined to the ruling classes, where it literally helped "keep the money in the family." When a citizen of Egypt called someone "sister" or "brother," he or she was likely to be using the term to mean "wife," "husband," or "lover." Thus, "my heart leaps to see my sister coming" means nothing more than "my heart leaps to see my lover coming."

Opposite: A stucco head of Anubis, the god of the dead. It was Anubis's job to oversee the mummification of the deceased, supervise his journey through Duat, the terrifying underworld filled with fire and monsters, and finally present the deceased to a jury of gods headed by Osiris. If the deceased was found unworthy of life everlasting, he was devoured by the monster Ammit.

Below: A limestone funeral stele shows an Egyptian couple. Within the Egyptian family the couple enjoyed an equality that was unique in the ancient world; women enjoyed rights and privileges, unusual at the time.

The most famous literary products of the Empire were the poems of the pharaoh Akhenaten. This pharaoh's poetry was the direct result of his religious innovations, which brought about the reformation of the entire priest class of Egypt and the elimination of polytheism. He replaced the old priests with new priests with different powers and ordered that henceforth there would be only one god in the Egyptian pantheon: Aten, the god of the sun on the horizon, the sun in its purest form. He offered only one bit of compromise to the old faith—he determined that it was not that the old gods did not exist at all but that they were simply different manifestations of Aten. In the end, he came close to preaching a kind of pantheism—the essential tenet of his poems is that everything is not only caused by the sun but is also a part of the sun.

A close look at Akhenaten's poems leaves one with the impression that he and his wife Nefertiti were the only true believers—everybody else is left out. In Akhenaten's words, Aten

> Has made Akhenaten wise in his ways.
> There is no one else that knows thee.
> You made the world possible.
> Where You shine there is life.
> Where you do not there is nothing.
> All men measure their existence by you.

> You make things beautiful when you rise.

> You made the world.
> You brought forth the ruler of it
> You created Akhenaten, ruler of the two lands,
> And his beautiful queen,
> The queen of the Two Lands,
> Who together will live and prosper for ever.

As pharaoh, Akhenaten had the power to enforce his will, which in this case meant the re-creation of the Egyptian religion. People obeyed because he was the pharaoh, but they did not necessarily believe, and Akhenaten apparently made no move to "sell" the people on his new faith. Important as religion was in his life, he forgot the important part that it played in their lives. When they had troubles—when they lost a loved one, for instance—or were faced with a hard decision, they wanted to turn to their old gods for help. When their pharaoh eliminated worship of the old, familiar gods, he took away the people's support. He compounded his error by making no move to include his people in the new faith. It is no wonder, then, that when he died all Egypt revolted against his ideas. The people, led by the old priest class, tried to destroy every trace of him, including his beautiful new city at Amarna. His name and that of his queen were chiseled from every monument in Egypt.

About 200 feet (60m) north of Rameses II's great temple at Abu Simbel is another temple commemorating Rameses II, again with four statues of the pharaoh and two of his favorite wife, Nofretari.

Nearly every Egyptian tomb held a funeral papyrus to guide the deceased. This one shows the dead man in a special funeral boat. The papyrus also shows the deceased plowing a sacred furrow as part of his journey to the court of Osiris, where his life will be judged.

Religion and Death Rites

f all the aspects of ancient Egypt, the one that most fascinates the modern world is its religion. It is, however, neither the polytheism nor the fantastic gods with human bodies attached to heads of jackals, hippopotami, hawks, crocodiles, or rams that attracts people's interest, but the Egyptian attitude toward death and the emphasis on mummification. Central to Egyptian theology is the belief that the soul survives the death of the body, and, most important, you really can take it ("it" being your worldly possessions) with you.

During the time of the Old Kingdom, life after death was a privilege that was limited to the pharaoh and those intimates he wanted to share eternity with. The idea of life after death played no part in the religious life of the commoners. But eleven hundred years later, at the height of the Empire, the afterlife was a goal that anyone might attain. A noble from this period might have a well-stocked tomb that upstaged the peasant's humble hole in the ground, but both men believed they would have to make the same dangerous journey through Duat, the underworld, to justify their bid for eternal life before the Judge of the Dead, Osiris, who always appears on tomb paintings with a green face, signifying the early stages in the decay of a corpse.

Before a person's spirit could make the journey to the Hall of the Two Truths, where the dead were judged, his or her body had to be embalmed. This was a complicated process and varied with the ability of the deceased family to pay. For a poor man, embalming involved simply burying the body in a box of hydrated sodium carbonate—natron—for a short period, until this chemical dried out the body. For the wealthy, the process, called mummification, was more complicated and supposedly preserved the body better. It was Herodotus who provided historians with this gruesome picture of the embalmer's craft, as well as other details calculated to both fascinate and repel his readers. He reports that embalmers were outcasts of society and that families who took a young daughter to the embalmers did not do so until the body had begun to decay—"to prevent indignities," as he euphemistically put it.

Mummification was a complex process. First, the body was eviscerated—the liver, intestines, lungs, and stomach were drawn out through a small hole in the abdomen and placed in special containers called canopic jars. The heart remained in the body, and the empty abdominal cavity was stuffed with myrrh and cassia. Next the embalmers packed the body into the box of natron and left it there for forty days. Finally, the body was wrapped in linen—yards and yards of it. Some of the bodies of wealthy clients were swathed in as many as twenty

The mummy of an Egyptian woman. Ironically it was not the process of mummification that preserved so many Egyptian bodies, but the dry, hot climate of Egypt. Had the bodies of dead Egyptians merely been buried in the sand, they probably would have been every bit as well preserved as by the most elaborate and expensive embalming.

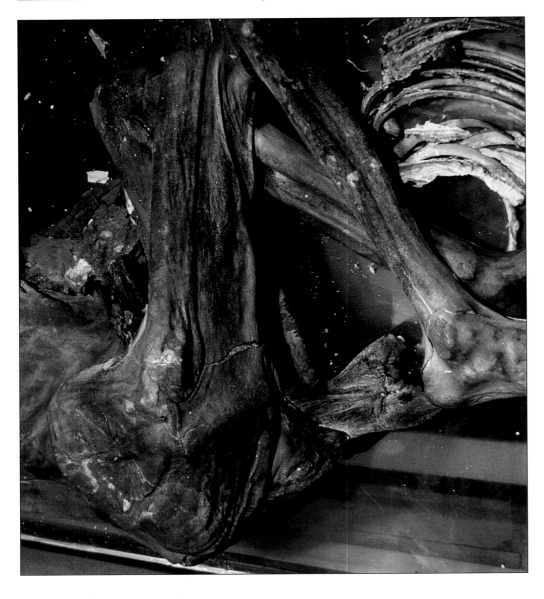

layers of linen, totaling nearly 79 square feet (850sq m). Twice during the wrapping process, the body and the linen were covered in melted resin. Medieval Arabs who knew about this process mistook this resin for bitumen; in their language, bitumen was called "mummiya," and this is where we get the word *mummy*. This resin treatment, which was so costly that only the rich could afford it, was supposed to be a foolproof way to preserve the body. In reality, it often caused a chemical reaction that burned away the flesh. Ironically, the bodies of the poor, who could not afford this treatment, are often better preserved than those of the rich. In fact, the best-preserved bodies are those that were buried in the sand under a covering layer of stones with no embalming whatsoever. The extremely dry climate of Upper Egypt was the best preserving medium of all.

Once the process of embalming was complete, the body was placed in a coffin shaped and painted like the god Osiris (if the deceased was wealthy) or merely covered with a painted shroud (if the dead person was poor). The body was then placed on a funeral sled and drawn through the desert to its resting place. A poor man's tomb might be a simple hole in the ground; a prosperous commoner or a court official could have a tomb cut out of rock, with a small chapel. At the burial site, the *Sem*, or mortuary priest, symbolically reanimated the corpse in a ceremony called "opening the mouth." This was to prepare the dead for their journey across the desert to the Hall of the Two Truths. Meanwhile, the women of the family shrieked in sorrow, poured dust on their heads, and rolled in the dirt. Wealthy families often augmented the number of grieving women with professional female mourners. The male family members stood nearby and watched the show.

Once the burial was over, the soul of the deceased began his or her journey to the west in a special solar boat, a model of which was always buried with the dead. Poor people often had only a drawing of this craft, whereas pharaohs had full-size vessels buried with them. In this craft, the soul traveled to the west until it found the entrance to Duat. Once there, the soul sailed on through a world of monsters and fire. To defeat these monsters, the soul needed a collection of spells from *The Book of the Dead*, at least a portion of which was always buried with the mummy.

The soul of an Egyptian (the figure on the left) pleads his case for eternal life before Osiris. The bird-headed figure is Thoth, the god of writing and wisdom, who prepares a transcript of the appeal. The god Anubis manages the scale that sees if the man's heart outweighs a feather. If it does, the supplicant is considered too evil to be admitted to the bliss of eternal life, and is killed on the spot by the monster Ammit. The scene has been painted on a canopic container with three compartments that hold the viscera of the dead man.

Finally, after many trials, the soul reached the Hall of the Two Truths and made a plea for immortality to Osiris and an assembled jury of forty-two gods and goddesses. The plea was silent, for it consisted of the god Anubis placing the deceased person's soul on one end of a balance, while a feather was placed on the other end. To gain immortality, the soul could not be heavier than the feather. A soul too heavy with sin would outweigh the feather, dooming the petitioner. If this happened, the supplicant was immediately seized and eaten by Ammit, the Devourer of Souls, a fearsome creature with the head of a crocodile, the body of a lion, and the rear end of a hippopotamus. This second death ended all hope of resurrection.

If a soul earned eternal life, it spent its time sailing back and forth between the tomb and the underworld. During the day, it lived in the tomb, enjoying all the bounty that was provided for it and being served by *shapti*, small sculpted figures that the Egyptians created for just this purpose. (*The Book of the Dead* included spells and chants designed to make the *shapti* work harder.) When nighttime approached, the departed got into his or her boat and sailed off to the west to enjoy the company of Osiris until morning.

Egyptian Society

So far we have discussed the upper classes with only an occasional glance toward the commoners. That is usually the way it is with surveys of ancient Egypt, because the rich have left the most impressive monuments. Egypt, however, was also a land of many small farmers.

When examining ancient cultures, it is often hard to find surviving examples of lower-class dwellings because the sites where the common man lived have been built on over and over again for centuries, with one period blending into another. But it is different in Egypt, at least for the period of the New Kingdom, because across the Nile from Thebes is a site that is unique to that era. Nobody lived there before or after that time—the site is a frozen time capsule of the common man during the New Kingdom. Deir el Medineh, as the site is now called, was

the village for the workers who built, decorated, and supplied the tombs in the Valley of the Kings and the nearby Valley of the Queens. It was not a logical place to build a village (there is no supply of water); dwellings were put up there only because it was close to the work sites. Once Thebes ceased to be the capital of Egypt, the workers simply moved elsewhere to find work. The French excavated Deir el Medineh more than twenty years ago, and most of what we know about the common man at that time comes from there.

The houses there were small. Most of them had only three or four rooms, which were arranged in a line. Each house faced the street, which was only five feet wide, and each shared a wall with the house on either side. Clearly, these were purely functional structures. The first room off the street was a place to greet guests and hang up one's tools—a combination foyer and utility room. The second was the main room of the house, where the family lived, worked, and frequently slept. A raised platform in the center served as a combination table and sleeping platform (residents would unroll sleeping mats on it when it was time to go to bed). This "table" was high enough to discourage all but the most determined of scorpions, which were always a problem. Directly behind this room was a kitchen with a small earthen oven and a shelf for jars and pots.

Most of the rooms featured reed mats on the floor and other brightly colored mats on the walls. Furniture consisted of low chairs and stools, storage chests of wood and woven rushes, and large jars set on wooden stands to hold water and oil. Some of the bigger houses had separate bedrooms where there were platforms for permanent wooden beds with leather webbing for springs. These beds were slightly inclined and had a footboard but no headboard. The "pillow" was a block of wood with a concave top that roughly fit the head. Such a device does not sound very comfortable, but one Egyptian diplomat, who had been away from home for a long time, wrote about how he dreamed of returning to Egypt where he could at last sleep comfortably on a "real" pillow, and not one of those cushions found in Crete.

The roofs of such houses were always flat, and access to them was provided by stairs leading up from the center room. On the roof, a reed shade protected the area from the hot desert sun. These ancient Egyptians spent a great deal of time on their roofs because the air flowed more easily there than inside, and roofs were probably a common place for visits with neighbors.

The workday for the Egyptian farmer or craftsman was adapted to the hot desert climate: they worked for four hours before lunch, at which time they took a long nap. After resting, they worked four more hours before returning home. The Egyptian day contained twenty-four hours, just like the modern day, and the work week ended after nine days, with a day of rest at the end. The year was split into twelve months of three "weeks" each, for a total of 360 days in a year. A special five-day period at the end of each year marked a holiday during which all of Egypt celebrated the birthdays of Osiris, Isis, Set, Horus, and Nephthys. That made a total of 365 days in a year (one quarter of a day short of the actual length). The Egyptians, whose year started when the star Sirius rose a few minutes before dawn on the eastern horizon, quickly

learned that their year was too short, but they felt no need to periodically correct it—they knew that the problem would correct itself every 1,460 years (365 x 4).

Beer and bread formed the basis of the Egyptian diet. Both were made from barley and/or wheat, and Egyptian beer was actually made using baked loaves of unleavened bread. From each batch of bread, the Egyptian housewife would set aside several loaves, add yeast to start the fermentation process, and put them in a large jar of water. She then climbed into the jar and mashed the bread to a pulp with her feet. In a few weeks, this mash would ferment; when it was done, it would have a 7 percent alcohol content. This brew was then filtered through a large sieve, but the final product was still extremely thick and chunky—it had to be drunk through a straw held near the bottom of the jar to strain out the remaining mash. The Egyptians could have filtered the brew more finely to eliminate these chunks, but it seems that they enjoyed

Nineteenth-century A.D. Egyptian peasants use an age-old device called a *shaduf* to draw water from the Nile and pour it onto cropland above the level of the river. This device, which is nothing more than a long pole balanced on a cross beam with a bucket on one end and a weight on the other, was practically the only "mechanical" device the ancient Egyptian farmer enjoyed to ease his labor.

chewing them occasionally as they drank. At local taverns, working Egyptians could buy fourteen grades of beer, as well as a more expensive imported product.

Besides bread and beer, staples of the common Egyptian diet included figs, dates, grapes, lettuce, pomegranates, onions, leeks, cucumbers, beans, and papyrus shoots. Some people ate fish, but some groups felt that this was not an appropriate food for humans. Only the wealthy regularly ate beef, mutton, or fowl.

Egyptian clothing was simple, and the differences in clothing for commoners and for the upper class resided more in quality than in style. Men wore white linen kilts and women wore long, tight-fitting dresses. The fine linen that the upper-class women wore could be quite sheer. Children went naked until the onset of puberty, but it was not uncommon for men and women of the lower classes to work naked in the fields. One of the main changes in fashion that came with the advent of the New Kingdom was the popularity of pleats in the clothing of the upper classes. Most Egyptians went barefoot, and only the wealthiest people regularly wore sandals, which were made of leather or papyrus.

Wigs were a major fashion statement during the Empire period. Egyptians disliked body hair, and many shaved their heads bald with copper razors. Wigs came in a variety of styles for both men and women, although by the New Kingdom period, most were made in short styles. An especially popular style for women was one in which all the hair was pulled sharply to the side of the head and worn hanging down over the left ear in a thick column that extended to the shoulder. A decent Egyptian woman kept her bald head covered except on rare occasions; during a party, for instance, she might expose her head, but such an act was considered daring, if not indecent, much as we view the exposing of the breasts in most societies today.

For important social occasions, men and women of all classes wore jewelry and makeup, and, as with clothing, differences between the classes were likely to be reflected in the quality of the makeup, not the style, for then as now the lower class aped their "betters." The most common decoration for both men and women was a wide collar made of row after row of bright, cylindrical beads strung end to end. The top of this necklace lay tightly against the throat and the bottom extended to the middle of the breast. For the rich, the beads of these necklaces were made of shell and semiprecious stones like carnelian, turquoise, garnet, feldspar, crystal, and lapis lazuli, interspaced or accented with gold or copper ornaments. The Egyptians did not use emeralds or diamonds. On their rare formal occasions, the lower classes wore the same style of necklace, except the beads were made of faience (glazed earthenware). During the New Kingdom period, Egyptian men also began to wear earrings for the first time.

Wealthy men and women regularly used cosmetics, though commoners restricted their use to very special occasions. Both sexes might wear heavy black eyeshadow made from galena or green eyeshadow made from malachite. The popularity of eyeshadow may have been the result of the then-current medical opinion that it prevented eye infections. Both men and women used iron oxide for lipstick and colored their cheeks with rouge made from red ochre. Both sexes also enjoyed oiling themselves, not only for the sake of beauty, but to counteract the damaging effects of the desert sun, which could be quite severe.

The parties and social gatherings to which the Egyptians wore these items were joyous and boisterous affairs. Spiced wine, served by young female servants whose only clothing consisted of a stylish wig and a single

Egyptian workers stomp on grapes. As the men tramp on the fruit, the juice flows into a lower basin. The workers are shielded from the desert sun by a roof, from which hang ropes for them to hang onto to keep their balance. To the right are representations of grape leaves. Next to these are the distinctive jars, common throughout the eastern Mediterranean, in which the wine ferments. The picture was found on the wall of a tomb of Nakht, a scribe under the Pharaoh Thutmose III (1479–1425 B.C.).

strand of jewelry around the thighs, flowed freely. Instead of one great dining table for guests to gather around, each had his or her own small table to which a never-ending stream of waiters brought course after course. Harps provided most of the music, although during the New Kingdom period oboes, lutes, and lyres entered Egypt from Asia. The most prestigious harpers were blind, a convention for which archaeologists have no explanation. Other musicians were likely to be young women in a seminude state. Additional entertainment came from dancers and acrobats who were usually, but not necessarily, young women.

Perhaps the most bizarre custom, from our point of view, involved the host placing a cone-shaped piece of perfumed fat on top of each guest's head. As the party progressed and the temperature of the party room rose, this cone melted and covered the head and shoulders with a sticky, sweet-smelling mass that was considered quite appealing.

Although the Egyptians did not condone public drunkenness, it was considered socially acceptable and a compliment to the host to leave a party completely inebriated, especially if the guest was too drunk to get home by himself or herself and needed the aid of servants.

A fresco from the Eighteenth Dynasty shows two female musicians and two dancers entertaining at an Egyptian party. The musicians, one playing a flute, the other clapping, wear the distinctive cones of perfumed fat on top of their heads.

Chapter Three

Assyria

"Like the Wolf on the Fold," 744–627 B.C.

Assyria offers the clearest evidence that in the ancient world military success was ultimately responsible for a dynamic, growing cultural and literary environment. Assyria had been a force in Mesopotamian politics since the twentieth century B.C., but Assyrian arts and culture flourished only during the period from 744 to 627, when Assyrian armies held sway over most of the eastern end of the Mediterranean and Assyrian governors organized and passed along the plundered wealth to Nineveh.

Opposite: Assurbanipal (reigned 669–627 B.C.), the last great king of Assyria, rides his chariot in a relief sculpture designed to hang along the halls of a king's palace to impress visitors with the king's power and brightly painted to dramatize the actions of the king. Not only is the king bigger than the other people in the chariot, but he wears a distinctive two-tiered headdress. He also wears a wrist band with a rosette on his right arm, a symbol of Assyrian royalty.

A wall relief from the palace of Sennacherib (r. 704–681 B.C.) at Nineveh showing Jewish war captives from Lachish in Judah during the reign of King Hezekiah (726–697 B.C.). The Bible records these Assyrian attacks in Isaiah 10 and II Kings 19. Although Sennacherib captured forty-five cities in Judah, he never took Jerusalem. Sennacherib was murdered by his own son, Esarhaddon, while praying in his private chapel.

Interestingly, although the Assyrians have a legitimate claim to greatness in the arts, their reputation for cruelty is among the worst in the ancient world. The Assyrians may in fact have had the nastiest reputation of any ancient civilization. In large part this is due, no doubt, to the bad press they have received from such divergent sources as the Bible, Herodotus, and Lord Byron. Accounts from all these sources dwell on the cruelty of the Assyrians and are practically gleeful over their misfortunes. In 723 B.C., the Assyrian king Shalmaneser V (reigned 726–722) conquered the town of Samaria and sent the inhabitants into exile, creating the famous Ten Lost Tribes of Israel. He then attacked the northern Hebrew state of Judah, laid siege to Jerusalem, and left only when King Hezekiah paid him an immense ransom. Still later, King Sennacherib of Assyria (r. 704–681) attempted to take Jerusalem but was driven away by a plague (II Kings 19:35–36)—an embarrassment immortalized in Byron's "The Destruction of Sennacherib." An even more picturesque tale of Assyrian woe comes from Herodotus, who reports that when Sennacherib tried to invade Egypt in 700, mice ate the strings of his troops' bows, leaving them defenseless against the attacks of the Egyptians.

The Assyrians themselves, however, actually have done the most harm to their reputations; their own chronicles seem to revel in recounting Assyrian deeds of cruelty, carnage, and mutilation against subjugated people. When the Assyrian army under Sennacherib sacked Babylon in 688 B.C., the conquering Sennacherib boasted that he had filled the streets of the city with corpses, burned the city to the ground, torn down the temples, and then diverted the Euphrates over the site to obliterate all signs of the place. Other Assyrian kings did similar things to hundreds of other towns that resisted Assyrian attacks. Assurbanipal (r. 669–627 B.C.) is precise in boasting that he thrust living men and women into ovens; cut off the hands, heads, or penises of others; had enemy generals impaled on stakes; personally poked out the eyes of soldiers with his dagger; and ordered other captives skinned alive and their skins nailed to posts.

Gruesome as these accounts are, they are not unique in the annals of warfare in ancient Mesopotamia. Their noteworthiness lies in the Assyrian insistence on publicizing them. Other contemporary kingdoms practiced similar atrocities, but those atrocities were recorded only by foreign observers or the victims themselves, not by those who committed them. Perhaps, as some historians have suggested, the Assyrians were open about their cruelties because they hoped to quell rebellion or discourage opposition by publicizing the fate of losers. After all, these terrible punishments were meted out only to those people who resisted the Assyrian armies. Cities that surrendered without a fight were not sacked; they suffered only the indignity of an Assyrian governor and a yearly tribute.

However cruel the Assyrians might otherwise have been, their soldiers were forbidden to rape captive women, although they were certainly encouraged to seek wives from among the hostages. Whereas captive men were pulled back to Nineveh attached to chariots by chains that connected to metal rings thrust through their lips, captive women were politely loaded in carts and were not subjected to violence on the journey. Consideration of this kind was a unique mercy in this brutal age.

The Assyrians apparently occupied the area of the upper Tigris around the Greater Zab River since the early part of the third millennium B.C.. Because they were surrounded on three sides by fierce mountain dwelling barbarians, the earliest Assyrians developed into tough, aggressive warriors—much tougher, it seems, than the Sumerians who lived farther south along the Tigris and Euphrates. Assyria's first period of greatness was a brief era, around the time of Hammurabi of Babylon, during which they were ruled by a man named Shamshi-Adad.

Soon after the fall of the Old Babylonian Empire, Assyria became a constant target of the Hurrians (called the Horites in the Old Testament), who lived north of Assyria proper around Lake Van, in modern southwestern Turkey. The Hurrians were especially troublesome because of their skill with the war chariot. By the middle of

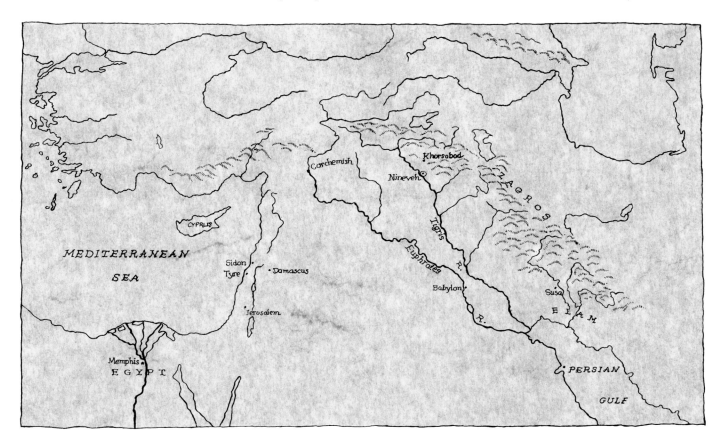

While Assyria centered on the upper Tigris and Euphrates Rivers, the empire's boundaries were ever-fluctuating, depending on these fierce warriors' fortunes on the battlefield.

the second millennium B.C., the Hurrians had established an empire, which historians call Mitanni, and the Assyrians had been subordinated by them.

Assyria enjoyed a brief period of independence under Assur-uballit I (r. 1363–1328 B.C.) when the Hittites destroyed the Mitanni Empire. No sooner had Assyria escaped being a subject than she attempted to become a conqueror. The Assyrian king Tukulti-Ninurta I (r. 1243–1207 B.C.) actually conquered Babylon and dragged the Babylonian king home as a war prize. After this brief moment of triumph, the Assyrians were content to stay home and battle the local barbarians instead of looking for trouble to the south.

Under Tiglath-Pileser I (r. 1114–1076 B.C.), Assyria once more moved into the Middle Eastern spotlight. This leader pushed the border of Assyria all the way to the Mediterranean coast, where the city of Byblos entertained him, not as a conqueror but as a guest. They thrilled Tiglath by taking him on a whale hunt, and if we can believe his later reports, he actually slew one of these mighty mammals. He was a mighty hunter—it was expected of Assyrian kings—and claimed to have killed 120 lions on foot, another 800 in a chariot, and 10 elephants. We must, however, be careful of accepting the numbers cited in Assyrian histories. The scribes regularly added a zero to any count of a king's kills (whether human or beast)—for 10 read 1, for 100 read 10, for 1,000 read 100, etc. If, however, the number of lions reported killed by Assyrian rulers throughout their history is even fractionally true, it helps explain the extinction of this species in the Middle East.

As soon as Tiglath-Pileser died, however, the people he had conquered rebelled, and the Assyrians had a hard time holding on to even their own homeland. They faced

King Assurnasirpal II (r. 883–859 B.C.) engages in the favorite pastime of Assyrian kings—lion hunting. The Mesopotamian lion, now extinct, was driven toward the king's chariot by beaters banging on their shields, where the animal was killed with arrows, a spear, or a skillful dagger thrust.

war not only from former subjects, but also from the Aramaeans, a group of barbarians who, intent on greatness, invaded Assyria from the west. By the time this threat was quelled, 160 years had passed, and the Assyrians were ready for another period of expansion of their empire.

This time the Assyrians conquered with more thoroughness—they had come to stay. Between 911 and 824 B.C., four Assyrian kings laid the foundation of a lasting empire based on efficient government and a standing, professional army. Around 910 B.C., Adad-Nirari II secured the northern and southern borders of Assyria and nearly annihilated the Aramaeans in the Assyrian homeland. The next ruler, Tukulti-Ninurta II (r. 890–884 B.C.), added northern Babylon to the Assyrian Empire, and finally the father-son team of Assurnasirpal II (r. 883–859 B.C.) and Shalmaneser III (r. 858–824 B.C.) moved west toward Aleppo to garner a share of the rich caravan trade from southern Anatolia. After these successes, the Assyrians were once more content to settle in for nearly a century.

The Empire's Foundations for Success

D uring this latest period of conquest, the Assyrians, who had stopped being raiders bent on booty, became empire builders. They developed an appreciation for economics and evolved a professional colonial bureaucracy, with the army becoming a protector of the new empire's achievements, rather than a tool of continuing aggression.

The first factor that helped them to achieve their new goals was the invention of the province, an administrative unit that allowed them to control the various portions of their vast empire and effectively funnel resources back to the central government. To the modern ear, this concept sounds so basic that it hardly seems to merit discussion, but the idea of dividing a large area of land into smaller components, each governed by one specific individual who was responsible to the central government and subordinates who were responsible to him, was a startling innovation for government. With this achievement, there

appeared to be a way to supervise a large empire without the king actually having to be everywhere at once.

With this provincial system, manned by trained staffs and officials, an Assyrian king could expect tax collection to go smoothly, and he could rest easy knowing that he had regional representatives who could administer the law and deal with local matters of defense. The earliest reports of the establishment of provinces are from the reign of Shalmaneser III, but these provinces were so well developed by this time that they must have been created sometime earlier. During his time, Tiglath-Pileser III

T his relief from Nimrud shows King Shalmaneser III (r. 858–824 B.C.) on the right greeting King Marduk-zakir-shumi of Babylon (854–819 B.C.). Shalmaneser III had helped Marduk-zakir-shumi regain his throne.

Assurbanipal fights pursuers from his chariot during the war against Elam. Assurbanipal was devoted to learning and gathered a huge cuneiform library at his capital at Nineveh, yet he was also a warrior who led armies and enjoyed fighting lions with a dagger.

nates were members of the local nobility who had been trained in Assyria. Generally, these men would leave home around the age of fourteen and go to the homeland to serve the king in the manner of an "intern" or "apprentice." During this time, the future leader/bureaucrat would be given an education—with courses of study that included reading and rendering accounts, diplomacy (by watching diplomats work with foreign visitors), and the law. He also became familiar with the most important aspect of Assyrian government: divination. After a few years, the most promising could be sent out as assistants to provincial subordinates known as *rab alani*, or town chiefs. The *rab alani* were local representatives of the provincial governors, and it was their duty to collect taxes, oversee the town's courts of law, and organize local levies of troops in time of danger. Once a youth proved his worth on this level, he might be appointed to the position of *rab alani* and might later be promoted to governor of his own province.

The second important ingredient in the successful building of the Assyrian Empire was the establishment of the first large-scale professional army. This was the ancient Assyrians' second masterful innovation.

Before Assyria's ascendancy, ancient armies in Mesopotamia were organized rabbles. Although Hammurabi seems to have maintained a small group of professional soldiers around his person, this army was very small, and they probably functioned more as bodyguards than as a true army. Because their environment was much more hostile than that of Babylonia, the Assyrians evolved a different type of army. Each large town had a permanent garrison, and the soldiers in these garrisons served under regular officers who had been trained to command and fight since childhood. In times of war, these officers also commanded the regular army.

These officers were "paid" for their services much like medieval European knights: they held an estate from the king in return for military service. Unlike their medieval descendants, however, they were expected to be full-time soldiers. In times of crisis, they raised a levy of troops from their estates, which they led into battle.

Local levies were not, however, the only source of soldiers for the Assyrians. Captured enemy soldiers made up the majority of soldiers in Assyria's army from the middle of the eighth century B.C. on. Intense feelings of patrio-

often reduced the size of a province to prevent local governors from having too many troops under one command; this may also have helped to discourage rebellion.

The province system presupposed a well-developed system of messengers. Provincial governors were under standing orders to send any and all scraps of information to the capital, no matter how trivial they seemed. One way to gain the king's favor was to spy on neighboring provinces and to send information about conditions there before the local governor could do so—a kind of internal espionage.

Efficient provincial governments depended on a well-trained bureaucracy. Governors and their subordi-

tism comparable to that in the modern world most probably did not exist in the ancient world. Survival, it seems, was more important. People might resent an invasion of their homeland, but if a successful invader offered the defeated soldiers steady employment—the alternative being execution—most men would be tempted to accept. In time, the Assyrian armies came to be composed almost entirely of foreigners, and there is no indication that these foreign soldiers fought with less zeal than native Assyrian troops. Sargon II (r. 721–705 B.C.), for instance, formed a *kisru*—a company of fifty chariots—from the captured population of Israel, and he did the same thing with men that he captured at Carchemish in central Syria. He incorporated both groups into an army that included Medes, Chaldeans, and Babylonians and led it successfully against the Urartu at the other end of the empire.

The success of the Assyrian army depended on the Assyrians' unique combination of tactics, mobility, and supply. According to the English poet Lord Byron, until neighboring nations learned to copy Assyrian methods, the Assyrians continued to "come down like the wolf on the fold."

The largest parts of the Assyrian army were the cavalry and the chariotry, with chariots composing about two-thirds of the total forces. The Assyrian chariot was a light and highly maneuverable fighting platform with wheels mounted across the rear to facilitate quick turning. A chariot crew consisted of two men, a driver-fighter and a shield bearer, although in the mid-seventh century B.C., the size of the chariot was increased to accommodate two fighters and two shield bearers. The driver fired a composite bow at the enemy while he guided the vehicle with the reins passed around his buttocks. The shield bearer's sole job was to protect the left side of the fighter with a large wicker shield. The two horses that drew the vehicle wore heavy leather barding that covered the chest and shoulders.

Assyrian cavalry also operated on the team principle. There were two men in each mounted combat team: one would ride into battle with a composite bow or, more rarely, a spear, while the other would ride to his left, controlling both horses with reins and covering the bowman with a shield.

The smallest portion of the Assyrian army was the infantry. Each infantryman was armed with a sling, a lance,

or, most commonly, a bow. His armor consisted of a pointed helmet and a long leather robe to which overlapping metal scales had been attached. Each infantryman was protected by a squire who ran beside him carrying a large square shield.

Assyrian generals never varied their tactics; they did not need to because they almost always won. Attacks began with a headlong chariot charge against the enemy line. If the charioteers' concentrated arrow fire disrupted the line enough, the chariots were able to break through; if the line held, the chariots could circle around for a repeat attack. Meanwhile, the Assyrian cavalry would launch an attack against both ends of the enemy line, pelting their opponents with arrows and attempting to get around the flanks. This dual attack was backed up by the infantry, who also guarded against counterattacks. This system, first developed around 1000 B.C., ensured victory for nearly four hundred years.

The other major contributing factor of Assyrian military success was their well-developed supply system. The organization of the empire into provinces ensured that the state received a constant stream of materials. These sup-

A relief panel from the palace of Sennacherib at Nineveh shows archers and slingers attacking Lachish, the second largest city in Judah. The soldiers are protected from counterfire by a large, thick wicker shield. Note the extra pairs of legs and feet at the bottom. These figures were originally sculpted on the lower part of the panel and then recut higher up. No investigator has effectively explained this mistake. Perhaps the floor level in the hall where the relief hung was changed.

and they wisely withdrew to fortified towns when the Assyrians approached. This tactic, however, did not avail for long. The talents of the Assyrian combat engineers extended beyond roads and bridges to siege equipment for use against fortified towns. The sieges led the Assyrians to experiment with siege towers, battering rams, fortified ramps, and mining techniques.

Assyrian generals were particularly noteworthy in their ability to quickly grasp an advantage and exploit it. In 671 B.C., King Esarhaddon of Assyria invaded Egypt, which at that time was ruled by the Nubian Dynasty under King Taharka. To do this, the Assyrians had to cross the desert near present-day Gaza, which meant encountering scorpions, snakes, and other unpleasant obstacles. The Egyptians hoped that the long crossing in the fierce summer heat would sap the Assyrians' strength. Esarhaddon's solution was to mount his entire army on camels and sweep across the desert in record time, saving the strength of both men and horses. His move caught the Nubians so completely by surprise that they had neither sufficient troops to fight the invading army in the open nor adequate fortifications to prevent Memphis from falling to a direct assault.

Architecture, Art, Literature, and History

ith their innovations in governmental administration and the first professional army in Mesopotamia, the Assyrians created the largest empire the world had seen so far. Furthermore, the steady flow of wealth from the provinces to the coffers of the Assyrian rulers fueled a tremendous outburst of creative energy in architecture and the arts.

The first king of this dynamic new phase in Assyrian history was Tiglath-Pileser III (r. 744–727 B.C.). He was not content merely to plunder new provinces; he conquered with an eye to building economic resources to sustain the Assyrian state. This king reinforced Assyrian rule in Syria, conquered Damascus, and swept on into Israel and Judah, all the way to the Egyptian frontier.

Sculpture like this relief of an Assyrian battle scene adorned the halls of Assyrian kings. Brightly painted, they were meant to impress and intimidate visiting representatives of subject or allied people with the prowess of the Assyrian military machine.

plies were not all sent to the capital; they were stored in warehouses throughout the empire, ready to support an Assyrian army no matter where it marched.

In addition to these more obvious aspects, there were less apparent factors that contributed to the Assyrians' great military success: specialization and the talents of the generals. The Assyrians trained special groups of soldiers to do specific jobs. Lightly armored archers, for instance, were used as skirmishers—they would advance to within bow shot of an enemy line and snipe at them—and the Assyrians had special units of combat engineers who were designated to build bridges and roads in front of the advancing army. Because of these factors and the highly successful Assyrian tactics, the enemies of the Assyrians soon learned that it was folly to oppose them in the open fields,

These invasions were expensive, and with each new advance came more and more resentful subjects. By 722 B.C., the conquered people of Assyria were in revolt, and the new king, Sargon II (r. 721–705), spent much of his time punishing rebels. He also found time, however, to build an impressive new capital city at Khorsabad. Sargon died in battle, a rare thing for an Assyrian king, and his son Sennacherib took over. Sennacherib was renowned for acts of destruction as well as creation: he was infamous for sacking Babylon and for forcing the Jews to pay a heavy tribute to save Jerusalem, but he was justly famous for his building of a new capital at Nineveh, along with numerous temples, roads, and aqueducts. He was also reputed to be a man who loved literature and art; indeed, sculptures he commissioned show a sensitive awareness of nature. He was a rare combination of brutal conqueror and aesthetic prince.

The next king, Esarhaddon, successfully invaded Egypt, but he could not hold it, and the expense of trying hurt the empire economically.

The last great king of Assyria was Assurbanipal (r. 669–627 B.C.). He repeated his father's mistake of spending time and money attacking Egypt, and he further bankrupted the empire by fighting a murderous civil war against his twin brother Shamash-shuma-ukin. The war between the brothers divided the empire, and the victorious Assurbanipal spent the rest of his reign trying to restore its fortunes. Although he restored its boundaries, the empire had grown too large, too fast, with too much brutality to survive for long. It stretched over 992 miles (1,600km) from the Upper Nile to the Zagros Mountains in modern Iran. It was a hopeless task to restore vitality to such a huge area, especially when the cruelty of the Assyrians had created the potential for rebellion in each and every town. Besides, the subject people had learned the military lesson that Assyria had to teach, and when the Medes and Chaldeans, with Scythian auxiliaries, marched on Nineveh in 614, they used the Assyrians' own military techniques against them. In 612, the allied army finally took Nineveh and sacked it with a thoroughness that would have done credit to an Assyrian army.

The Assyrians matched their overwhelming military deeds with similarly impressive works in stone. Their architecture and sculpture were second only to that of the New Kingdom in Egypt. The city of Khorsabad, some 12

miles (19km) from Nineveh, is a fine example of the scale on which the wealth and tribute of the Assyrian Empire allowed its rulers to build. Sargon II had spent most of his reign living in other king's palaces. First, he lived in Ashur, the ancient and traditional capital of Assyria. Then he moved to an old palace of Assurnasirpal II, which he restored and gave to his son Sennacherib. Finally, he moved on to Nineveh and restored that ancient city. But by 712 B.C. he wanted a place of his own to show off not only the wealth brought by his victories but also his own aesthetic tastes.

He chose a site on which nobody had ever built. He began by building a square curtain wall measuring 5,905 feet (1,800m) on each side. Crenelated battlements spanned the top, 183 towers reinforced the walls, and

A relief shows Sennacherib's soldiers returning with loot from the conquered Judean city of Lachish. Although the Assyrians did not succeed in taking Jerusalem, the war is portrayed as a complete victory. Assyrian reliefs never recorded defeats. Our knowledge of the defeat comes from the Old Testament's Isaiah 10:12–17.

eight major gates controlled access to the interior. At the base, the walls were 66 feet (20m) thick. These walls were constructed of mud bricks, with the bottom of each wall sheathed in stone and set on a thick stone base. The city, which housed thousands of subjects, was organized in a rigid grid of square city blocks. Hardly anything remains of the residents' mud-brick houses, but the palace and temple complex, built directly across from the main gate, has been a rich source for archaeological digging since 1843. On that site, Tab-shar Ashur, Sargon's architect, built a palace for his king. This fortress covered 25 acres (50ha) and was surrounded by a wall with 63 square towers—it is almost as if the king expected an attack from within the city itself.

The main entrance gate to this palace, which archaeologists have named the Citadel, was covered with painted reliefs, vividly colored tiles, and sculptures of mythical stone monsters called *lamassu*. These creatures are famous throughout the world as the characteristic sculpture of the Assyrians. A *lamassu* is a stone carving of a winged bull with the head of a bearded man wearing a fezlike hat. In Assyrian mythology, the *lamassu* were friendly demons that protected the Assyrian monarchs. These curious figures have five legs arranged so as to create a certain effect: when the creature is viewed from the side, it seems to be striding forward, but when it is viewed from directly in front, it seems to be standing solidly in place. The figure's stance and fierce gaze were meant to convey a warning and sense of power to anyone entering the gate.

The entire perimeter of the Citadel walls was covered with stone reliefs that were once painted or, in some instances, glazed. Some of these reliefs depict battle scenes, and various heroic animals such as lions, eagles, and bulls, all of which symbolize the king's power. Other, gentler motifs such as plants, palm trees, and a relief of the king wandering through a forest of palms toward a small Greek temple with Ionic columns seem out of place.

The main entrance into the Citadel is on a long inclined ramp that leads up through the main gate. Through that gate, one enters a large courtyard surrounded by walls 39 feet (12m) high. Three of the walls were painted, and the wall opposite the entrance was done in stone relief. Whatever the medium, the subject was the same: the power, ancestry, and victories of King Sargon. The most prominent relief is of the hero Gilgamesh strangling a lion. The royal genealogists portrayed Gilgamesh as the direct ancestor of King Sargon. In the same relief sequence, Phoenician and Median ambassadors bring tribute, captives are tortured, and battles are fought in Syria.

Archaeologists have discovered that a throne once sat against the relief wall; with this knowledge, it is reasonable to conclude that this is the room in which Sargon conducted official duties. This conclusion is further supported by the presence of a staircase behind the throne that ascends to a roof, leading to another staircase, and finally to another, smaller courtyard, which was the center of the king's personal residence area. Two suites of rooms, which probably were used by the king's two wives, open off this area. The Assyrians had no prohibition against polygamy, though the practice seems to have been confined to the wealthier classes.

Outside and to the east of the throne room lies the Temple of Sibiti (the Assyrian Ishtar), which has the general form of a ziggurat, but with a circular ascending ramp that runs up seven levels to the top, where there are two

This fragment of a diorite stele commemorates the Great Akkadian King Sargon (2334–2279 B.C.). Even though Sargon was not Assyrian, and lived fifteen hundred years before the age of Assyrian greatness, the Assyrians revered his memory as a great conqueror. The Assyrian King Sargon (r. 721–705 B.C.) numbered himself the second Sargon out of respect for this earlier empire builder. The scene portrays bound prisoners being herded by an ax-carrying guard who roughly pushes one captive along.

This view of one of the two great *lamassu* that guarded the entrance to the palace of King Sargon II at Khorsabad shows the fifth leg of the half-man, half-winged bull, which makes it seem to the viewer that the creature is standing still if viewed from the front, and walking forward if viewed from the side.

tiny temples. Each of the seven levels of the tower was painted in a different color to represent one of the seven heavenly bodies (five known planets—Mercury, Venus, Mars, Jupiter, and Saturn—the sun, and the moon).

Two other temples stand in the Citadel. One was dedicated to the honor of Nabu, the god of scribes, and the other to Sin, the moon goddess. These temples were well decorated, but they do not compare with the palace. Unlike the Egyptians, whose temples were generally more impressive than their homes, the Assyrian kings built palaces for their own use and comfort, and these palaces were much grander than the temples.

The Citadel also contains a pleasant residence for the officials of the court. There are many rooms within this residence; some were certainly living quarters, and a number of them might have been audience chambers for Assyrian officials. The walls of the audience rooms were covered with paintings, most in reds, whites, and blues. A common feature of such room paintings is King Sargon

standing before the god Ashur with his right hand raised and his index finger pointed directly at the god—the traditional means of making a humble request in Assyria.

Unfortunately, Sargon's Khorsabad did not survive the king. When he was killed fighting hill tribes in the Zagros Mountains, his son Sennacherib assumed the throne. Wanting nothing to do with his father's city, the young king abandoned the site and moved his court to Nineveh, where he spent lavishly on its decoration throughout his reign. His one sign of appreciation for his father's good taste was the removal of many of the Khorsabad reliefs to the walls of his own palace.

The largest collection of Assyrian relief sculpture comes from the palaces of Assurbanipal in Nineveh and Nimrud. As expected, the main subject of these works is the king—sometimes he is engaged in battle, sometimes he is hunting, and, more rarely, he is involved in various activities in the palace. These sculptures are monumental. They were supposed to inspire and they still do. On a

Lions riddled with arrows were a popular motif from all periods of Assyrian history. Lions were the prey of choice for Assyrian kings, and every Assyrian ruler was expected to hunt them as a sign of his virility and power.

purely artistic level, however, the artists found a vehicle for creativity in the animals and plants that form the background to these reliefs. The best examples of this come from a number of reliefs from Nineveh that portray a royal lion hunt.

The lions for these hunts were captured alive in the wild and then released into an arena. Lines of soldiers would arrange themselves in the form of a huge square and interlock their tall shields. The king would then enter the square in his chariot or, less typically, on foot, and he would slay the trapped beast with arrows. This may not seem particularly sporting, but then neither is bullfighting or hunting birds with dogs and shotguns. In such scenes, the attitudes of the king and his attendants are stiff and formal, almost Egyptian. Real grace exists in the details, however, especially among the movements of the lions as they leap at their attackers.

Assyrian artists were masters of portrayal when it came to depicting dead or dying animals. In the Assurbanipal reliefs, there is a wonderful depiction of a dead lion, lying on the floor with four arrows in its body—particularly noteworthy are the positioning and detail of the paws of the animal. The skill of the Assyrian relief artist is perhaps best shown in the most famous Assyrian relief—the dying lioness. Again the representation is gruesome: three arrows have pierced the lioness, and one has apparently caused paralysis in the hind quarters. With great care, the unknown artist has made apparent in the animal's face the tension and confusion it feels as it drags itself forward to attack on its two good front legs. The viewer sympathizes with the lion.

Assyrian artists also excelled in representations of plant life. Again from the Nineveh reliefs comes a famous scene that shows Assurbanipal reclining on an elbow while he drinks wine. His wife, Assursharrat, sits bolt upright in a chair beside him. Musicians play in the background, and slaves wave fans to cool the king and his wife. Although the humans are stiff and formal, the garden background behind them is not. The artist has captured the shape of the palm fronds, the rough texture of tree trunks, the distinctive leaf patterns of surrounding shrubs, and the bunches of grapes that hang over the couple. The severed head of the defeated king of Elam, which hangs from a tree in the background, almost escapes the viewer's notice.

Great sculpture, however, was not the only artistic treasure that Khorsabad held, for Sargon II created there the first library devoted solely to literature. Libraries had existed before, but they were collections of business documents and records of tribute collected. The Assyrian royalty and nobility were great lovers of literature. Assurbanipal even boasts that he learned to read and write the language of the scribes—a claim that many modern historians doubt, given the difficulty of cuneiform. Certainly, none of Assurbanipal's contemporaries questioned the claim.

When assessing the intellectual achievements of a people, one might assume that the creation of literature is usually held in higher esteem than the collection of it; however, the Assyrian royalty's institution of formal libraries of the creative literature of other cultures was indeed a creative act in its own right. This act preserved the best of Mesopotamian learning for later generations. Scholars have studied the Assyrian library primarily to reconstruct the lost literature of Babylon. Had it not been for the collecting efforts of Sargon and his descendants, little of the ancient Babylonian and Sumerian literature would have survived.

This decorated ivory tablet, which once adorned the end of an Assyrian bed, is from the palace of Assurnasirpal II at Nimrud and shows four men holding a pail and anointing a tree with what looks like a pinecone. Archaeologists have found hundreds of small ivory statues and reliefs in Assyrian ruins.

Part of a scene from Assurbanipal's palace at Nineveh details a day of hunting. The panel begins by showing the release of the great hunting dogs and ends with the hunters returning loaded with game. This is from the middle of the panel and shows a group of gazelles becoming nervous at the approach of the hunters.

Regarding creations of the Assyrians themselves, we can attribute to them one completely original literary form: recorded history. Historical writing had certainly existed before in Babylonia, but these were the barest of statements, consisting, for instance, of the names of a few temples, the name of a king, and a list of goods received as part of a treaty. The Egyptians had been a bit more detailed, but their histories concentrated exclusively on the actions of the pharaoh. The recording of details such as the exact route the army followed, the amount of grain the army took with it, or even the name of the enemy commander seldom occurred in scribes' writings before the Assyrian period. The warlike Assyrians, however, wanted their scribes to preserve every detail of their wars: the portents of the soothsayers before the campaign started, the route of the army, its organization, the size of its baggage train, the battlefield disposition of the enemy forces, and the tactics the Assyrians used to achieve their inevitable victory. This new way of writing history was to a large extent the result of the invention of the hexagonal cuneiform table, which allowed for a greater writing area than the old two-sided clay tablet. Of course, the Egyptians' favored medium—papyrus—was much easier to work with than the Assyrians' clay, but the Egyptians never concentrated on details the way the Assyrians did.

Nevertheless, the new Assyrian "history" had limitations of it own: the only subjects that were deemed worthy of reporting were military campaigns; also, there was no attempt at impartiality. The scribes were royal employees, trying their best to please their king, which meant that they reported only the successful and triumphant campaigns. In July 714 B.C.., for instance, Sargon II led an expedition east into the Zagros Mountains to collect tribute from the Munnai, who were led by King Ullusunu and lived near the southern end of Lake Urumia, near present-day Tabriz, Iran. The Assyrian king's scribe

Nabu-shallimshunu carefully recorded their route, and he explained that when Sargon arrived he found that Haldians under King Rusash had been conducting raids against the Munnai. Sargon set off in pursuit, and his faithful scribe wrote a detailed route of the trek, including the amount of supplies carried by the army and the difficulties of marching at high altitudes. Nabu-shallimshunu describes how Sargon successfully negotiated the high passes and sped on ahead with the cavalry to defeat Rusash. A detailed account follows of Rusash's retreat to his capital at Masasir, its siege by the Assyrians, and its inevitable capitulation.

The royal archives at Khorsabad, Nineveh, and Ashur are filled with these kinds of historical reports. Perhaps if other ancient nations had kept records as precisely as the Assyrians did, the Assyrians would not appear as gruesome and as cruel in contrast. Their evil reputation may be nothing more than the precise, if sometimes exaggerated, recording of their scribes.

Religion and Medicine

The Assyrians' religion mirrors their violent and troubled history. Neither solace nor compassion are facets of their belief system. Instead, their religion is one that, according to their own records, revels in cruelty, delights in myths that stress violence and gore, and is dominated by awful demons who constantly attempt to do mankind harm.

The chief god is Ashur, or Assur, from whence comes the name Assyria. He was originally a sun god, and just like the sun in this desert land, he was cruel and merciless. He stands at the head of the Assyrian pantheon—the other gods are clearly his inferiors. Even Marduk, whom the ancient temple texts call his brother god, is less powerful than he.

Ashur's chief function, it seemed, was to encourage the expansion of the empire by demanding victims from the king. The minimal theology of this belief system stressed that the king was the servant of Ashur and that his chief duties were to please the god by observing numerous ritual taboos and by bringing prisoners of war to the temple of Ashur for execution; the god apparently

A relief carved on the base of a throne shows the Assyrian King Tukulti-Ninurta I (1243–1207 B.C.) praying to the fire god Nusku. The king is shown in two postures, one upright and the other kneeling. The god Nusku is never shown; only his symbols, in this case a throne, indicate his presence. Tukulti-Ninurta I was the earliest Assyrian king to attack Babylonia, but later Assyrian kings repeated his performance.

A tiny part of a much larger relief dramatizing the conquest of the Judean city of Lachish by Sennacherib shows three men impaled on stakes, one of the Assyrians' favored modes of execution for their enemies. Another was thrusting a living enemy into a furnace.

Luna Sin, the moon god, was an important Assyrian deity. This relief shows the traditional crescent that was the sign of Luna Sin. Sargon II's palace at Khorsabad included an elaborate temple dedicated to Sin.

took joy in the torture, mutilation, and murder of captives. These customs seem uncomfortably similar to those of the Aztecs of Central and South America, whose brutal gods Huitzilopochtli, Tlaloc, and Tezcatlipoca demanded human sacrifices from the tops of their pyramid temples.

The seventh, fourteenth, nineteenth, twenty-first, and twenty-eighth days of each month were taboo days for the king; on these days, it was forbidden for him to eat cooked food, change his clothing, or use a chariot. These days also had restrictions for others: on pain of offending Ashur, no priest could make a prophecy and no doctor could treat a patient. On new year's day (the vernal equinox), the king had to fast until the new moon made its appearance.

The Assyrians borrowed much of their religion from the Babylonians, including their myths. However, they seemed to have preferred those myths that stressed violence and conflict. The most popular was the *Enuma elish* or Creation Epic. In this story, the god Apsu, angry with the people on earth for the great noise that they were making, suggests to his wife Tiamat that she find a way to destroy all mankind so that he may get some rest.

Assyria 81

When news of this reached Ea, the god of wisdom, he called a meeting of the gods and asked them what he should do. The assembled gods told Ea that he should cast a spell and kill Apsu. Ea followed this advice and afterward built a palace where he buried Apsu.

The grieving Tiamat held her anger but promised herself she would get even with Ea. She used her skills as a magician to create an army of demons, monsters, and snakes so terrible that the mere sight of them was enough to kill mortal men. When she had finished with her creations, she sent them to attack Ea and the rest of the gods. Terrified, the gods milled around in confusion; none of them felt strong enough to destroy this terrible army. Finally, Marduk, the son of Ea, offered to kill Tiamat if the gods agreed to name him their king after the deed was done. They readily agreed and gave him a royal standard, a bow, a mace, and a net. With these weapons, he challenged Tiamat to single combat. For fear of being called a coward, she accepted and was killed by Marduk.

In one version of the story, as a memorial to his victory, Marduk then sliced up Tiamat's body and used it to make the earth, the constellations, the calendar (which to Assyrians was a physical thing), the polestar, and the sun and the moon. From her eyes Marduk created the sources of the Tigris and Euphrates rivers. From her breasts he made the mountains, and from the blood that flowed from them he created the tributaries of the two rivers. Finally, from her tailbone he made the Milky Way, using her pelvic bone to hold up the sky. This brutal tale, with its emphasis on dismemberment and bloodshed, became the most popular story in the "theology" of the Assyrians.

Gruesome as the Assyrians' mythology was, the demonology aspect of their religion was even more disturbing. Ancient Assyrians believed that they were continuously surrounded by literally thousands of demons. They believed that demons populated the dark and forbidding places of the world, especially ruined cities, graveyards, crossroads, and the desert. Demons were especially active around the birth of a child, especially when their queen, Lamashtu (the Assyrian Lilith), led them in search of babies to eat. The Assyrian Lamashtu is much more terrible to behold than her Babylonian counterpart: she is usually depicted standing on a horse and holding a snake in one hand, with two pigs suspended from her nipples.

Assyrian demons came in all shapes and sizes. They could even change shape and size at will, ranging from seductive maidens to donkeys and snakes. They could be large enough to blot out the sun yet suddenly become small enough to squeeze under a door. Their most common evil act was infecting people with diseases in retaliation for some real or imagined slight. They caused the disease by entering the person's body. The only way to cure the victim was to get the demon to leave. This was the domain of a special priest called a *mushmushu*.

The *mushmushu*'s course of treatment was almost always the same. The first stage consisted of making an effigy of the afflicted human. To do this, the priest collected dirt from isolated places such as cemeteries, ruined buildings, or abandoned canals; he mixed the dirt with bull's blood, and, as he recited prayers to the god Shamash, formed the mixture into a small human figure. Finally, he placed a small carnelian stone around the figure's neck. The second stage consisted of getting the demon to leave the sick person's body and enter the figure. The *mushmushu* accomplished this by ritual chants and/or feeding the sick person disgusting mixtures of blood, dirt, fecal matter, and rotted meat. If the chants did not succeed in scaring the demon from the infected body, the "food" would sicken the monster so much that it would leave of its own volition. Such treatment lasted three days, after which the *mushmushu* would examine the person to see whether the demon had left his or her body and entered into the figure. Once the demon was inside the effigy, the red carnelian stone prevented it from leaving. If the *mushmushu* determined that the cure had worked, the figure was placed in a jar and buried. If not, the "doctor" declared the patient incurable.

Sometimes clay models of this kind were also used to dispel bad luck. According to H.W.F. Saggs, one of the foremost Assyriologists, being urinated on by a dog—apparently a common occurrence in Assyria—was considered the height of bad luck and was certain to cause a lifetime of disaster. The only way to lift the "curse" was to hire a *mushmushu* and have him prepare a clay model of a dog that would attract the bad luck away from the person who had been urinated on.

Some Assyrian medical texts report that demons were often nothing more than ghosts. By Assyrian definition, a ghost was somebody who had either been buried improp-

protective spirit, represented by a winged and eagle-headed figure, pollinates a sacred tree in a wall relief from Assurnasipal's palace at Nimrud. He holds a pinecone in his right hand that is probably covered with the male pollen of the date palm and may be involved in fertilizing a female date palm flower. Other archaeological authorities believe he is gathering the sap of the palm tree that will later be used to anoint the king and protect him from evil spirits.

erly or had suffered a violent death. Hanging was considered an especially terrible way to die and almost certainly guaranteed that the deceased would return as an unhappy spirit. Proper burial was not complicated. As in Babylonia, it generally consisted of the body being buried under the floor of the family dwelling and provided with a dish of food and flask of wine. A coffin was not required, although some people were buried in two large pottery jars joined together and sealed at the lips.

The last but most important function of Assyrian religion was predicting the future. Nothing important, from marriages to invasions, was allowed to go forward unless the omens were considered right. The most popular form of divination was the traditional Babylonian method of reading sheep's livers. In fact, the Assyrians added nothing new to this method; they simply used the numerous books of divination prepared by the Babylonians. But this is not to say that the Assyrians did not improve on other forms of divination. For them, astrology became progressively more important. Six of the seven planets—the sun and moon were considered planets—were associated with a particular Assyrian god: Venus was identified with Sibiti, the goddess of love; Mercury with Nabu, the god of learning; Mars with Nergal, the war god; and Jupiter with Ashur and the king. Saturn was the star of justice. It was believed that by watching the course of these planets through the constellations the astrologers could predict the course of future events. For instance, any strange behavior of Mars as it traveled through the constellation of the hunter (Orion) could be interpreted as predicting the success or failure of the current war—if one considered the activity of Saturn.

Ultimately, however, the Assyrians believed that the most meaningful messages from the sky concerning the success or failure of the current king would be divined from the behavior of the moon and its relationships to eclipses. The Assyrian astrologers watched each night for the appearance of an eclipse (they had not yet realized there was an eighteen-year cycle for this phenomenon). They had divided the sphere of the moon into four quarters, known successively as very good, good, very bad, or bad. The astrologers estimated the success or failure of the current king's reign based on which quarter or quarters the eclipse's shadow passed through.

A basalt statue (65 inches [165cm] high) of the god Hadad or Adad, the Assyrian god of thunderstorms. An inscription on the statue threatens the well-being of anyone who damages it. Hadad-Adad is usually shown riding on the back of a bull.

Everyday Life

f the world of Assyrian astrology seems somewhat esoteric, the everyday existence of the average Assyrian was much more down to earth. The Assyrian city was organized into square grids of streets, and the typical Assyrian home was a one-story, mainly mud-walled house. For a number of years, the main Assyrian cities of Ashur, Nimrud, and Nineveh lacked an adequate water supply because the Tigris was slightly brackish at this point, as were wells. Around 705 B.C.., Sennacherib solved this problem for Nineveh by building a thirty-mile (48km) aqueduct that brought fresh water from the mountains in the northeast to that city.

Typically, all Assyrian houses looked much the same. From the outside, nothing distinguished one from another, and there were no house numbers or street names. Once past the door of the house, a visitor knew immediately that Assyrians liked their privacy. The front hall turned a corner and then went back on itself before it opened into the first room—it was impossible for someone passing on the street to gain even a glimpse of activity in an Assyrian house. In wealthier houses, privacy was further guaranteed by primitive pin tumbler locks that opened with keys. The lock and key was an Assyrian invention and seems to have spread from Assyria in the late eighth century.

The individual rooms of the Assyrian home had walls that were covered with a layer of gleaming white gypsum, and a band of red on top of a band of black circled the room just above the floor. The floors and some walls were covered with brightly covered rugs—the so-called "Persian rug," which actually goes back much further than Persia. There were no closets, but each room had a number of shallow niches for storage. Furniture consisted of chests for storage, along with chairs and stools with woven reed seats.

The most important area of the Assyrian home was the central open-air courtyard onto which a number of rooms opened. People spent most of their time in this courtyard, retreating only when it rained or when the noon sun was directly overhead—the noon break or siesta comes naturally to residents of the Middle East. The Assyrians decorated these center courts with small gardens or with small trees in planters. King Sennacherib was a particularly avid gardener. He ordered his invading armies to send back interesting trees and plants to Nineveh. One of his ambassadors to central India is credited with sending the first cotton plants to western Asia. Other standard features of this courtyard were a small grinding stone, a fire pit, and a number of blackened clay pots that the housewife, or in more affluent homes the slaves, used to prepare meals.

The Assyrians were simple in their food tastes. The main staple of their diet was a thin unleavened bread made from barley. The cook formed the dough into a thin sheet and then laid it across the side of a clay pot which had been turned on its side on the ground and filled with a hot fire. It "baked" in a few moments and was added to a mainly vegetarian diet of olives, garlic, onions, lettuce, turnips, cucumbers, and lentils. For important meals, the more affluent Assyrian might eat pork or mutton. His less fortunate neighbor might celebrate with an occasional duck or goose. Only the nobility and the royalty ate beef. To cook whatever kind of meat or poultry, the cook built a fire of dried thorns and tinder in a clay pot until the vessel became extremely hot. She then removed the fire and thrust in the food, after which she stopped up the mouth with a cap and let this primitive oven do its work.

The common drink was beer, although visiting Babylonians considered it much weaker than their native brew. Assyrians and Babylonians also differed in their opinion of milk: the Assyrian drank goat's milk with relish and considered cow's milk a real delicacy; the Babylonians believed that milk was poisonous and useful only as medicine. Richer Assyrians drank wine and brandy made from fruits. It seems that the Assyrians may have invented the process of distillation.

Assyrian dress was much more modest than that of either the Egyptian Empire or Babylonia, where women's breasts and men's legs were often bare. The Assyrians covered their upper bodies completely. Both sexes often wore an undergarment on their upper bodies, with a long robe thrown over the left shoulder and belted at the waist. Workers left their legs exposed below the knees, but the upper classes usually covered their legs to the ankles. For the lower classes, clothing was made of wool, which must

have been uncomfortable in the desert climate. For the upper classes, clothing was made of imported linen. At the beginning of the seventh century B.C.., however, Sennacherib's gardeners began to grow cotton, and cotton clothing became an extreme luxury item. By the end of that century, it had begun to diffuse through society.

oldiers in the field before the besieged city of Hamanu enjoy a meal. Assurbanipal II carried on a long siege of this city during his conquest of Elam. When the city fell, the head of the Elamite king was brought to Assurbanipal while he was eating dinner with guests. He ordered the severed head fixed to a pole so his guests could enjoy it during the meal.

pposite: Assurbanipal holds a mace of authority in one hand, while with the other he holds a cord that is connected to rings set in the noses of Ushanakhuru, the son of the Nubian Pharaoh Taharqa, and Adbimilkutti, the king of Sidon. Assurbanipal's father, Esarhaddon (r. 681–669 B.C.) had conquered Egypt between 674 and 670 B.C.

All classes favored solid, bright colors for everyday clothing. The nobility often added fringes to the edges of their robes, but commoners were strictly forbidden to do so. During state ceremonies, the nobility wore spotless white clothing. Purple pigment, made from the shell of the Mediterranean murex, was also reserved for the nobility. Red shoes seemed to have been reserved for the king alone.

The Assyrian men wore distinctive kinds of sandals that covered the heels with leather. This heel was a military innovation that was supposed to make the shoe adhere more firmly to the foot to prevent it from slipping. Women's shoes, which looked very much like modern espadrilles, covered the toes.

No matter what they wore, Assyrian men were proud of their beards and moustaches, and the nobility had them dressed so that they hung in curls off the face.

Assyria was truly a man's world. Women of all classes had virtually no rights. When a husband died, everything became the property of his eldest son, unless he had specifically willed it to his wife. Social pressure required that the son give his mother shelter, but no law compelled him to do so. As soon as possible, a widow was married off to a male relative of her husband. Should a husband tire of his wife and simply abandon her, the law required her to wait five years before remarrying. During this time, she was supposed to return to her father's house, but he was not required to take her back; if her family refused to take her in, then her only recourse was to go to the local ruler, swear she was destitute, and receive a tiny allowance from the state treasury. In the case of either abandonment or formal divorce, the husband was not obliged to return the marriage dowry to her family. It goes without saying that divorce could be initiated only by the husband.

Looking at seventh-century B.C. Assyrian male-female relations from a late twentieth-century A.D. perspective, the only positive thing we can find is that their laws punished men and women equally. A woman who stole was punished by the loss of her hand, just as a man was, and adultery was a capital crime for both men and women. That was a step forward from Babylonian or Egyptian society, in which adultery was a capital crime for a woman but a mere "lapse" for a man.

The End of Empire

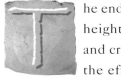

The end for Assyria came suddenly and at the height of her creative energy. The success and creativity of the country was based on the efficiency with which the nation conquered, held, and administered foreign territory. Unfortunately for the Assyrians, efficiency meant cruelty that inspired rebellion in their subject people.

The last important king of the Assyrians, Assurbanipal (r. 669–627 B.C.), found his empire surrounded by foreign enemies and greatly troubled by internecine strife; he was, it turned out, unable to meet all the challenges at once. In 663, the Assyrian provinces of Egypt, Lydia, and Babylonia revolted. Around the same time, the Medes and Cimmerians on the northern and eastern borders began to conduct raids against the empire.

Added to this chaos was a good deal of trouble that the Assyrians had brought on themselves. Every victory of the Assyrians had resulted in new peoples being brought into the empire. Many of these were recruited into the Assyrian army and government. Over time, the organization of the Assyrian Empire had become dominated by foreigners, who could be expected to be loyal only so long as they saw an advantage for themselves. When the empire began to unravel in the 660s, these "recruits" took advantage of the situation. This was certainly the case in Lydia and Babylonia, where the local leaders saw the barbarians at the gates and decided that they could defend themselves without help from Nineveh.

The death of Assurbanipal destroyed the last vestige of effective central control. In 612 B.C., an allied army of Babylonians and Medes captured Nineveh and destroyed it. In an instant, the nation of Assyrians vanished.

Chapter Four

The Athenian Empire

War, Conquest, and the Pursuit of Culture, 490–404 B.C.

In 490 B.C., Athens was a tiny Greek enclave, smaller than many counties in the United States. Thirty years later, she ruled the Aegean Basin, sent armies to invade Egypt and Sicily, and was the artistic and intellectual leader of Greece. All this happened because her tiny army and navy had, against all odds, decisively beaten Persia, the mightiest military power in the world.

Opposite: The Parthenon was the crowning jewel of the Acropolis, and the spiritual center of the city. It is appropriate that many considered it the most perfect building of the ancient Greek world. It certainly typified the Greek spirit of seeking perfection in all things.

A portion of an Attic red-figure vase showing a fight between an Athenian hoplite and a Persian cavalryman. Greek infantry sometimes fought naked (especially against fast-moving cavalry) since they knew, without knowing exactly why, that pieces of clothing carried into a wound by a penetrating sword or spear point were more likely to cause infection.

Since 550 B.C., the Persian Empire, with its capital at Susa (located in present-day southwestern Iran), had been gradually expanding both toward the east and toward the west, until Persian territory stretched from the borders of India to the Mediterranean. In 546, the Persian king Cyrus conquered Lydia in central Asia Minor (modern Turkey), and for the first time, the Persians came in contact with the dozens of tiny Greek city-states on the Aegean coast—an area called Ionia. Resistance seemed futile, and these cities gave Cyrus earth and water, the traditional Persian token of submission, and tried to go on about their business.

The Persian rule was not especially oppressive, but it irked the independent-minded Greeks, who resented any interference in their affairs. Many of their leaders whis-

pered—none too loudly—about staging a revolt if the opportunity ever came. In 513 B.C., the time seemed right. Earlier that year, Darius, Cyrus's successor, attempted to conquer the Scythians, who lived in modern-day Rumania. To everyone's surprise, the Scythian horsemen beat the Persian army and forced it to retreat. If a bunch of barbarian horsemen could beat the mighty Persian army, the Ionic Greeks reasoned, perhaps they could, too. The first Greek state to try was Naxos, an island in the Aegean. When its revolt succeeded and the Persian garrison was massacred, the entire coast joined the revolt. One of the cities, Miletus, asked for help from the Greek states across the Aegean, and Athens and Eretria responded by sending twenty ships. The fleet helped secure the coast, and when it seemed the crisis was over, it sailed home.

Unfortunately, the revolt in Ionia failed. The Persian response was overwhelming: they sacked Miletus and exiled the citizens en masse to the desert interior of Mesopotamia. King Darius rested his army on the ruins of Miletus, where he decided to make an example of Athens and Eretria. He sent messengers to Athens to demand earth and water. The Athenians received the messengers, heard their message, and summarily executed them for even suggesting that free Greeks become subjects of a foreign prince. When Darius heard of this diplomatic affront, he began organizing the largest army his country had ever assembled. He decided that he would not only punish Athens but also add the entire Greek peninsula to the Persian Empire.

From City-State to Empire

On September 16, 490 B.C., a huge Persian fleet sailed into the Bay of Marathon and landed forty thousand troops on the beach, only 26 miles (42km) from Athens. The army was fresh from victory over little Eretria. In just six days, the Persian army had taken Eretria, burned the city to the ground, and sent its inhabitants off to permanent exile in Mesopotamia. A few survivors escaped to Athens with the news. The Athenians sent their runner Philippides to Sparta to ask for help. He covered the 140 miles (225km) that separated the two cities in a single day. The Spartans agreed to send an army

but not immediately; they were celebrating the religious festival of Apollo Carneius, and their religious laws forbade instituting military action until it was over. Philippides carried this message back, again in one day, and arrived just in time to join his regiment for the coming battle.

The Athenians, thinking they would have to fight alone, formed their regiments and marched over the mountains to Marathon. At the last moment, a contingent of one thousand Plataean Greeks arrived to reinforce them. Together, the Athenians and Plataeans numbered nearly eleven thousand men. They would be outnumbered nearly four to one.

The combined Greek army was made up exclusively of heavily armored infantrymen called *hoplites*. Each hoplite wore a bronze helmet, breastplate, and greaves (shin protectors). Every hoplite also carried a hoplon, a wide, heavy wooden shield reinforced with bronze, and was armed with a sword and a six-foot (1.8m) spear. In battle, these troops lined up shoulder to shoulder in compact lines, with each man holding his shield in front of his body with his left arm so that it protected both his left side and the right side of his immediate neighbor. Each soldier held his spear in the right hand and thrust it out between his shield and his neighbor's so that from the front the enemy faced a solid line of shields bristling with spear points. Behind the first line was a second line arranged in the same way. This line pressed their shields against the backs of the men in the first line, and their spears also projected out beyond the first rank. A third line of spear men did the same. Depending on tactics and terrain, a Greek phalanx—for this was what this in-rank formation was called—might be seven ranks deep. As this deadly bronze-spear-tipped "hedge" advanced, it literally ground into the opposition.

When similarly armed Greek armies met in the middle of the battlefield, they stopped as spear points met shields, and began pushing and shoving against each other, while every soldier tried to maneuver his spear point between the shields of the enemy line and into the flesh of an opposing soldier. If a Greek soldier fell, the man behind him stepped forward to take his place. Victory usually came to the phalanx best trained to endure this strange pushing-and-shoving match until the opposing phalanx gave way and collapsed. It was a deadly,

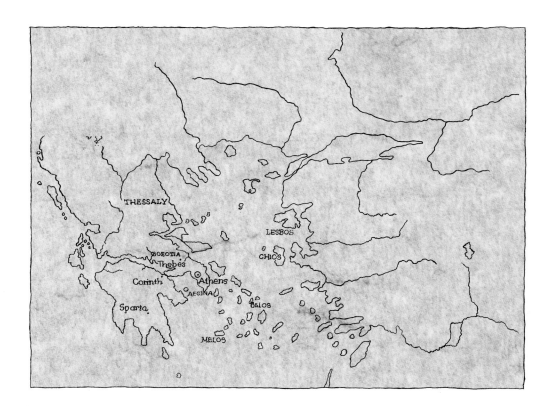

stressful form of fighting, and Greek commanders often strengthened their troops' courage with a liberal ration of wine just before the advance across the battlefield. Often, once the two armies locked together, the press of man against man was so tight that a soldier killed by a spear thrust could not fall to the ground and his corpse would be carried back and forth across the field by the press of battle until one line or the other finally gave way.

The Persians had nothing like this system of warfare. Their infantrymen were lightly armed and protected with a wicker shield, leather cap, and armor made from bronze or iron pieces sewed to a leather jacket. According to Persian tactics, the front line of their infantry was generally used only to hold the enemy momentarily while Persian archers behind the line fired arrows over their own infantry and onto the heads of the enemy. Meanwhile Persian cavalry worked around the enemy flanks and attacked from the rear. The Greeks had neither cavalry nor archers to counter these maneuvers, and with their spears facing to the front, they had difficulty quickly turning to face an attack on their flanks. Both the Greek and the Persian armies had strengths and weaknesses; victory would go to the side that best used its strengths and capitalized on the enemy weaknesses.

Nevertheless, when the outnumbered Greek army emerged on the mountain trail above the Plain of

The Athenian Empire began as a collection of city-states that banded together to defend themselves against the invading Persians.

Marathon to look down on the huge Persian army, they must have questioned their ability to win, for the area near the beach was nearly black with Persian troops. The Greek army was deployed on the bottom slope of Mount Kotroni, partially hidden from Persian view by some scrubby trees. Its flanks were protected by two small streams that made cavalry attacks difficult. In this position, they were relatively safe from the Persians, but, conversely, they could not leave it to attack without exposing themselves to encirclement by the cavalry.

The Greek leaders called a meeting to decide what to do, and they soon took to arguing. The Greek army had no commander-in-chief because each regimental commander took charge of the army for a single day. This system ensured that no one man could use the army to become a tyrant, but it also made it difficult for an army to follow a unified strategy—anything accomplished by a particular general on one day could be undone by another leader the next.

For the next two days, the generals argued while the armies eyed each other across the plain. Five generals wanted to attack the Persians, and five wanted to retreat and defend Athens from its walls. Finally, after the leaders remained unable to decide on a single strategy, one of the generals, Miltiades, persuaded two others who wanted to attack to give him their day of command. Counting his own day, he now had three days of command. He laid out a carefully conceived plan of attack that would capitalize on the Greek's superior armor and would prevent the Persians from using their cavalry and archers. Miltiades had noted that the Persians did not keep their cavalry horses saddled during the night but instead pastured them to the north near good grass and water. Furthermore, the Persian army and archers dispersed to scattered camps at night. Miltiades therefore determined to attack at dawn and gamble that he could destroy the Persian infantry before the fearsome cavalry and archers could organize to attack.

Another portion of an Attic red-figure vase showing Athenian hoplites putting on pieces of metal armor. The man on the left is putting on a greave, or shin protector, while the man on the right is fastening his breastplate. Soldiers also wore helmets and armor around the waist and carried large round shields.

The day before the attack he ordered the Greeks to cut timber and build some defensive positions. He hoped this would convince the Persians that he had no intention of attacking and intended to stay on the defensive. That night he ordered the army to new positions. He purposely took troops away from the center of the Greek line and used them to strengthen the Greek army on the flanks. He then ordered the Greeks to bed down for the night in these positions but to keep their armor and weapons nearby, ready for instant use.

The next morning, at a prearranged signal, the Greek army sprang into battle position and launched their attack downhill before the Persian divisions could form completely. Nevertheless, a group of Persians managed to break through the weakened Greek center as they came down the hill. However, the Greek flank, strengthened with row after row of hoplites, easily pushed through the surprised Persians on either end of their army. Suddenly, the Greeks on the flanks stopped their advance, raised their spears momentarily, executed a turn, reformed their battle line, and drove into the startled Persians. The Persian cavalry did not have time to form, and the archers were mixed in with the infantry. For a time, the Persian center, unaware of what was happening on the flanks, continued to advance through the broken Greek center until, looking backward, they saw the Greeks approaching the Persian ships on the beach. Fearing that the Greeks would destroy their ships and trap them, they panicked and ran back to the beach to save the ships. Some reached the beach, pushed the ships into the water and escaped, but many were captured, and over six thousand lay dead on the field; the Greek dead numbered only 192. The next day a Spartan relief army arrived, intending to help the Athenians; instead, they simply complimented them on their victory and marched back home.

Everybody was stunned by the victory. Darius could not believe that his mighty army was beaten, Sparta realized that she might possibly have a military rival, and the

Athenians swelled with pride. To have fought at Marathon became the proudest memory of many Athenians and Plataeans, and any soldier's involvement at Marathon was always mentioned on his tombstone with more prominence than any other act of his life.

Suddenly, Athens found herself the leader of a group of Greek states that feared another Persian invasion. There was need for fear, because now, more than ever, the Persians wanted to punish the Greeks. Darius immediately started to rebuild his army, and he instituted a special tax to fund the construction of a gigantic fleet. When he died in 486 B.C., his son Xerxes (reigned 519–465 B.C.) inherited both the throne of Persia and the planning for the final conquest of Greece. By 481, Xerxes had assembled an army of two hundred fifty thousand men and a fleet of twelve hundred ships and was on the move. The army and the navy moved in parallel to each other along the coast of Asia Minor. When the massive army reached

The Athenian General Miltiades defeated the Persians at the Battle of Marathon in 490 B.C. Legend holds that his brilliant and original tactics resulted in the death of 6,400 Persians but only 192 Athenians, who are buried under a mound that is still evident on the battlefield. However, it is possible that Miltiades only took credit for the victory, and the real architect of the battle was Callimachus, who died in the battle.

the Hellespont, it was supposed to cross on two massive pontoon bridges, but a storm destroyed them both. Enraged, Xerxes had his executioner lash the body of water with a whip before he built another bridge. This time the Hellespont was more complacent, and the army crossed without incident. Slowly, the force wound its way south through Thrace and Macedonia and into Thessaly. Most of the Greek states, thinking it hopeless to resist, made the symbolic offerings of earth and water to Xerxes and sent military contingents to serve with the Persians.

Meanwhile the Athenians led the drive to create an anti-Persian alliance with the remaining Greek states. Many were reluctant to join, either because they feared the might of Persia or because they disagreed among themselves on how best to fight them. In Athens, a new leader, Themistocles (r. 514?–449? B.C.), assumed command over the preparations for the coming invasion. He correctly assumed that the next Persian invasion would rely heavily on sea power, and he persuaded the Athenians to earmark a large part of their treasury for the construction of *triremes*—large battleships with three banks of oars that gave them tremendous ramming power. By the time the Persians arrived, the Athenians had built two hundred new *triremes* and were the predominant naval power in Greece.

By August 480 B.C., the Persian army had reached the pass of Thermopylae on the coast near the border of Boeotia and Thessaly, and their fleet lay fifty miles northeast up the same coast at Artemisium. The Greek forces that Athens had assembled decided to engage in battle at both these points. To get Sparta to join, Athens had had to agree to their leadership of both the army and navy, but the Spartans wisely let the Athenians under Themistocles lead the fleet. On August 17, 480, the Greek army and navy met the Persians at both Artemisium and Thermopylae. The results were Greek losses at both places. The fleet lost seventy ships to the Persians, and a small Spartan, Theban, and Thespian infantry force that tried to stop the Persians at Thermopylae was annihilated. Still the victories cost the Persians dearly. More than twenty-two thousand Persians died at Thermopylae, and a storm after the battle at Artemisium sank two hundred Persian ships. At Thermopylae, the Spartan king Leonidas won eternal fame and gave the Greeks a rallying cry when three hundred Spartans and seven hundred

Thebans refused to surrender and died to the last man. Before the battle, the Persians had told Leonidas that his position was hopeless because the Persian archers could darken the sun with their arrows; Leonidas had grandly replied, "Good, then we can fight in the shade."

Despite the moral victory at Thermopylae, the huge Persian army disheartened the Greeks, and their army retreated south to the Peloponnesus, where they began to prepare defenses at the Isthmus of Corinth. At same time, the fleet sailed to the Bay of Eleusis, near Athens. The Spartans wanted the Greek fleet to defend the Peloponnesus against Persian amphibious landings, but Themistocles and the Athenians said no. They were reluctant to abandon the city of Athens without a fight. Among the Athenians, however, there were two opinions on how best to defend against the Persians. Some wanted to strip the fleet and use the sailors to man the wooden palisade around the city. Others, led by Themistocles, felt that the best way to defeat the Persians was to maintain the fleet and attack the invaders at sea. They argued that the enemy could not feed its huge land army without a secure supply route across the Aegean; if the Persian fleet

Part of a mosaic, now in the National Archaeological Museum in Naples, that portrays the Persian King Darius III attempting to flee from Alexander the Great after the battle of Issus in 333 B.C. Although this picture is of an event long after the days of Athen's greatness, it does dramatize the long-standing and bitter relations between the Greeks and the Persians.

could be defeated, the army would have to retreat into northern Greece where they could depend on supplies from Greek cities that had elected to support Persia.

Until the matter was decided, the Greek fleet lay at anchor in the Bay of Eleusis. This bay is formed by a large, roughly semicircular indentation in the Attic coast; the island of Salamis nearly blocks off the southern part of that semicircle, for extremely narrow channels at the east and west end of the island restrict entrance into the bay. Themistocles saw these narrow channels as the perfect place for the 380 Greek ships to make a stand against the more than one thousand ships of the Persians. The problem for Themistocles was to hold the Greek fleet in the bay, because most of the Athenians wanted to leave and join the Spartans to the south. His dramatic solution

would have been considered treasonous if he had been discovered. He secretly sent his trusted slave, Sicinnus, with a message for the Persians. One cannot help but marvel at this servant's bravery as well as his incredible ability to lie: Sicinnus convinced Xerxes that Themistocles secretly favored an alliance with the Persians and felt that he could convince the Athenians to abandon the Greek alliance if they felt their cause was hopeless. Why not trap the Greek fleet in the Bay of Eleusis by blocking both exits at either end of Salamis? This would force the Athenians to seek terms. Xerxes believed Sicinnus and divided his fleet, placing the largest part at the wide eastern entrance and a considerably smaller force at the western end.

Themistocles gambled everything on the ability of the allied fleet to defeat an enemy three times its size. He had supreme confidence in the tactical ability of his captains and the design of the Greek *triremes*. The Greek shipwrights had constructed vessels that lay low in the water and had extra timbers for strength, a design that made them more maneuverable and strong enough to ram enemy ships without suffering any real damage. The Persian ships were designed to maneuver alongside an enemy vessel so that archers could fire down into an enemy ship and marines could jump aboard and fight hand to hand. As at Marathon, the battle would be won by the side that used its tactical abilities most successfully.

Themistocles had chosen his "ground" wisely, for in the narrow waters at the entrance of the bay, the Persians could not bring their whole fleet to bear on the smaller Greek fleet. In fact, the Persian numbers might prove a disadvantage, because as their ships crowded forward toward the entrance, they might become fouled in the oars of other ships or run into each other.

At about 8 A.M. on September 23, 480 B.C., the Persians began their advance into the bay. The Greek fleet was drawn up in the channel leading into the bay, out of sight of the Persians. The Persians apparently expected the Greeks to block the channel. In fact, as the battle began, the Greek ships sailed down the right side of the channel next to Salamis. When the Persians entered the bay, they found that the Greeks were to the left of their own fleet. The Greek ships began to turn left so that the heavy bronze rams mounted on their prows were aimed directly at the sides of the advancing Persian fleet.

They were in a perfect position to ram. The Persian captains frantically tried to turn their ships to face the enemy so that they could shear off their oars and grapple the sides of the Greek ships, thus allowing their archers and marines to attack from above.

But the turning maneuver caused the ships to run into each other. In a matter of minutes, the Persians were locked together in a mass and other Persian ships in the rear crashed into the leading vessels, packing them together even more tightly. The Greek fleet swept in, rammed holes into the sides of the foremost Persian vessels, backed water, and rammed again. The ensuing slaughter lasted for several hours. When the battle was over, the Persians had lost six hundred ships, the Greeks, seventy. The Greek sailors from sinking ships swam easily to Salamis only a few hundred yards away. Most of the Persian sailors, who strangely could not swim, drowned.

Xerxes, who had ordered his throne set up on the shore of Attica so that he could watch the battle comfortably, was enraged. He vented his fury by ordering the execution of a few Persian captains who had arrived on shore safely from their sunken ships. Later that day, fearing that the victorious Greeks would sail into the Aegean, capture the Hellespont, and cut his supply lines, he ordered what remained of his navy back into Asian waters. Once more, as if by a miracle, the Greeks, and most specifically the Athenians, had won an incredible victory. The next year a combined Greek army pushed the last Persian army out of Greece. As it turned out, this effectively ended the power of the Persian king, but the Greeks, who could not be sure that this last battle was entirely decisive, did not stop there.

The Persian Empire still dwarfed the Greek states, its potential for war was still strong, and everybody on the Greek peninsula was certain that the Persians would be back. To prevent that from happening, Cimon, who succeeded Themistocles to political leadership in Athens, proposed the creation of an offensive-defensive league in 477 B.C. This organization, called the Delian League because its treasury was located on the island of Delos in the southern Aegean, was to be a voluntary association of free Greek city-states. Each state contributed either ships or money to create a fleet. This new allied fleet, led by Athens, would patrol the Aegean, launching preemptive strikes against the Persians. Never again would Persians fight Greeks on Greek soil.

The Spartan king Leonidas (standing with outstretched arms) took his duty as king so seriously that he did not hesitate to pronounce the grim sentence of exile against his own brother Cleombrotus (seated), as shown in Benjamin West's painting of the sentence being delivered.

Almost immediately, the League proved effective. Its fleet cleared the coast of Asia Minor of Persian ships, suppressed piracy, and captured Byzantium—a move to forestall any future Persian invasion of Greece by land. It was not long, however, before cracks began to appear in the League. As time went by, Athens took more and more of a leadership role, until the League began to function as an Athenian Empire. In 473 B.C., the Athenians forced the city of Carystus on Euboea to join the league against its will. In 470 B.C., the island of Naxos tried to leave the League, but the Athenians attacked the island, forcing it to remain. Most telling, however, was the Athenians' use of the League's treasury to enhance and beautify Athens instead of to maintain a fleet. In a short time, the League had become a dictatorship led by Athens.

Curiously, when modern people think of Athens and her beautiful buildings, dramatic sculpture, classic dramatists, and philosophers, they forget that it was all built on the money and power that Athens extracted from member states of the Delian League. It is strange that Athens, the symbol of democratic freedom to many modern people, was in reality the often brutal leader of an empire that ultimately became more oppressive to some Greek states than Persia had been. In a particularly horrible example dating from 416 B.C., the tiny island of Melos in the southern Aegean declared herself neutral in a war between Athens and Sparta. The Athenians landed troops, stormed the city, massacred all male inhabitants, and sold the women and children into slavery. By comparison, Darius and Xerxes seemed benevolent. In time many Greek city-states would look to Sparta for help against Athens and would join with that state in 431 to destroy Athens in the Peloponnesian War (431–404 B.C.).

In 479 B.C., however, when the last Persian troops left Boeotia and retreated north, all that lay in the future. For the next seventy years, Athens celebrated her victory with a burst of creativity in literature, art, sculpture, and architecture that has seldom been equaled.

An Athenian hoplite on his way to battle. For his time the Greek hoplite represented the epitome of military technology. A hoplite's equipment included a bronze helmet, a bronze corselet, and a pair of greaves covering his shins. He also carried a shield with a wooden core covered with bronze. His principal weapon was a spear 8 to 10 feet (2.5–3m) long.

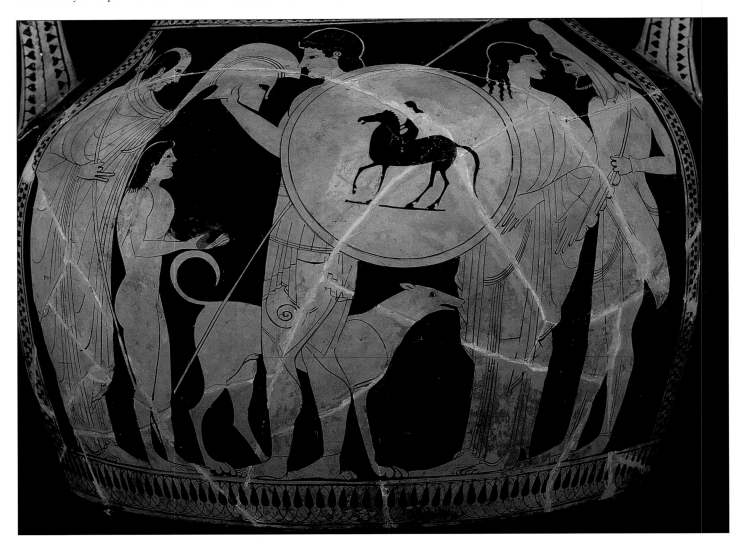

Arts and Sciences

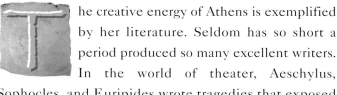he creative energy of Athens is exemplified by her literature. Seldom has so short a period produced so many excellent writers. In the world of theater, Aeschylus, Sophocles, and Euripides wrote tragedies that exposed the short comings of gods and men, and Aristophanes wrote comedies that made the audience laugh at these foibles. In the field of history, Herodotus and Thucydides wrote the first historical accounts that sought to explain why things happened, instead of merely recording what had happened. In science, Hippocrates began the first truly scientific study of disease, far surpassing anything the Egyptians had done. Last but not least, Athens at this time witnessed the first stirrings of philosophical investigation with the speculations of Anaxagoras and Socrates.

Drama

Drama had existed before the Persian Wars, but it did not become a truly dynamic form of literature until after the near miraculous victories at Marathon and Salamis. Western drama had begun in the late sixth century B.C., when Athenians used religious presentations to thank the god Dionysus for a successful harvest. In these thanksgiving celebrations, choruses commemorated with songs and dances the sufferings of the god Dionysus. Each Athenian tribe sponsored a chorus, and the best won a prize. Over time the spirit of competition created performances that became more and more elaborate, until by the first decade of the fifth century B.C., there was not only a costumed chorus, but an actor who interpreted the songs and dances of the chorus for the audience, along with a formal theater to house the performance.

In the early fifth century B.C., the Athenians constructed in the center of their city a seventeen thousand–seat theater for the presentation of these tragedies (the word comes from the Greek *tragos oides*, or goat singer, perhaps because in the earliest days the victorious chorus won a goat). The theater was built into a hillside with an ascending semicircle of stone seats looking down on a circular floor called the *orchesis* ("dance" in

Greek; the origin of the word *orchestra*). Behind the *orchesis* and facing the seats was the *skene* (from whence we get the word *scene*), a one-story building that had doors for the entrances and exits of the chorus and the actor, rooms where they could change into costumes, and structures that supported scenery. By the time of the Persian Wars, the annual performances had moved away from material strictly about Dionysus to stories featuring other gods and their interactions with mankind. The performances usually lasted an entire day and consisted of three tragedies built around a single theme. At the end of this trilogy, there was always a comic play to lighten the mood.

AESCHYLUS

This was the environment in which Aeschylus (525–455 B.C.), the world's first great master of tragedy, practiced his craft. He was born at Eleusis, just up the coast from Athens, into a noble family, and most of his writing betrays a sympathy for the upper classes. He fought at Marathon and considered that to be his proudest achievement in a life filled with honors. His grave at

The Theater of Dionysus on the south side of the Athenian Acropolis, the ruins of which are shown here, was attached to the shrine of Dionysus Eleuthereus, since drama was originally a religious celebration. In this picture one can see the base of the *proskenion*, on which the *periakta*, or scenery screens, wood panels painted with buildings, forests, and seascapes, rested. Above the *proskenion* was the *logeion*, the platform on which much of the action of the play took place.

The playwright Aeschylus founded a virtual dynasty of playwrights. His sons Euphorion and Euaeon made a living by restaging their father's plays, and a nephew, Philocles, started a family that wrote plays for over a century.

Gela in Sicily was marked with an epitaph that he composed for himself. Surprisingly, it does not even mention his plays, but simply states: "This is the Tomb of Aeschylus, to whose bravery the field at Marathon bears witness, and many a long-haired Persian, too."

Aeschylus brought a number of innovations to the Athenian theater. He introduced a second actor, making dialogue possible for the first time. He also was responsible for the use of masks and costumes that helped an audience to know an actor's identity and character. For instance, a mask with light hair identified the wearer as either a goddess or a young person; brown hair told the audience that the actor was a god or a person of middle age; white hair was reserved for old people; and entities from the underworld wore masks topped with black hair.

First and foremost, Aeschylus was concerned with teaching his audience that the best lives are lived by those who respect the natural order and justice of things. This message runs like a red thread through his six surviving plays. Evil results when men do things in defiance or ignorance of what is natural and just. In *The Persians*, written around 472 B.C., Aeschylus presents a simple and straightforward message: the Greeks beat Xerxes, the Persian king, because he refused to accept the natural division of the world between Persians and Greeks. This natural division is symbolized throughout the play by the sea that divides the two nations. When Xerxes builds a bridge across the Hellespont, Aeschylus condemns the action as unnatural. Later, in a vision, Xerxes' mother, Atossa, sees her son try to harness two statuesque women, magnificently garbed, to a chariot. One is dressed as a Persian, the other as a Greek. Xerxes' apparent intention in the dream is for both women to draw his chariot, thereby signifying his conquest of both nations. The Persian woman submits to the yoke, but the Greek woman struggles, upsets the chariot, and tosses Xerxes to the ground. The meaning is clear: Xerxes is supposed to rule the Persians, but he violates the natural order of things when he tries to rule the Greeks.

Aeschylus makes the point a second time in the play when he demonstrates that the pride of Xerxes is unnatural. Excessive pride angers Zeus, who does not like for men to forget their place in the world. When Xerxes returns to Susa, the Persian capital, he is dirty, disheveled, and in rags—the result, we are told, of Zeus's displeasure with his pride. The dialogue of the play leaves no doubt that had Xerxes behaved himself and not sought to expand his empire beyond its natural limits, he would have enjoyed a successful reign.

As Aeschylus matured in his writing, he took on more complicated themes. He remains the apostle of order and justice, but he begins to ask what happens when order and justice conflict. Sometimes, he posits, the natural order of things leads to more disorder and wickedness. The perfect example of this dilemma is the trilogy of plays entitled *The Oresteia*, written in 458 B.C. This series of plays, the only complete trilogy that survives from the classic era of Greek drama, includes *Agamemnon*, *The Choephori* (Libation Bearers), and *The Eumenides* (The Kindly Goddesses).

These three plays present a gruesome chain of events revolving around Agamemnon, the leader of the Greek army during the Trojan War. At the beginning of *Agamemnon*, this respected general sacrifices his own daughter, Iphigenia, to gain the goodwill of Artemis, who has sent an adverse wind that trapped the Greek fleet on the east coast of Greece at Aulis. To restore the natural order of things—normal winds—Artemis requires the sacrifice of Agamemnon's virgin daughter. Realizing that his wife, Clytemnestra, would never agree to send the girl to Aulis to serve as a sacrifice, Agamemnon lies to her and claims that Achilles wants to marry the girl. Clytemnestra joyfully sends her daughter to Aulis. Of course, once Iphigenia gets to Aulis, Agamemnon kills her, freeing the fleet but earning the hatred of his own wife. Ten years later, when Agamemnon returns home, Clytemnestra and her lover Aegisthus murder him in his bath. There is justice in what Clytemnestra does, for she is following the dictates of the Erinyes, the goddesses of vengeance who demand retribution for violations of the natural order—and killing a daughter certainly qualifies. Unfortunately, in seeking a justified revenge, Clytemnestra violates the natural order by killing her husband, an act that in turn requires rectification.

The next play in the trilogy, *Choephori*, turns to Orestes, the son of Clytemnestra and Agamemnon, who is duty bound to seek justice by killing his mother for the murder of his father. This presents Orestes with quite a dilemma, and he struggles against the urge to slay his mother; the god Apollo, however, urges him onward. When Orestes finally yields to the god's urgings and carries out the murder, he violates the natural scheme of things, laying himself open to further vengeance.

In the final play of the trilogy, *The Eumenides*, Zeus, the ruler of the gods, decides to take a hand to end this hopeless cycle of killing and vengeance. He arranges for the Areopagus, the high court of Athens, to determine the fate of Orestes. The goddess Athena presides over the trial and also acts as prosecution, while Apollo defends Orestes, who has, after all, only carried out the god's will.

Once the arguments have been made, the court votes, but the results are a tie. Strangely, Athena is moved by the testimony to break the tie by casting her vote to free Orestes from the cycle of vengeance.

This presents the Erinyes with an unheard-of complication—they have never before been thwarted by the gods. Furious, they refuse to accept the verdict. They must see to the punishment of Orestes, for vengeance is the very purpose of their existence. Prevented from doing so by the gods' will, they swear vengeance against Athens for "having destroyed the old laws." Zeus, working his eloquence through Athena, persuades the Erinyes to pursue their natural thirst for vengeance not by attacking Orestes, but by defending the state through beneficial acts of justice to mankind. Through the intervention of Zeus, the Erinyes undergo a kind of metamorphosis and become the Eumenides, or Kindly Goddesses.

In this play, Aeschylus presents a positive message about the gods: they are ultimately beneficial to mankind. This message is consistent with the very positive feelings with which the Athenians viewed themselves after the Persian Wars, for certainly there was no other explanation, other than beneficial, timely, divine intervention, that could explain their victory in the face of such odds and their subsequent rise to power and control over a large and prosperous empire. Aeschylus's works made him the most popular playwright in Athens. However, soon after the production of *The Oresteia*, he apparently became disgusted with the democratic excesses of Athens and left for Sicily, where he died in 455 B.C., reportedly when an eagle dropped a tortoise on his bare head. Nevertheless, long after his death, the dramatic judges of Athens automatically voted him a special prize every year in commemoration of his skill. Furthermore, the state paid for productions of his past plays.

According to the great German archaeologist Heinrich Schliemann, this was the golden death mask of Agamemnon, the leader of the Greeks at the siege of Troy. Aeschylus used the legend of Agamemnon to create *The Oresteia*, a gruesome trilogy of plays that examines the consequences of revenge.

SOPHOCLES

The next great dramatist after Aeschylus was Sophocles (496–406 B.C.). He was born in Colonus, a small town near Athens, and grew up in comfortable surroundings, for his father was a shield maker at a time when Athens pursued an aggressive foreign policy. With his very first dramatic entry into competition in 468, Sophocles not only won first prize but also defeated Aeschylus. Over the course of his writing career, he won the first prize twenty times and the second prize thirty times. Unfortunately, only seven of his 123 plays have survived the centuries. He lived to the ripe old age of ninety, in full possession of his faculties, and wrote his last play the year before he died. Legend says that he died during the Spartan siege of Athens when he choked to death on a grape during dinner. The Spartans agreed to a truce with the Athenians so that they could bury the famous dramatist at Colonus, which was inside the Spartan lines.

Of all the Greek tragedians, Sophocles is the most sympathetic to women. Many of his female characters are strong, dynamic women whose lives are strangely at variance with the life of most Greek women in ancient Athens.

Sophocles was a more complex writer than Aeschylus. He not only added a third actor to many of his plays, but also developed the personalities of his characters to a greater degree than earlier writers, making the characters' motives clearer to the theatergoer. For instance, Aeschylus's Orestes hates his mother, Clytemnestra, and her lover, Aegisthus, because they killed his father—the fact of the patricide is all the excuse for hatred that Aeschylus gives us. Yet Sophocles, in *Electra*, a play about the second daughter of Clytemnestra, creates a detailed explanation of why Electra hates Clytemnestra and Aegisthus—how the death of her father, Agamemnon, has robbed her of the joys of young girlhood, ruined her chances to have children, and forced her to live as the wife of a dusty, dull peasant. Her hatred is more understandable because Sophocles has laid out the reasons for it in full detail. The undeserved misery of poor Electra makes her desire to see her mother dead more understandable.

One of the keys to understanding the dramatic message of Sophocles is that he insists that his characters perform the right action, regardless of the consequences. Those who do are heroes or heroines; those who do not are knaves and cowards. This theme is clear in all of his surviving plays, but its most eloquent presentation is in *Antigone*, which he first presented in 440 B.C. This play deals with the conflict between an individual doing the right or moral thing in the face of an immoral law enforced by the power of an unjust government.

Antigone is the niece of Creon, tyrant of Thebes. As the play begins, a civil war over the throne of Thebes has just ended, and Antigone's two brothers, Eteocles and Polynices, have died fighting each other. Eteocles had fought to preserve the rule of his uncle Creon, and Polynices was a rebel fighting against the tyrant's rule. Creon decrees that Eteocles shall have an elaborate funeral but orders that the body of Polynices be left to rot in the fields. He further orders that anyone who attempts to bury him will be executed. This was a terrible punishment, for in ancient Greece it was believed that the souls of the dead could not go to Hades unless the body received a proper burial. The burial could be cursory, involving only the sprinkling of a handful of dirt over the corpse and a hurried prayer, but it had to be done. Antigone did not actually support Polynices in the war—

in fact, she seems apolitical—but the unfairness and cruelty of Creon's decree offends her, and she determines to bury her brother, regardless of the law, simply because it is the decent thing to do.

A soldier catches Antigone in the act of burying Polynices and takes her before Creon. He invokes the law, and her defense is simply that an unjust law is no law at all. Her sister Ismene and her fiancé Haemon, Creon's son, try to intervene on Antigone's behalf, but this only earns them punishment from Creon. He orders Ismene executed along with Antigone and decrees that Haemon must watch the execution of his intended bride.

Antigone goes bravely to her death, through the streets of Thebes; a crowd of citizens follows her in sympathy. Creon, too cowardly to kill her outright, has the girl walled up alive in a cave to die of starvation. When Creon returns to his palace, he meets the blind soothsayer Tiresias. The prophet tells the tyrant that he has had a dream in which he has learned that the gods are displeased over the harsh treatment afforded Polynices and Antigone, and they are going to punish the king by causing the death of his son Haemon. Knowing that Tiresias's predictions are never wrong, Creon quickly orders a tomb prepared for Polynices and hurries back to the cave to release Antigone. The gods, however, cannot be bargained with, and when Creon breaks into the cave, he finds that Antigone has hung herself with her robe. Haemon arrives at the scene soon afterward, curses his father, and kills himself in grief, thus fulfilling the decree of the gods. Creon's wife, distraught at the death of her son, also kills herself, and Creon is driven out of Thebes by the people. The villain lives on, miserable and despised by all, in contrast to Antigone, who died a noble death, beloved by all and assured of a heroine's welcome into Hades.

Sophocles' *Antigone* reflects the optimism of an Athens proud of its democratic institutions, just as Aeschylus's plays reflected the city's earlier pride in the defeat of mighty Persia. *Antigone* won the prize at the dramatic contest in 440 B.C. in part because of its brilliant writing and characterizations but also because of its implicit warning to a democratic audience about the perils of a tyranny. The people of Athens were sensitive to any sign of dictatorship, and this play, which showed the wicked consequences of one man's rule, was sure to find a responsive audience in the citizens of Athens. They

would all have agreed with Haemon's statement: "There can be no freedom in a city where one man rules."

EURIPIDES

The plays of Athens's last great dramatist, Euripides (484–406 B.C.), reflect the atmosphere of a much less idealistic Athens. Most of the surviving plays of Euripides were first performed during the Peloponnesian War, that long twenty-seven-year conflict between Sparta and Athens. It was not a glorious war with victories to match Marathon and Salamis, but a long, tough, grinding conflict that wore away at the liberties of various parts of the Athenian Empire and created bitter factional fights in Athens that seemed to kill the idealism which had characterized Athenian life throughout much of the fifth century.

Euripides was born on the island of Salamis, and legend has it that this birth took place on the very day of the great sea battle. According to tradition, his father owned a tavern and his mother sold herbs. Yet there must have been money in the family, for he received a first-class education in a school designed to prepare athletes for

Euripides was an Athenian playwright who delighted in plays that stressed the evil and loathsome side of mankind. Aristotle wrote in his *Poetics* that whereas Sophocles portrayed men as they should be, Euripides wrote about them as they really were.

Cassandra, shown in a statue by the German sculptor Max Klinger, was the beautiful but tragic daughter of King Priam of Troy and his wife Hecuba whose curse was always to be able to predict what the future held, but whose warnings nobody would believe. She was taken captive by Agamemnon at Troy and then murdered by his wife Clytemnestra when she reached Mycenae, although another tradition has it that she escaped this evil fate.

won a prize in 441 B.C. He was never as fortunate in winning as Aeschylus or Sophocles; in fact, he won only four prizes in his long career, during which he produced about ninety plays. Much of this can be laid at his feet, for some of his plays are poorly crafted, and others are convoluted and hard to follow.

Unlike the works of Aeschylus and Sophocles, Euripides' plays do not seek the answers to great questions, nor do they try to resolve philosophical dilemmas. Instead, these stories concentrate on the mundane aspects of life, especially the personalities of people. Euripides was good at evoking emotions from his audience about his characters by creating emotional situations which tug at heartstrings.

In one of his earliest plays, *Alcestis*, written in 438 B.C., he tells of the plight of Alcestis, the long-suffering wife of Admetus. Admetus has learned that he will die unless he can supply another to take his place. He asks his parents if one of them will die for him, but he is told, "Life is sweet even for the old." He then turns to his wife, Alcestis. A traditional Athenian wife, she is totally under the dominance of her husband, and she agrees to die in his place. In the heart-wrenching death scene, the noble Alcestis bids good-bye to her children and husband, and the audience realizes what a fine and noble person she is. Conversely, after the funeral, an argument between Admetus and his father shows what a wretched person Admetus is. This situation gives the audience the chance to reflect on the randomness of death, where honorable people die and unworthy people live. In a surprising twist, the play ends with the fortuitous arrival of Hercules, who wrestles Thanatos, the god of death, forcing him to give up the soul of Alcestis, thereby allowing her to return to life.

Euripides' masterpiece is probably the *Troades*, or *The Trojan Women*, the sad story of the noble Trojan women captured by the Greeks after the fall of Troy. Seldom has a dramatic work taken such an unremitting toll on the audience's emotions. The action of the play takes place on the beach where the victorious Greek fleet has been drawn up. A group of women wait near the ships to learn their fate from the Greek messenger, Talthybius. The leader of these captive women is Hecuba, queen of Troy and wife of Troy's dead king Priam. When Talthybius approaches, she asks him what is to be the fate of her two

competition. Supposedly, this was because his parents had misinterpreted a fortune-teller's prediction that the infant Euripides would grow up to wear the victor's crown. He was, of course, destined to win the crown for drama, not athletic competition. Euripides had a reputation as a difficult man to get along with. He had a number of close friends, including the philosophers Anaxagoras and Socrates, but he was not so lucky in his relationships with women: he divorced his first wife for infidelity, and his second wife left him.

He presented his first play for the dramatic competition in 455 B.C. but did not win a prize. He continued to submit work for the next fourteen years before he finally

daughters, Polyxena and Cassandra, and of her daughter-in-law, Andromache. Talthybius tells Hecuba that Polyxena has been designated a human sacrifice to placate the spirit of the dead Achilles; Cassandra, the virgin seeress, will become the concubine of Agamemnon; and Andromache will serve a similar role for the Greek warrior Neoptolemus. Hecuba herself will spend the rest of her days spinning at a loom in the house of Odysseus.

Enter Cassandra, the half-crazed prophetess who has predicted all the important events of the last ten years, only to have no one believe her. Even now, as a prisoner, she speaks of the future, telling all those around her that Agamemnon and his family will soon die and that Odysseus is fated to travel for ten years before he can return home.

Talthybius leaves and returns later with terrible news. The Greeks have determined that they cannot allow Little Astyanax, the son of Andromache and Hector, to live, for someday he will grow to manhood and seek vengeance on the Greeks. They have therefore decided

to toss him off the battlements to his death. The only solace that Talthybius can offer—and to his credit he takes no pleasure in these announcements—is that if the women do not make too much of a scene, the Greeks will return the baby's body for burial.

As if this is not horrible enough, Euripides continues to present the women with trouble and tragedy. It is at this moment that Helen makes her first appearance in the play. To the captured Trojan women, Helen is the vixen whose lust started all this misery, for when Paris brought her to Troy, the Greeks followed. Helen is determined to worm her way back into the affections of her husband, Menelaus, the king of Sparta. She kneels before him and asks forgiveness, depending on her beauty, reinforced with excuses, to save her. Her excuses are clever and eloquent. First, she pleads that she is not to blame for Paris's abduction of her; it was Hecuba and Priam, she says, who were really to blame. At Paris's birth, they ignored an oracle who encouraged the royal couple to kill their child because he would be the cause of the destruction of Troy.

The decorated bottom of an Athenian red-ware kylix, or wine cup, portrays a Greek soldier about to kill a Trojan while Cassandra watches helplessly. On the right, however, Andromache, the wife of the Trojan hero Hector, attempts to attack the Greek soldier. Behind her is her son Astyanax, whom the Greeks want to execute for fear that if he grows to manhood he might some day seek revenge.

Then she blames Aphrodite, for the goddess bewitched her into falling in love with Paris. Finally, she blames the soldiers who guarded her in Troy during the long siege and prevented her from returning to the Greeks. Menelaus is about to accept these excuses when Hecuba mocks Helen's arguments. It was not Aphrodite's enchantments, says the Trojan queen, but Helen's own lust that made her fall in love with Paris. As for breaking away from her captors, she could have "escaped" from Troy by taking her own life, which would have been the honorable thing for a faithful wife in her position to do.

Hecuba warns Menelaus not to take her aboard his ship for the long voyage home, saying that instead he should kill her on the spot. Not surprisingly, Menelaus does not kill her, but he does agree to send Helen home on another ship and thus avoid prolonged exposure to her feminine wiles. He will make his final decision once he gets back to Greece.

The misery of the Trojan women continues as Talthybius returns with the dead body of Astyanax. Andromache is not allowed to bury her baby, however; she is dragged aboard a ship, leaving the burial to Hecuba. The Trojan queen nearly breaks, and she contemplates suicide. Yet even the solace of suicide is denied her, for Talthybius restrains her. The play ends with the walls of Troy crashing down, probably the most unremittingly tragic sequence in the history of dramatic literature. Throughout the whole play, there is not one moment of humor. One longs for the gatekeeper in *Macbeth* or the gravediggers in *Hamlet*—anything to break the gloom.

Euripides could not have expected the Athenians to like this play, and much speculation has revolved around his motive for writing it. Its only saving dramatic grace is that Hecuba serves as an inspiring model of strength in the face of adversity—one cannot help but admire the old woman. Totally defeated and powerless, she somehow still finds the courage to provide emotional support for her fellow captives, and she bravely tries to seek revenge against Helen. That would be one justifiable goal of writing the play, yet most historians see another reason: Euripides was seeking to arouse the guilt of his fellow Athenians for their recent unjustified sack of the city of Melos—the Athenians had punished the city, whose only wish was to remain neutral in Athens's war with Sparta, by killing all the men and selling the women and children into slavery. The parallel between Troy and Melos was too clear to miss.

The Athenians, however, did not like Euripides' mirror. A few years later, Euripides left Athens, perhaps as a result of public pressure. He wandered for a time through Greece before settling at the court of King Archelaus of Macedonia, where, some years later, he was torn to pieces by a pack of dogs as he staggered home drunk from a party. Somehow, this was a fitting end to the bitter, angry, and caustic genius who saw too clearly the cruelty and brutality that was typical of Athens in the last years of the fifth century B.C.

ARISTOPHANES

Among the others in Athens who objected to the course the city was taking was Aristophanes (450–380 B.C.), who presented his objections in comedic dress. Comedic plays were as much a part of the yearly festivals as dramas, and Aristophanes contributed forty-four such works throughout his career. Many of his plays attack

Aristophanes is the only classical Greek comic playwright whose plays have survived. While much of his humor strikes the modern reader as slapstick and the plots of his plays are usually beyond the realm of possibility, most of them, even the most ribald, have a serious message.

Athens's participation in the war against Sparta or direct criticism toward Cleon, the political leader of Athens during the later days of the war. Cleon was a particularly violent man who manipulated the government by appealing to the baser instincts of the electorate.

In *The Knights*, Aristophanes attacks Cleon, the demagogue of Athens, using a character named Cleon the Leather Tanner. The fictional Cleon is the slave of Demus (a name that is an adaptation of the Greek word *demos*, meaning "the people"). Aristophanes presents Demus as slow-witted, easily led, and completely taken in by his unscrupulous slave Cleon, who steals him blind and confuses him over any number of details. The allusions to the Athenian government under the real Cleon were too clear to miss. At one point, two enemies of Cleon, Demosthenes and Nicias, try to enlist a butcher in a plot to undermine Cleon in the eyes of his master. When the butcher protests that he is too stupid to understand politics, Demosthenes and Nicias assure him that stupidity is an admirable qualification of politics, in fact a positive necessity of the craft.

Aristophanes' most famous play is *Lysistrata*, in which the women of Athens and Sparta, sick of the war, band together to refuse their husbands sexual favors until the men agree to a peace treaty. The leader of the Athenian "peace party" is Lysistrata, a humorous, earthy woman who organizes the women and keeps them to their task. She is the master of the double entendre, and the play is littered with such veiled references to sex and/or the male member as: "Do you grasp the meaning? Oh, yes it is thick with meaning." There is also slapstick throughout the show. At one point, the women barricade themselves on the Acropolis and defy the attempts of their husbands to get them to come down, pouring water on the men at every opportunity. Holding the Acropolis, the women also discover that they hold the treasury, and so the Athenians are hamstrung in their attempts to fight the war. Finally, in spite of many problems and threatened defections, the women bring the men to their senses. Diplomats from Sparta and Athens gather at Athens to agree on terms. Fearful that the men may prove difficult in the negotiations, Lysistrata arranges for a beautiful young woman, representing the goddess of peace, to stand naked before the men—who by now are desperate to end their enforced abstinence—as they negotiate. There is, needless

to say, a hurried conclusion of the terms of peace, the men are reunited with their women, and everyone goes off to make amends.

The fact that Aristophanes could use his plays to poke fun at both the political leaders of Athens and the foreign policy of the state demonstrates that ancient Athenians enjoyed a remarkable amount of freedom of speech, at least when it came to political matters. Although Athens was somewhat brutal as a ruler of an empire, it seems that citizens of the city itself were able to criticize and debate their country's policies without fearing any formal state action against them. This freedom was one of the greatest legacies that Athens left to the modern world.

History

The great literature of ancient Athens was not limited to theatrical works. The art of writing history also reached a new level of creativity in the work of Herodotus of Halicarnassus (480–420 B.C.) and Thucydides (c. 460–400 B.C.). Herodotus may well have been an inspiration for Thucydides; tradition holds that in about 445, when Herodotus was giving a public reading of his work on the Persian Wars at Athens, the young Thucydides was moved to tears and promised himself that one day he would also be an historian.

Herodotus was born in Halicarnassus, on the coast of Asia Minor. His father, Lyxes, and his uncle, the poet Panyasis, had both been political leaders of their home city, until their democracy was overthrown by the tyrant Lygdamis about 454 B.C.

For some reason, Herodotus left his home city and traveled to Athens, where he gained popularity by giving public readings of his work. Although he was not a native Athenian, the city was an inspiration for him because he loved its freedom, which stood in stark contrast to the tyranny he had experienced at home under Lygdamis. Being a nobleman, Herodotus moved in the very highest circles of Athenian society; he counted the powerful politician Pericles and the great Sophocles among his friends. About 443 B.C., he left Athens, possibly as the personal representative of Pericles, with a group of colonists who went settle in Thurii, on the southeastern

During antiquity many Greeks criticized the Greek historian Herodotus, the "Father of History," for being too sympathetic to the Persians. In reality, he was merely living up to his belief that an historian should be impartial.

coast of Italy. At Thurii, Herodotus wrote much of his history; during this time, he also traveled in Sicily and Italy, returning at least once to visit Athens. Sometime in his life—nobody is quite sure when—he visited most of the countries that border the eastern Mediterranean, traveling up the Nile as far as Elephantine, across the Tigris and Euphrates to Susa, the capital of Persia, and along the Black Sea coast to Colchis. All these places served as background for his great work *The History*.

What makes *The History* unique and gives Herodotus the title "Father of History" is that for the first time a his-torian chose to explore the reasons behind historical events, not just to present the events, and to write with a clear thesis: that the Persian Wars resulted from a clash of cultures between men who believed in freedom and those who allowed themselves to be ruled by one man. Although Herodotus occasionally diverges from his theme to tell this or that legend, he always returns to this thesis. Even though this makes him seem more or less modern in his method, there is an accompanying theme that firmly fixes him as a devout man of the ancient world. Herodotus firmly believed that the world was ruled by the gods, who helped those who respected the normal order of things and punished those who were impious, overly ambitious, or conceited.

Herodotus brought to his work at least two attitudes that have since become tenets of the historian's craft. First, he was impartial to a remarkable degree. Although he felt that the Greeks were the chosen of the gods, this did not prevent him from seeing admirable aspects in the Persians, respecting their bravery, and even praising aspects of their culture. He also recognized that the Greeks often did disreputable things, and freely stated these realizations—he was never a propagandist. One of the most famous passages attesting to this impartiality is that "an historian must be a stranger in his own land." Second, he took great care in citing his sources and trying to determine what was true. If he could not determine which source gave the true account, he said so.

Nevertheless, his book does contains many "tall tales," especially about lands on the edge of the known world. The most famous is the one about dog-sized domesticated ants that the Persians used to mine gold dust. Herodotus tells his readers that he does not believe such stories but reports them because "I have an obligation to record what people report to me, but I have no obligation to believe it. Let that be the basis for this history."

In the *History of the Peloponnesian War*, Thucydides, the second great historical talent of fifth-century Athens, certainly preserves the impartiality so prized by Herodotus. For instance, at one point in the narrative he reports that the admiral Thucydides was relieved of his command and exiled because he failed to take the city of Amphipolis. Nowhere does he mention that Thucydides of Amphipolis is in fact himself. He reported the incident without rancor or an alibi and accepted his exile quietly.

In fact, this exile served his purpose as an historian, for being free of involvement in Athens's war effort, he was able to visit Athens's enemies, including Sparta, her Peloponnesian allies, and Sicily, in search of material for his book. He returned to Athens in 404 B.C. under the general amnesty of the peace treaty. A few years later, however, he was killed by an assassin in unknown circumstances; he was buried in Athens.

Thucydides wrote his *History of the Peloponnesian War* because he anticipated the magnitude and historical importance of the war. This was a conflict between the ancient Greek equivalent of the mid-twentieth century's superpowers, and he believed that posterity would gain something by knowing about it, especially because he believed that human nature was constant and therefore what had happened once could certainly happen again. Fear was a great motivator, and he believed that the cause of the war was Sparta's fear of the growing power of Athens after the Persian Wars.

Perhaps his greatest observation, and the one that is most valuable with hindsight, is that the Peloponnesian War was decided neither by reason, by logic, nor by the actual military power of the two major combatants. The end was essentially the result of chance—the uncontrolled interplay of events. Although he may have been inspired by Herodotus to begin his career as an historian, Thucydides did not believe Herodotus's thesis that the gods play a role in the outcome of a war. For Thucydides wars were caused by men, and their outcomes depended on a throw of the dice.

Thucydides was not only a solid historian but also a fine stylist. His writing is, in and of itself, a masterpiece of grace, flow, and organization. One of the foremost historians of ancient Greece, N.G.L. Hammond, drew a memorable analogy about Thucydides: he said that the words of this ancient historian are like the blocks that form the Parthenon, in that they were deliberately shaped and fitted to give a precise effect in meaning and sound.

When Thucydides describes an event, he does so clearly and well. On occasion, he dramatizes a moment in history by putting a speech in an historical character's mouth. Often, as he himself admits, the speech is not what was actually said—indeed there may have not been a speech at all—but it is a way of emphasizing a particularly dramatic moment. When Thucydides grants a speech to the Spartan king Archidamus just before his army of Spartans and their allies begin their invasion of Attica (May 431 B.C.), he is careful to have the king review why the army is invading Attica, place the invasion in its historic context, warn his men about the potential power of Athens, condemn the Athenians for their aggressiveness, and caution his troops that victory is very much a matter of chance. In this short speech, we not only get an encapsulated summary of the war so far and its possible outcome, but we also get a repetition of Thucydides' favorite thesis that victory is a matter of chance. Like Athenian drama, Athenian history is always written with a clear message.

Thucydides was the famous historian of the Peloponnesian War between Athens and Sparta. Since the nineteenth century he has been considered the finest of the ancient historians.

Medicine

The inventive atmosphere that allowed great literature and history to flourish also encouraged science. Hippocrates of Cos (460–380 B.C.), the "Father of Medicine," would have agreed with Thucydides, who doubted the role of the gods in the political affairs of man, for Hippocrates doubted divine intervention as a cause for the diseases of man. His single greatest contribution to medicine was to see disease as a purely natural process. This attitude is evident in his famous analysis of epilepsy, wherein he states clearly that the gods have nothing to do with the disease. In this analysis, he accurately diagnosed epilepsy as a disorder of the brain and speculated that its cause was hereditary. He was also firm in his belief that the cure for the disease was to be found not in chants and prayer but in proper diet and lifestyle.

Hippocrates' treatments are usually logical, although his theories on causation are frequently in error. Take his analysis of hemorrhoids, for instance. He determined that their cause was an overabundance of bile and phlegm accumulated in the blood of the veins near the rectum. This, he said, heated the blood so that more blood from throughout the body was attracted to the area, and the veins, being unable to accommodate the extra blood, swelled out into the anal track in the form of nodules. As fecal matter passed by these nodules, it irritated them and caused bleeding. Although this may not have been exactly right, his suggested cure was somewhat "more scientific." Hippocrates recommended forcing open the rectum and burning the nodules off with a red-hot iron. He directs that the patient should be tied down, so that his movements do not disturb the operation, but he should be allowed to scream because screaming naturally

opens the rectum wider, giving the doctor better access to the inflicted area.

Perhaps Hippocrates' most famous contribution to the practice of medicine was his insistence on high ethical standards for physicians, as reflected in the famous Hippocratic Oath. Under this oath, physicians were (and are) enjoined to live a moral, ethical life, to do nothing harmful to patients, to keep confidences, and to treat patients and their families with respect. Physicians still work to accomplish these goals today, although elements of the oath have been dropped, for instance, the promises not to accept money for teaching medicine and to accept no students except for one's own sons and the sons of one's teachers. Other parts of the oath state that physicians should not operate to remove kidney stones from the bladder or try to seduce women or men while visiting the house of a patient. Although some have claimed that the Hippocratic Oath forbids physicians to perform abortions, in fact, it forbade only those abortions performed via insertion of a suppository. As far as we know, Hippocrates had no specific feelings against abortion, although one can question the safety and effectiveness of the methods he suggests. His favorite is the Lacedaemonian leap, which consists of repeatedly jumping high into the air and lifting the heels quickly up to the buttocks and then landing firmly on the ground on one's feet.

As strange and probably ineffective as some of Hippocrates' methods were, his recognition that disease is due to natural causes and his suggestion that it can be cured by rational treatment was a giant step in medicine.

Philosophy

During the same century that saw the rise of great drama, history, and medicine, Athens saw the first stirrings of that greatest study of mankind, philosophy, wherein man asks such important questions as where did we come from, where are we going, and why are we here. When we think of philosophy, we think of Plato and Aristotle, but these men were not part of Athens's golden age, and the impetus toward philosophy actually belongs to two others: Anaxagoras of Clazomenae (c. 500–428 B.C.) and Socrates (469–399 B.C.), who actually set the stage for Plato and Aristotle.

The earliest philosophical pioneer in Athens was Anaxagoras. This thinker came to Athens from Clazomenae, a town on the west coast of Asia Minor, between 480 and 456, and soon after his arrival, he had befriended well-known citizens of all stripes, from Pericles to a difficult stonecutter named Socrates. Although only fragments of his writings survive, there are enough to re-create the main parts of his philosophical system. The basis of Anaxagoras's system was a theory that the world is made up of matter, which in turn is made up of an infinite number of particles that are in turn infinitely divisible and different. The objects of the world

Dozens of stories surround the activities of Hippocrates, an exceptional physician. One is that he ended the great plague of Athens by ordering great fires lit throughout the city. Another is that he traveled to Rome to practice medicine.

ANAXAGORE.

point had existed as a great, single, undifferentiated mass. This movement caused the great mass of matter to fly apart, combine, and fly apart again in different combinations so that all the things of the universe were formed. Everything from the sun and the moon to the creations of nature are therefore nothing more than accidentally formed arrangements of matter.

Anaxagoras's universe had no place for gods, and that may have gotten him in trouble. About 433 B.C., he was accused of impiety because his philosophy seemed to deny the existence of the Greek gods. He was acquitted through the intervention of his friends, but he had to leave Athens. He emigrated to Lampsacus, at the western end of the Dardanelles, where he died at the age of seventy-two. In a sense, it was he who got the philosophical ball rolling.

The man who "caught the ball" was Anaxagoras's friend Socrates. He was by all reports a difficult and unique individual whose greatest gift seemed to be framing questions that made people angry. Some people have speculated that his difficult nature had something to do with the shrewishness of his wife, Xantippe, who supposedly made his home a living hell. Most probably, however, Socrates had a higher motivation for his thorny and irksome questions—he really was in search of the truth. He was rebelling against the teachings of the sophists, a group of intellectuals who denied that there was any discernible meaning to life—an idea that Socrates vehemently disagreed with. The sophists taught that we can know nothing for certain, for knowledge comes to us through our senses; Socrates, however, believed that this message was too imperfect to depend on. The most famous of the sophists, Protagoras (490–420 B.C.), who lived in Athens as a contemporary of Socrates, taught that nothing was true. Truth, he said, resided only in the individual, and what was true for that individual was true only for that individual. This was an attitude that Socrates could not abide, and he set out to prove the sophists wrong and to discover what the truth really was.

Socrates began by assuming nothing and then attempting to learn by building on everyday specifics and examples. He wandered throughout Athens questioning everyone from Pericles down to the lowest sod carrier. If his subject used the word "justice," for instance, Socrates questioned him to discover exactly what he meant by the

An eighteenth-century print portrays Anaxagoras of Clazomenae, the first philosopher at Athens, who offered an early theory of the origin of the universe.

are made up of these particles in different combinations, and it is these combinations that account for the diversity of things around us. The one exception to this matter-particle concept is *nous*, or Mind, which is unmixed with any other particles and is therefore pure and can exist by itself. This concept allowed Anaxagoras to make his speculation on cosmology, the origins of the universe. According to him, the universe came into being when Mind, acting as the first cause, created movement, which in turn caused movement within matter, which up to this

word. This is called inductive argument: taking specific examples and examining them in detail to find universal truths. He took numerous examples of justice, for instance, and from them created a universal concept of justice applicable to all instances.

Certainly, many people he questioned must have thought he was playing with them, for his close questioning of their every word was irritating. But from this irritating method Socrates determined that knowledge led to virtue and hence to what was right. He firmly believed that evil could be cured by learning what was right, teaching it, and, if anyone asked, proving it. Unfortunately, his constant quest for knowledge from other people convinced him that although a few people knew something of importance, most people did not. That in turn led him to the belief that his fellow Athenians were incapable of making the right decisions in the important business of governing. He did not hesitate to make this opinion

known, and in time it earned him enemies. The specifics are not clear, but eventually some of his enemies were able to get him accused of impiety and corrupting the youth of Athens. When the court found him guilty and sentenced him to death, he accepted the verdict and refused to try and escape from Athens to avoid the penalty—one of the truths he had discovered was that a man had a duty to his city, and it was incumbent on that man to obey its laws, even if those laws decreed his death.

The dramatic nature of his death inspired his friends to continue along his path to the truth. Plato, one of his pupils, began this movement, and Aristotle continued it. Although both men came up with philosophies that were radically different from that of Socrates, they both saw Socrates as a noble example, and they both learned much from his methods. Indeed, it is only through their writings that we are able to learn anything about Socrates, for throughout his whole life, he never wrote anything down.

In Jacques Louis David's famous painting *The Death of Socrates*, Socrates is shown about to drink the poison that was the means of capital punishment in ancient Athens. Even though, according to legend, his disciples had arranged for his escape, he refused to take this way out because, true to his philosophical principles, he had respect for the laws of Athens.

A view from the south side of the Acropolis looks up toward the west end of the Parthenon. The Acropolis was a high rocky mass that stood in the center of Athens. Originally it was a place of refuge in time of danger, and it continued to fulfill this function throughout the history of the city. In time, however, the Athenians beautified the Acropolis and placed some of their most sacred buildings on top of it, including the Parthenon, the Erechtheum, and the Propylaea.

Architecture and Art

he glory of Athens after the Persian Wars was not confined to the intellectual triumphs of her people. The architecture and sculpture with which the city was decorated were just as magnificent. When the Persians took over Athens for a short time before the Battle of Salamis, they burned a good portion of the city and its civic and religious buildings. Afterward, in the full flush of victory, the Athenians determined to rebuild their city on a grander scale than ever. At first, they used the resources of Athens and the revenues of the silver mines of Laurium to finance this reconstruction. But it was not long before they began to use the tribute that the subject cities of the Delian League paid into the league treasury—money that supposedly went to protect Greece from Persia.

Pericles decided to make the Acropolis the showplace of Athens, and during his rule, he spent lavishly to decorate this area. The masterpieces of his spending spree were the Erechtheum, a temple dedicated to Athena and Poseidon; the Propylaea, the entryway into the sacred precinct atop the Acropolis, through which religious processions passed; and the Parthenon, the great temple to Athena, the protector of the city. All these buildings are triumphs of architecture, but the most perfect example of architecture in the golden age of Athens is the Parthenon.

The Parthenon was designed by two architects, Ictinus and Callicrates, between 447 and 433 B.C. The design of this building, which was dedicated to Athena Parthenus, or the Virgin Athena, was simplicity itself: two rooms arranged back to back to form a rectangle called the *cella*. The larger room, called the *naos*, or sanctuary, held the statue of the goddess. The other room, called *theoposthodomos*, or treasury, is located directly behind the naos but is accessible only through its own door on the west end of the temple. This room is where the city's treasury and the tribute money of the Delian League were kept. The cella is surrounded by marble columns, eight on each end and seventeen along each side.

The foundation of the Parthenon is a flat platform of marble, called the *stylobate*, that measures 228 feet by 101 feet (69.49m x 30.78m). The columns rest on this platform and support the roof, which rises 78 feet (23.77m) into the air. Perhaps the most interesting fact about the Parthenon's design is that the stylobate and the columns are constructed with horizontal and vertical deviations to help correct optical illusions. Had the stylobate been built to lie absolutely level and the columns been erected absolutely vertically, the temple would have appeared distorted to the eye—the edges of the stylobate would have seemed to dip in the middle and the columns would have seemed to lean outward. To correct this, the stylobate is 4.25 inches (10.79cm) higher in the center than at the sides and the columns lean inward 2.26 inches (5.73cm) off vertical. The result of these deliberate errors is that the Parthenon appears to be built with perfect right angles.

The Parthenon was constructed of the whitest Pentelic marble and must have gleamed with a striking brightness in the light of the moon or the sun, making for a stunningly beautiful building. This simple beauty and magnificence were enhanced by sculpture and reliefs that were a stone textbook of mythology and Athenian religious life.

On the east end of the temple was a triangular pediment, much of which is now in the British Museum, decorated with the monumental sculptures of Phidias, which recounted the birth of the goddess Athena. Legend has it that she sprang full grown from the head of her father, Zeus, after he had devoured her mother, Metis, because of a prophecy foretelling that Metis would bear a son who would grow to be more famous than his father. Most of this sculpture does not survive, but we do have a number of descriptions of it. Apparently, there was a statue of Helios (the Sun) driving his horses up over the horizon; a monumental figure of Theseus, an early king of Athens; and statues of Iris, the special messenger of Zeus, and Hebe, the goddess of youth. After Phidias finished these sculptures, painters colored them to make them lifelike. More than one ancient observer wrote that the musculature under the clothing and the stance of the figures made it seem as if they were just at the moment of initiating movement.

The equally impressive western pediment, now gone, portrayed the contest between Athena and Poseidon to see who would watch over the city of Athens. In ancient Greece, it was customary for each city to have a particular divine protector. According to legend, Athens, in the earliest days, had no such patron deity. The gods competed

In Greek a *propylon* is a stone gateway, but in Athens there is only one Propylaea, the famous entrance to the Acropolis. It was designed by the architect Mnesicles and built between 436–432 B.C., during the height of Pericles' power.

for the honor of ruling such a fine city by offering advantages to the citizens. Poseidon, noticing that there was little water in Attica, promised a copious supply of water if the people would choose him, and he struck the ground with his trident to bring forth a spring of fresh water to show his potential. Athena, on the other hand, promised the people immense wealth through cultivation of the olive tree, a plant that was sacred to her. The burghers of Athens, knowing the mercurial and violent nature of Poseidon and the contrasting gentleness and sweetness of Athena, chose the goddess. Before he left, the angry Poseidon cursed the spring, making it produce only foul-smelling, bad-tasting water. On the pediment, Athena and Poseidon were sculpted in a pose as if struggling, with their rearing horses on either side restrained by the lesser goddesses Nike and Amphitrite.

The drapery on the figures of both pediments was sculpted in a new style: the folds were cut more deeply than ever before so that when light and shadow play off the folds, they appear to be moving.

The sculptures of the Parthenon, however, were not and are not confined to the pediment. Below the cornice of the pediment was the *architrave*, the top half of which was decorated with 92 *metopes*, small squares of stone measuring about 5.7 inches (37cm) square with relief sculptures on them. These metopes, which were separated by *triglyphs* of similar size and ran all the way around the temple, portrayed various scenes from Greek mythology. Those on the east side show battles between gods and giants, and those on the west dramatize the mythological struggle of Athens with the Amazons. The metopes on the north side show scenes of the Trojan War, and those on the south portray the battle between the Centaurs and the Lapithae (mythical early inhabitants of Greece). The quality of the carving on the metopes varies—some are clearly the work of novices, others are true masterpieces—for they represent many hands working under the general direction of Phidias.

The sculpted masterpiece of the Parthenon's exterior is the frieze that runs along the top of the outer wall of the cella. Most of this sculpture still exists, either on the building itself or in various museums. Despite centuries of damage and neglect, the sculpture remains impressive to this day. It originally extended 525 feet (160m) and

The Erechtheum just north of the Parthenon on the Acropolis housed a number of sacred objects and places. Inside there was a statue of Athena Polias, the spot where Poseidon's trident struck the ground and produced a saltwater spring, and altars to Poseidon and Hephaestus, plus ones commemorating Cecrops and Erechtheus, early mythical kings of Athens. It was built between 421 and 407 B.C. A detail of the porch is shown on page 10.

showed the details of the Panthenaic Festival. This ceremony, which took place every four years, celebrated the gift of a new robe *(peplos)* to the goddess Athena. The frieze began on the west side of the Parthenon, where it showed people gathering and forming a procession. In this scene, some figures fiddle with their robes, while others tighten their sandal straps. Also present are the parade marshals, who keep order and make certain the marchers do not bunch together as they start moving. In the next scenes—on the north and south walls—the marchers pass through the Propylaea, the entrance to the Acropolis, on the way to the Parthenon. At the head of the procession are the priests and political leaders of Athens, followed by maidens carrying baskets of food on their heads. Next come the foreign residents of Athens carrying baskets of fruit and cakes; they are anxious to make offerings to Athena for the good fortune they have had in the city. At first glance, many of the basket-carrying figures seem to be merely the same sculpture repeated over and over again, with the same clothes and the same type of basket, but closer inspection reveals that the figures have a slightly different tilt to the head or a minutely varying grasp on their jars. Such details are surely the work of the master Phidias or of some of his best students. Then there are the sacrificial goats and cattle, followed by horsemen—

the cavalry of Athens, made up of young men from the city's wealthiest families. Many of the horse sculptures at one time had bridles and accoutrements made from bronze and attached to the sculpture. The final scene of the frieze, on the east wall, depicts Athena seated with her divine guests, awaiting the arrival of her worshipers. As with most of the sculpture on the Parthenon, there is the illusion that the figures have stopped for just a moment and are about to shift their weight forward to begin moving again. Originally, each figure was brightly painted against a background of blue.

The magnificence of the Parthenon does not stop with the exterior; the dimly lighted interior has and had its own grandeur. Inside the naos stood the great statue of Athena Parthenus. Although the statue has not survived the centuries, there are numerous descriptions by ancient visitors that tell us what it looked like. Counting its carved pedestal, which bore a relief depicting the legend of Pandora, this most famous work of Phidias stood between 29.5 and 39.4 feet (9 and 12m) high. In her left hand, the goddess held a spear, and leaning against the spear was the huge round shield of Zeus depicting the fight between the Greeks and the Amazons. One of the figures was carved in the likeness of Phidias, an act that led some to accuse him of impiety. Draped around the

Athena is shown emerging from the head of Zeus. Having learned of a prophecy that any son born to Metis would be greater than the father, Zeus swallowed Metis to prevent the birth of a rival. A short time later he began to suffer from a monumental headache and asked the blacksmith god Hephaestus to relieve the pain by splitting his head open. When Hephaestus complied, out popped Athena.

neck of the goddess was the *aegis*, a goatskin with the head of the Gorgon on it. When Zeus shook the aegis, it brought the thunder, and he entrusted it to Athena as a special sign of his favor.

The body of the goddess was made of ivory. Athena's floor-length gown was made of sheets of cast gold attached to the figure with pegs, so that in time of financial crisis, they could be removed and melted down—ancient Athenians were devout, but they were also practical. Ancient sources report that the gown weighed 44 talents, or about 2,547 pounds (1,154kg).

Directly in front of the statue was a shallow pool of water designed to reflect whatever light came into the temple from the east doorway—there was no other source of illumination inside the building. The perpetual lack of lighting, however, was not a hardship; it was, in fact,

desirable, because it contributed to the atmosphere of reverence and awe. Besides, no public religious ceremonies took place inside the temple. All actual ceremonies took place outside, on an altar in front of the temple. The inside of the temple was reserved for the priests and for those people who wanted to make a private appeal to Athena. The sanctuary was also a refuge for fugitives, and it was considered a great sacrilege to remove forcibly from the temple anyone who had sought the goddess's protection.

The great statue of Athena guaranteed Phidias a position as one of Greece's greatest artists. The beauty and perfection of the temple had been made possible by his ability, combined with the tremendous wealth of the Athenian state. But both Phidias and the vast expenditures had their critics, and these naysayers were determined to bring Phidias down. While he was in the process of creating the great statue, a small amount of gold and ivory designated for its construction disappeared from his workshop. His enemies used this fact to bring his honesty into question and indirectly to attack Pericles and his policies. Phidias was tried, found guilty of both impiety (the self-portrait on the shield) and theft, and fined the enormous amount of 40 talents (about a ton of gold). Happily, the people of Elis, a small city-state on the west coast of Greece, offered to pay his fine if the artist would move there and build a great temple to Zeus at Olympia. Phidias accepted their offer and, perhaps as revenge, created a temple and statue to Zeus that outshone the Parthenon. By common consensus, this new temple came to be considered one of the seven wonders of the ancient world.

Athenian society under Pericles excelled not only in drama, architecture, and sculpture, but also in painting. The fifth century B.C. was the great age of painters in Athens, for it was a basic tenet of architecture and sculpture that statues would be painted and walls would be covered with vast murals. Unfortunately, with the exception of a single splotch of blue paint at Delphi, probably from the brush of Agatharchus (flourished 440–410 B.C.), absolutely nothing remains of their work. Happily, a fairly large number of descriptions of their works does survive, along with biographies of the painters.

Painting in this era existed in three forms: tempera, where paint mixed with the whites of eggs was applied to boards or damp cloth; fresco, in which the artist applied the paint to wet plaster; and encaustic, wherein the paint was mixed with wax. One of the earliest painters to use all three mediums was Polygnotus of Thasos (fl. 490–460 B.C.), who arrived in Athens about 472 B.C. He became a friend of Cimon, one of the rising political stars in Athens, and seduced his sister, Elpinice, whose face he painted into several of his works. Apparently, Cimon had no hard feelings about the seduction, for he helped Polygnotus get a commission to paint some large murals on the walls of the Stoa, the large public marketplace in the Agora at the foot of the Acropolis. These paintings depicted the Sack of Troy, the battle between the Amazons and the Athenians, and the Battle of Marathon. Polygnotus's painting of the Sack of Troy was unique because instead of painting the wild carnage of the nighttime attack on the city, he decided to paint the morning after—a panorama of exhausted Greek soldiers and piles of corpses. Later, he went to Delphi and painted a huge fresco of Odysseus in the underworld and another treatment of the Sack of Troy—this time dealing with the captured Trojan women, one of whom, Laodicea, has the face of Elpinice. The painting in Athens may have inspired Euripides to write *The Trojan Women*—the chief "drama" of the painting is the hateful gazes that the Trojan women direct at Helen. Like many of these new painters, Polygnotus was adept at painting expressions, which apparently was an innovation of the era.

Another well-known painter of the period was Agatharchus, who got his start painting scenery for some

of the plays written by Aeschylus and Sophocles. Through the medium of stage painting, he pioneered a new style called chiaroscuro, in which the painter uses contrasts of light and shade to produce the illusion of depth. This was possibly the first step toward the achievement of perspective, although true perspective, with one precise vanishing point, was several centuries in the future.

The most famous painters of the time were Parrhasius of Ephesus and Zeuxis of Heraclea, both of whom worked in Athens between 430 and 390 B.C. Their exploits were infamous, and some of their paintings of women in "see-through" dresses shocked the older generation of Athenians. Most people, however, seemed to tolerate these artists' exploits in much the same way that modern people accept the Bohemian lifestyle of some painters today.

Zeuxis specialized in painting panels instead of huge murals; he adopted the chiaroscuro technique of Agatharchus, while his rival Parrhasius painted murals and some portraits. Parrhasius also painted small erotic pictures, which he said "relieved him." One such work, a picture of Meleager making love to Atalanta, survived for more than four hundred years and eventually became the favorite painting of the Roman emperor Tiberius (r. A.D. 14–37). Parrhasius was also famous for a huge fresco entitled *Demos (The People)*. In this work, he supposedly painted facial expressions with such skill that all who saw

Above: The sides of this *kylix* are decorated with a picture of Athena supervising Odysseus and other Greek heroes drawing lots for the armor of Achilles. The figure behind Odysseus is Ajax.

Left: A fifth-century B.C. Athenian red-figure *krater* (a bowl used for mixing wine and water) shows Greek youths preparing for athletic contests.

it marveled at the range of human emotions depicted. Legend has it that Parrhasius was fascinated with faces. He wandered the city studying faces, and he even went so far as to buy a slave and have the poor man tortured just to study the facial expressions peculiar to agony and pain; not surprisingly, this act got him into trouble with the city government, which had strict laws against mistreatment of slaves.

According to the Roman historian Pliny, Zeuxis and Parrhasius eventually had a contest to decide, once and for all, who was the best painter. As his entry, Zeuxis exhibited a painting of grapes that was so realistic that a bird tried to peck at the fruit. Seeing this, Parrhasius acknowledged the greatness of that painting and invited Zeuxis to step across the room and lift the curtain covering his own entry. When Zeuxis tried to do this, he found that the curtain was Parrhasius's painting. Pliny says that Zeuxis saw the humor in the situation and cheerfully acknowledged Parrhasius as the best painter.

Although none of these masters' paintings survive, their work did have an indirect influence on the paintings that decorated the famous Attic red on black, or red-figure, pottery, which was popular during the fifth century

F rom a very early time Athenian artists produced exceptional pottery ware, such as this example of Attic black-figure ware, which predates the period of Pericles by a hundred years. The two men are placing bolts of cloth on a scale.

B.C. as kitchenware. The figures done in red allowed a skilled artist to use darker colored lines to express the emotion of the figures, just the sort of thing that Zeuxis, Parrhasius, Polygnotus, and Agatharchus were doing in their larger formal paintings.

The Attic red on black ware was also unique in its subject matter. Although artists continued to decorate pots with mythological scenes, this era marked a movement toward portraying everyday scenes. For the first time, we see real people in everyday activities. There are vases featuring acrobats, dinner parties, soldiers, jugglers, lute players, and women combing their hair. There are even quite a large number of artworks that convey a message, such as the one done on the inside of a wine cup showing a young woman, probably a wife, holding the head of a young man throwing up on her feet—a visual invitation to temperance.

People throughout the Mediterranean recognized Attic red on black ware for its artistic merit, and it quickly became the pottery of choice for people of means. The Athenians exported it in bulk and also sold their high-quality olive oil in it.

Everyday Life

T he daily life of Athens is as fascinating as the city's artistic and cultural triumphs. The key to understanding ancient Athenian society lies in the degree to which it was a world dominated by men. More so than most of the Greek city-states, Athens relegated women to a secondary status far below that of women in Egypt in the New Kingdom centuries before and much below that in contemporary Sparta. Women were isolated in the *gynaeceum*, a special place in the rear of an Athenian home where visitors never ventured. Wives and daughters alike were isolated as completely from their society as Oriental women were in their harem. Shopping was done by the man of the house or his slaves, and on those occasions when women left the house to visit relatives or female friends, they were always heavily veiled and accompanied by a male relative. The freedom that Athenian men prided most was not something their wives shared. There do not even seem to have been close relationships between men and

women at home. Athenian men found companionship with other men, and their attitude toward women is neatly summed up in this famous quotation from Demosthenes, a fourth-century B.C. Athenian politician: "We have *hetairai* [prostitutes] for pleasure, concubines for health, and wives to bear legitimate offspring."

At the age of six or seven, boys left the care of their mothers and entered fully into the male world. They went to school with males, exercised in the male-dominated gymnasium, and went with their fathers to watch the debates in the law courts and to attend assembly. They rarely saw women, in the flesh or otherwise; even the sculpture viewed by fifth-century B.C. Athenian boys was almost exclusively male. Women stayed at home and managed the house.

Marriages of the time almost made the bride seem superfluous. They were arranged at every level of Athenian society, the primary requirement being that the bride and groom must both be Athenian citizens. A marriage between an Athenian male and a non-Athenian female was nothing better than concubinage, and a marriage between an Athenian woman and a non-Athenian male was simply unthinkable. Furthermore, the bride's father had to supply a dowry, for women were of such little worth that a male literally had to be bribed to marry. The fathers of two socially compatible families, often tied together by friendship, would make the arrangements. For men, the ideal marrying age was thirty; for women, it was fifteen.

Most weddings took place during the month of Gamelion, roughly the period between January 15 and February 15, and were preceded by formalized rites called *proteleia*. These rites included prayers to Hera, the protector of marriage, and a visit by the bride and her family to the Acropolis and the Parthenon, where they prayed for the favor of Athena and made an appropriate sacrifice. Only after these things had been accomplished did the two families meet for a formal exchange of the dowry, which took place at the bride's home, with witnesses present. A few days later, the marriage ceremony took place.

On the day of the wedding, the bride and the groom each sent a trusted friend to collect water from the spring at Callirrhoe, a few miles outside Athens. When both bride and groom had bathed in this water, the wedding ceremony could begin. At the bride's home, her father offered as sacrifice a cow or goat, depending on his wealth.

An essential part of this sacrifice involved burning the gall of the animal to ensure a lack of discord in the marriage. After the sacrifice came the banquet, for which much of the meat came from the sacrifice. This banquet was one of the few times in Greek social life when women and men ate together in groups. The men sat on one side of the room, the women on the other. After toasts and feasting, the couple, accompanied by the maid of honor and the best man, mounted a cart drawn by donkeys or oxen and traveled to the groom's home. The bride's mother trailed along behind the cart with two torches symbolizing the union. She was followed by a throng made up of relatives and friends who sang songs accompanied by flutes. One peculiar custom of this procession was a young

An Athenian red-figure vase shows two women preparing for a wedding. The girl on the left appears to be the bride, while the other woman seems to be holding up a mirror for her.

boy who wandered among the guests carrying a basket of cakes that he distributed as he chanted, "I fled evil to find a better lot." The significance of this custom is unknown.

Once the wedding party reached the groom's home, the couple got off the cart, and the groom carried the bride through a doorway decked with green branches. There she met her new in-laws, who welcomed her to the family and introduced her to the household gods. This accomplished, the wedding throng came into the house and showered the couple with presents, after which the bride ate a quince, symbolizing fertility. At this point there was usually a light supper, from which the bride slipped away to the bridal chamber. Soon afterward, the groom's friends led him to the bedroom door and remained outside, drinking, chanting, and singing until he opened the door to announce that the marriage was consummated.

The next day the relatives would gather at the groom's house to offer gifts and congratulations. Finally, a few days later, the last event of the wedding would be held: the male members of both families gathered for a banquet given by the groom's family.

In Athens, the new bride's only real purpose and responsibility was procreation. She might manage her house, but she was forbidden to make a contract or incur debts except for those related to basic household expenses. Even her role in procreation was diminished by the belief that children were fully formed in the male sperm, and the female served only as an incubator.

At the very end of the fifth century B.C., however, there was a change in marriage customs, brought about by the abnormally high casualties among the Athenian male population in the Peloponnesian War. Starting in 415, the Athenians began to suffer military defeats that threatened the stability of their society. As perhaps a quarter of the city's young fighting men perished in various military disasters, women were left widows in droves. The government recognized the seriousness of the situation by creating laws that sanctioned marriages between one man and two women. On a more practical level, widows, out of necessity, began to take greater control over their families and their households. It is no coincidence that it was about this time that the women in Greek drama became more than mere subjects to be manipu-

O n a red-figure kylix, Athenian women put on perfume and arrange flowers. Perhaps the woman who is seated is a bride to be, and the other women are her attendants.

lated. But an increasingly responsible role for women in Athenian society was still far in the future.

The average Athenian home was a humble, some would say squalid, dwelling. This was due in large part to the fact that its walls were built of "rammed earth." To construct such walls, the householder placed two parallel walls of wooden boards about 18 inches (45cm) apart and filled the space between with damp earth interlaced with loose straw. Periodically, he would take a heavy square beam and tamp the earth down, gradually building up an earthen wall. Finally, the boards would be removed, leaving only the earthen wall. The only wooden parts of the house were the doors and the window openings. This made robbing a house quite easy, for a burglar did not need to force the door—he could simply kick in the wall. Nevertheless, such break-ins were rare, for the simple reason that the average Athenian had very little of value in his house.

The interior of the house had an earthen floor, and perhaps the walls were plastered. The walls were usually whitewashed, and the floor had a rush mat on it. Furniture was sparse. There were a few chairs, and perhaps one or two three-legged tables called *trapezai*, used mainly for eating, along with a chest or two. In Greece, there was little need for heating a home, and if there was, people carried a small portable brazier from room to room.

The heart of the Athenian home was the kitchen. All cooking was done over an open fire built in a corner; cookware was made of iron or earthenware. The family ate two meals a day, and they generally ate together, but if there was a guest, the women retired into a room behind the kitchen. The main diet of the Athenian family was uninspiring but healthy. Grain, eaten in the form of flat loaves, porridge, and cakes sweetened with honey, was the basis of the diet. At most meals, the grain was helped along with figs, olive oil, grapes, and wine, and sometimes eggs. When it came to vegetables, the Athenian was limited to beans, peas, lettuce, onions, and cabbage. Salted fish was often added to this diet; beef was almost never eaten, except at the great festivals of the year, and on the rare occasions when other types of flesh were eaten, pork was usually the meat of choice. The people drank wine with every meal but always cut it with water, usually in a proportion of eight parts water to one part wine. It was considered barbarous to drink undiluted wine. At formal

dinner parties, the proportion of water might be three to one, but it was rarely any stronger than that.

Among the wealthier members of Athenian society, there might be differences in houses and in what was served to eat, but these differences were slight because it was considered inconsistent with the principles of democracy to advertise wealth. A rich man might have a house built with sun-dried bricks instead of rammed earth; in such a case, his house might even have a second story. There might even be a fountain or a shallow pool in an open courtyard immediately inside the front door. Inside, the walls would be plastered and whitewashed, and the furniture might include couches, made with an armrest on one end and laced with leather springs. During meals, males might recline on these couches, but the rest of the family sat in chairs or on stools. Additions to the table of a wealthy Athenian might include fresh fish instead of the

An Athenian vase from about 540 B.C. records a portion of a famous legend about Bacchus, the god of wine. Pirates had captured the young god and tied him to the mast of their ship and insulted him. When Bacchus finally became angry, he burst his bonds and magically turned the mast into a giant grapevine. The terrified pirates jumped overboard, and Bacchus changed them all into porpoises.

salted variety, perhaps a variety of cheeses, and more honey for sweetening.

The healthy diet of the Athenian certainly contributed to what was an exceptionally long life span, as demonstrated by the ages at death of many famous Athenian residents: Aeschylus, 71; Antisthenes, 90; Aristophanes, 62; Euripides, 80; Gorgias, 100; Herodotus, 64; Isocrates, 98; Miltiades, 69; Pasion, 61; Protogoras, 70; Socrates, 70; Sophocles, 91; and Xenophone, 76. We do not know about the average age or life span for women—nobody thought it important enough to preserve records of their life spans—but they probably lived nearly as long as men, allowing for the risk of childbirth.

For most of the golden age, the typical Athenian man spent much of his time in the company of other men, interacting with others at work, in the vibrant social center of Athens, or in the center of political affairs. He arose early in the morning, straightened the woolen *chiton* in which he had slept, ate a quick breakfast of bread and olives, and hurried to the Agora. He did not bathe often, for water was scarce and only the very wealthiest had bathing facilities in the house.

The Agora was at the very heart of Athenian politics, and Pericles had made involvement in politics both profitable and desirable by beginning the practice of paying citizens for performing the civic duties for which only the wealthy had previously had time. After Pericles' reforms, the state paid Athenians to perform jury duty, serve in the *boule*, or council, and carry out a number of other government duties. All Athenian male citizens could be members of the Assembly, the fundamental governing body of the city, and the state paid any citizen to attend its sessions: a drachma and a half for attending the boring regular sessions, but

A fine example of mid-sixth-century B.C. black-figure ware from Vulci in Italy features scenes of women gathered around the fountain, talking. This type of vessel, fitted with three handles (the third is on the back side of the vase), is known as a *hydria*. A hydria had a tight-fitting top and was used to carry water home from the public fountain.

only a drachma for attending a session deemed exciting or significant. Pericles also established the "theoric fund," out of which a citizen might draw a stipend to attend the festivals of Athens. As many as half of the male citizens of Athens may have drawn a salary from the public treasury of Athens during the empire period. When one considers these financial inducements along with the physical beauty of Athens and the generally mild climate, it is no wonder that Athenian men spent most of their lives outside, participating in some way in the local government.

The business of Athens was politics, and politics required social interaction on a grand scale. From dawn to dusk, Athenian males were in the Agora at this special "work." Usually the business was routine, but occasionally something really exciting happened. Often, at the end of a chief magistrate's tenure, his enemies might organize an ostracism vote. In this uniquely Athenian custom, the citizens would inscribe the official's name on a pottery fragment called an *ostrakon* (from which the word *ostracize* is derived). Should an official get a majority of votes, he was banished from the city for ten years. This custom was intended to be a check on excessively ambitious politicians; in reality, however, it became yet another tool in the battles between political rivals.

Women, of course, were absent from the Agora—except for the special class of prostitutes called the *hetairai*. These women were easily identified by their brightly colored flowery *peplos* (shawls), makeup, and assured manners. Their style and manners stood in sharp contrast to the other women of Athens, who scurried around the city dressed drably with their faces heavily veiled. The hetairai were the highest class of prostitutes in Athens. They were strictly differentiated by dress, background, and education from the regular whores, called *pornai*, who lived in special houses in Piraeus, the port city of Athens. Most hetairai were Athenian citizens who had rebelled against the traditional strictures placed on Athenian women. By one means or another, they had found the money to maintain a separate home, pick up at least a smattering of education, and cultivate refined and elegant manners. Although most hetairai were brunettes, they generally dyed their hair blond, for Athenian men found that color particularly attractive. In Athens's male-dominated society, the hetairai were the only women who mixed with men in anything approaching equality. Hetairai were the only women present at formal dinner parties, where they were included in the give and take of the conversation. The most famous hetaira was Aspasia, the consort of Pericles, who, according to tradition, was his political advisor. She is even supposed to have written his speeches, including the famous Funeral Oration of 430 B.C.

As most modern readers know, the Athenian male, like his Greek contemporaries in the rest of the peninsula, involved himself romantically not only with the hetairai but also with other men. The modern world has had trouble accepting this aspect of life in ancient Greece. Although formally censured in the law of Athens, love affairs between men, usually with quite a difference in age, were the norm. Plato makes this clear in the *Symposium* and even holds homosexual love as superior to heterosexual love. Some historians have speculated that this is due to the abnormally low position women held in Athenian society, which exempted them from any meaningful intellectual relationship with men. This seems an unlikely reason, however, because tolerance of homosexual love existed even in Sparta, where women traditionally held a much higher status than in Athens.

If the Athenian male did not choose to spend his day "politicking" in the Agora, he would certainly spend it engaged in business—Athenians were known throughout the ancient world as consummate businessmen. Athenians had become successful in business out of necessity: the peninsula of Attica produced only about a third of the food her population needed, and Athens turned to trade to survive. Her main export was olive oil shipped to destinations throughout the Mediterranean in the incomparable red on black Attic ware. Her main imported goods were grain, timber, and slaves. The commercial activity of Athens was further enhanced by her

coinage. In a time when most Greek city-states purposely adulterated their coins with base metals, the Athenians issued coins that contained 98 percent silver. This purity was facilitated by Athenian control of the silver mines at Laurium, on the very tip of the Attic peninsula. These mines were the richest in Europe. Its level of purity made Athenian coinage acceptable anywhere in the Mediterranean and even beyond—Athenian silver coins were honored even as far away as India.

The basic Athenian coin was the *tetradrachmon*, the four-*drachma* piece. A drachma was further divided into coins known as *obols*, which were issued in various denominations down to the *tetratemorion*, or one-quarter-obol piece. Below obols there were copper coins called *obeliskoi*, eight of which equaled a silver obol. Obols and

An Athenian *hetaira*, or high-class prostitute, adjusts her sandal strap. There was a great deal of difference between a hetaira and a *porne*, or simple whore. The term *hetaira* implied a degree of education and charm that men paid high prices for.

obeliskoi were what Athens went shopping with—a day's supply of bread and olives could be purchased for three or four obeliskoi—and because they did not have pockets in their chitons and peplos, Athenians carried their small change in their mouths. A day's wage for a skilled artisan, such as a stonecutter working on the Parthenon, was one drachma; the daily wage for an unskilled worker was three obols. A man and his family could just get by on about 40 drachmas a month, while 120 drachmas a month would support a family on the upper end of the social scale.

Because the city was so dedicated to commerce, it soon developed a formal banking system. The system was informally initiated by the professional money changers who specialized in exchanging the varied coinage of Greece. From there it was an easy step to lending money at interest, an act that the philosophers condemned as immoral, and then to acting as a depository for money. In a short time, the money changers gained associates in other parts of Greece and were therefore able to facilitate the transfer of funds or credit via letters of credit. Because they were experts in financial matters, the money changers began to function as commercial attorneys: they witnessed contracts, oversaw transfers of property, and drew up business agreements. Banking in a town as commercial as Athens was an important activity, but most Athenian citizens believed it was beneath them, so banking was the domain of resident aliens or freemen. Interestingly, a freeman known as Pasion (430–369 B.C.) served Athens so well in financial matters that the city granted him citizenship.

Politics, trade, and banking, however, were not the only industries in Athens; there was of course a great deal of blue-collar activity. Athens was filled with workshops large and small. The largest one we know of employed 120 workers to produce shields; the smallest, a shoe factory, had six employees. These factories, however, were not owned or operated by Athenian citizens, for there was just a hint of disdain toward an Athenian who owned or worked in a factory. Athenian citizens believed that work-

A silver tetradrachma carries a portrait of the seated goddess Athena leaning on the shield of Zeus. In front of the goddess is the name of the artist who designed the coin, Lisimachus.

ing with one's hands took up too much time and robbed a man of the leisure time needed to pursue important things like politics. A great many Athenian factories were therefore owned by *metics*, foreigners. These outsiders numbered perhaps twenty thousand, half the size of the citizen population of about forty thousand, and although they were discriminated against in the law and forbidden to marry Athenian citizens, their property was recognized and protected in the courts by the free Athenians.

The largest number of workers in Athens were slaves, who by some estimates numbered more than one hundred thousand. They were mostly foreigners because there was a prejudice against enslaving another Greek, no matter what city-state he or she came from. By and large, slaves in Greece were well treated, better than slaves in Rome. This was not true, however, of the slaves who worked in the silver mines at Laurium. They were forced to crawl through tunnels that were seldom higher than three feet (1m), and they worked in the smelters, where they were subjected to dangerous, often fatal fumes. The horrid conditions of the mines were well known, and slave owners throughout the city found the threat of being sent to these hellholes a much more effective deterrent than the threat of physical punishment. The law protected most slaves from excessive punishment, and an owner was not allowed to kill a slave. If an owner beat a slave excessively, the slave had the right to flee for sanctuary to any temple, make an appeal to the law courts, and if his or her case was upheld, force the owner to sell him or her. Slaves performed most of the clerical work of the government, and surprisingly, the Athenian police force was composed entirely of slaves. Many slaves went into business for themselves and earned enough money to buy their freedom.

If Athenians were enlightened in the treatment of their slaves in comparison to their contemporaries, they were even more advanced in their views and practices on education. Athens was unique in the ancient world in her

emphasis on education for her young men. Although there was no formal education for women, almost every free Athenian male learned to read, write, and do simple sums. In fact, the law required parents to provide for the education of their male children, along with formal instruction in music and gymnastics. Failure of the parents to comply with this law released a child from any obligation to care for his parents when they grew old. Having made the requirement, however, the state left the means of education entirely in the hands of the parents. There were two means available: parents could hire a private teacher, or they could send their son to any of the hundreds of private schools maintained throughout the city. Teachers varied in ability, and they set their own fees.

Elementary education began with learning to write by memorizing letter shapes in the correct order. For students in ancient Athens, the main means of learning was memorization. The teacher would write out the letters, and the students would copy them. Students would then be directed to memorize and copy passages from famous poems and epics. The city police would periodically sweep through a school to ensure that the passages used by the teachers were suitably moral and inspiring. By common tradition, the *Iliad* and the *Odyssey* were the basic texts, and most Athenian boys left school with most of these poems memorized. The *Iliad* was considered practically a holy book, and people regularly scoured it to settle arguments and make points.

The Athenians stressed physical education as well, and in this field, the state bore some of the expense. The law required that all free Athenian boys attend a school

specifically devoted to this subject. For boys between the ages of six and fifteen, this was a private school known as the *palaestra*, where the *poedotribes*, or boxing master, taught them to wrestle, box, and develop themselves physically. At sixteen, boys graduated to the *gymnasia*, where they honed the physical skills that would make them good soldiers. There were three gymnasiae in Athens; each had exercise arenas, baths, shaded parks, and covered porticoes. Wrestling, boxing, running, and jumping were the most frequent kinds of exercise. In practicing running and jumping, most students weighted themselves with metal spheres called *halteres* to build muscle. Foot races varied in length from one *stadion*, about 597 feet (182m), to longer runs of 3.1 miles (5 km). As the boys matured and grew closer to military age, it was customary for them to practice these runs in full armor. Javelin, discus, and sword practice further helped boys prepare for military service.

At the age of twenty, an Athenian boy completed his education at the gymnasia and entered a short period of regular military duty, usually in the form of guarding the frontier. This duty completed, the boy became eligible to assume the full rights of citizenship and to sit in the Assembly.

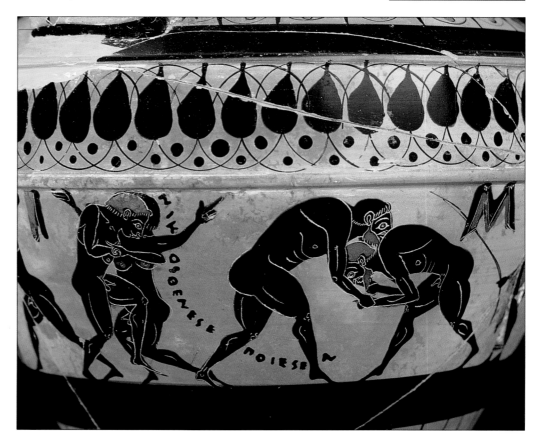

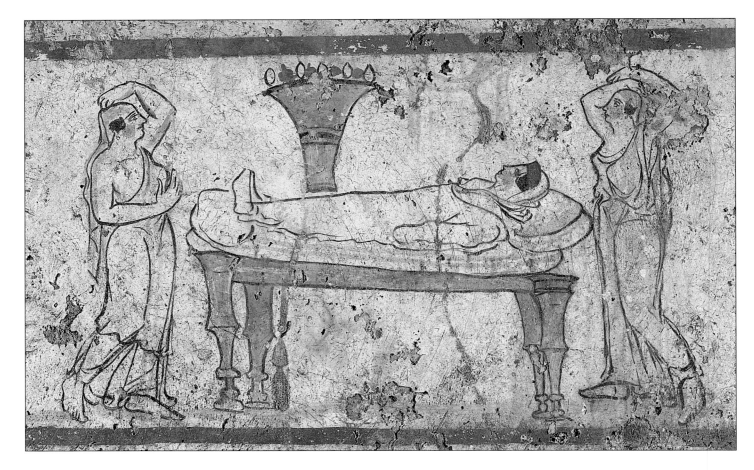

For the wealthy, education might be continued in the form of lectures on rhetoric and philosophy. In the fifth century B.C., these subjects were the exclusive domain of the *sophistae*, or sophists, whose goal was to train their students in the arts of argument and debate. These were necessary skills for an Athenian citizen, for at least twice in his life he would be called on to sit in the boule, or council, and help to govern the state. The limited size of Attica's population also made it likely that each male citizen would serve at least some time in the various magistracies of the empire. The most famous sophist, and the most expensive, was Gorgias (480–380 B.C.), who claimed that he taught his students so well that they could convince anyone of any point even without knowing anything about the subject.

The last, and in their own mind most important, duty of an Athenian male was to guarantee proper care for the dead. This was a sacred duty and neglecting it invoked the displeasure of the state and of the gods. So sacred was this duty that anyone finding a corpse was required to arrange for proper burial, and the victors in a battle, no matter how intense their hatred for the enemy, had to ensure honorable burial for each and every dead soldier.

For his play *Antigone*, needing an unimaginably wicked tyrant, one that no one in the audience could possibly sympathize with, Sophocles created Creon, a man so base as to refuse burial to his own nephew.

An Athenian funeral began with the women of the household washing the body, dressing the corpse in white, and laying it on a couch at the front of the house. They also placed an obol in its mouth so the soul could pay Charon for passage across the Styx to Hades. Law forbade excessive wailing and moaning, but the family usually hired professional female vocalists to sing sad songs. Near the door to the house, the host placed a jar of water so that all mourners could purify themselves when they left after the funeral.

Burial was always the next day. The corpse was carried to the tomb or funeral bier before dawn to avoid giving offense to the sun. Male relatives preceded the litter and female relatives followed. At the cemetery, the body would be either buried or burned. Cremation was considered more honorable but was also more expensive, for the simple fact that wood was scarce and usually imported. A body might be buried in a coffin in the ground or sealed in a tomb hollowed out of stone. In the case of cremation, the bier was lighted by the nearest male relative, and everyone attending the funeral threw something into the fire—either locks of hair or small objects that the deceased had favored in life. Afterward, the relatives would collect the ashes and place them in the family vault. The ceremony concluded with a meal at the deceased person's home, during which his or her virtues were recounted. On the third, ninth, and thirtieth days after the funeral, the family would make offerings at the tomb. During the month-long period of mourning, it was considered terribly impious to say anything bad about the dead.

Athens No More

he great age of Athens came to an end in February 404 B.C., when the Spartan fleet blockaded the Athenian port of Piraeus and subjected the city to three months of starvation. Finally, in April, Athens surrendered. The Athenians agreed to tear down the walls of the city, give up all the ships in her navy, allow exiles to return, and become an ally of Sparta. This end surprised the entire Greek world, for nobody had expected mighty Athens to be defeated. True, she had lost battles during the war, most notably the terrible defeat in Sicily in 415, but the city had rallied and beaten back her enemies

every time. In 407 and again in 405, however, the Spartans, in alliance with their old enemies the Persians, had destroyed two Athenian fleets. Athens could not make up these losses, and a Spartan fleet soon took control of the mouth of the Dardanelles—and with it Athens's grain supply. Once the Athenian fleet had gone, the various subject states of the Delian League declared their independence, annihilating the economic underpinnings of the Athenian Empire.

With this economic support gone, Athenian culture began to decline as well. Athenian philosophers and artists continued to generate impressive work, for this was the era of the great philosophers Plato and Aristotle and the outstanding sculptor Praxiteles (fl. 370–330 B.C.), but literature and painting were on the wane; the center of creativity in painting moved from Athens to Ephesus in Asia Minor. Athenian theatergoers continued to enjoy the works of Aeschylus, Sophocles, Euripides, and Aristophanes, but no new playwrights emerged to match these giants. The historian Xenophon carried the history of Athens down to 362 B.C., but he did not exercise the care with his sources that had typified the monumental works of Herodotus and Thucydides.

The conquests of Philip of Macedonia (382–336 B.C.) and his son Alexander the Great (356–323 B.C.) shifted attention away from Athens. By the beginning of the third century B.C., Athens was a quiet university town to which rich Romans sent their children to be educated.

Chapter Five

The Rome of Caesar Augustus

"I Found a Rome of Brick and Left It Covered in Marble," 27 B.C. – A.D. 14

Unlike Periclean Athens, which flourished culturally and artistically after a successful foreign war, Rome under Caesar Augustus experienced its golden age after a fierce and bloody period of civil war. Between 105 and 27 B.C., Roman fought Roman in a bewildering series of conflicts that saw the republican government of Rome break down, only to be replaced with an environment of uncertainty, violence, and periodic massacre.

Opposite: Built in 27 B.C. and reconstructed in the second century A.D., the Pantheon is the only building in Rome whose ancient arches and walls have been preserved. Even the huge bronze doors of its entrance are ancient. It was probably built originally to honor Venus and Mars, the principal deities of the Julian family, and the ancestors of Julius Caesar.

A modern fresco by Cesare Maccari in the Palazzo Maccari, Rome, dramatizes Cicero, the famous Roman senator, accusing Lucius Sergius Catilina, who is seated in the foreground, of treason against Rome in 62 B.C. The Senate, shown here, was the oldest governing body in Rome. When Caesar Augustus assumed power, he had to be extremely careful to preserve the fiction that the Senate still ruled Rome.

For most of its long history, Rome had been a republic ruled by an assembly of citizens called the *Comitia Centuriata* and an advisory body called the Senate. The Senate, made up of the oldest and most influential families of Rome, exerted considerable influence but had no legal legislative power. In addition, two officials, called consuls, elected for one-year terms, held joint executive power and led the army in time of war. This government was not a true democracy, for it was organized in such a way that the richest citizens held all the power, but it did give Romans the feeling that all citizens had a voice in the governing of their society. Had you polled the citizens of the city, they would have concurred that Rome was indeed ruled by the "Senate and the People of Rome."

During the third century B.C., however, Rome fought a long series of wars against the north African city of Carthage. In the process of fighting that war, the republican form of government was somehow inadvertently destroyed and replaced with a senatorial oligarchy. At the same time, economic processes brought on by the war destroyed the financial viability of Rome's small farmer class. Unable to make a living through agriculture, these farmers moved to the city, where they lived on a dole of cheap grain from the state and became a volatile mob controlled by unscrupulous political factions.

On separate occasions in the latter part of the second century B.C., two brothers, Tiberius and Gaius Gracchus, tried to improve the economic conditions of the urban poor by redistributing some of the land held by the wealthy so that the lower classes could grow food and not depend on the public granary. The Gracchus brothers also tried to return a measure of democracy to the government of Rome. For their trouble, they were condemned by the Senate, hunted down, and killed by enraged senators and their followers. In 133 B.C., Tiberius and three hundred of his followers were beaten to death with legs of chairs and benches. Twelve years later, his younger brother Gaius and three thousand of his followers were killed in an assault of enraged senators backed by a contingent of Cretan archers. For payment, these mercenaries received an amount of gold equal to the weight of Gaius's head hollowed out and filled with lead.

The brutal and extralegal deaths of the Gracchus brothers opened the floodgates of violence and ended any pretense to dignity and decorum in government. The century from 121 to 27 B.C. was filled with political violence, assassinations, and civil wars. From 107 to 87, for instance, Gaius Marius, a commoner from rural Italy, became a virtual dictator of Rome on the strength of his foreign military victories. Hating the pretensions of the Senate and backed by the army, he gained power by encouraging the lower classes to defy senatorial leadership. In 87, he singled out members of the Senate who had incurred his hatred, and he had a mob of his supporters hunt them through the streets and tear them to pieces. This mob removed the heads from the bodies, left the torsos on the streets, and decorated the speaker's platform in the forum with the severed heads.

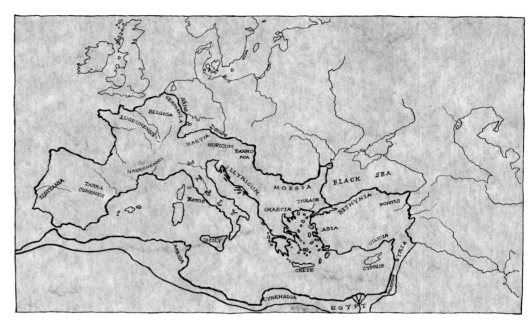

In 83 B.C., it was the turn of the senatorial class to take revenge. A poor but brilliant nobleman, Cornelius Sulla Felix, seized political power, led an army into Rome itself, and ordered the massacre of three thousand Roman citizens he believed had supported Marius.

Above: The Roman Empire spread far beyond Rome; at the end of Augustus' time, all the territory outlined was tied to the empire.

Left: Not only was the city of Rome the center of the Empire, but during Augustus Caesar's reign, it was the seat of the arts.

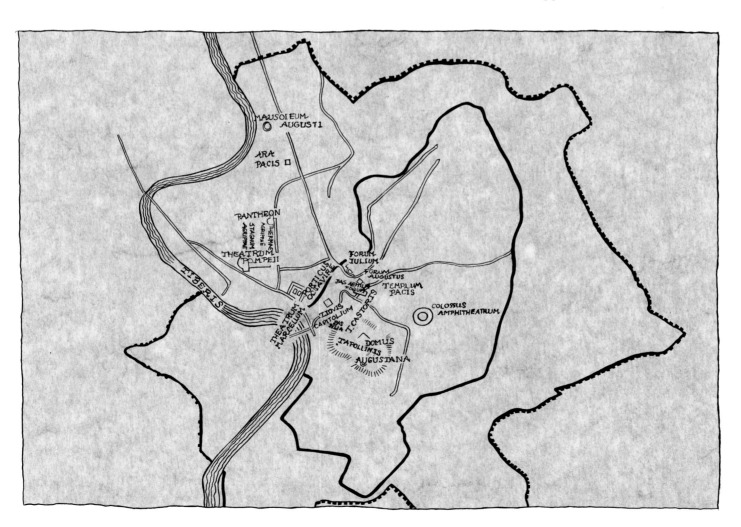

Julius Caesar (100–44 B.C.) was a brilliant politician whose gifts allowed him to emerge out of the chaos of civil war to seize nearly absolute power in Rome. His motives have been debated since antiquity. Was he attempting to restore the old Roman republican government, or was he chiefly concerned with seizing political power to feed his own giant ego?

Caesar and the First Triumvirate

The excesses of Marius and Sulla destroyed all pretensions to democracy in the Roman government. Between 80 and 44 B.C., a succession of Roman leaders, the most famous of whom was Gaius Julius Caesar, struggled to gain personal political power at each other's expense. Groups of noblemen formed temporary alliances with each other as they jockeyed for control of the government. In 70 B.C., Marcus Licinius Crassus and Gnaeus Pompeius Magnus (Pompey) put aside political differences in a political alliance of convenience. In 60, they added Gaius Julius Caesar to this alliance, now called the Triumvirate, when he became too powerful to ignore. In this atmosphere of chaos, the business of the Roman Republic lurched along from one violent confrontation to another. When, for instance, Gaius Julius Caesar, as consul, proposed a land reform bill for passage, and the other consul, Lucius Calpurnius Bibulus, attempted to oppose it in a speech, a supporter of Caesar sneaked up behind Bibulus and dumped a basket of turds on his head, to the vast amusement of the crowd. Bibulus was humiliated into silence, and Caesar's measure passed. In such an atmosphere, the proceedings of the Roman government became a circus.

Between 59 and 45 B.C., neither Caesar, Pompey, nor Crassus could gain an advantage in Rome, and so the three agreed on a truce. Pompey remained in Italy, prevented from taking control of the government by able lieutenants of Caesar and Crassus, while the other two left the peninsula to undertake overseas military conquests. Each one's plan was to gain enough booty and wealth through foreign conquest to finance his final push to establish absolute control over the Roman government. Crassus went to Syria and attacked the Parthian Empire east of the Euphrates. He died in 53, along with most of his army. Caesar, as most modern readers know, went west, where between 56 and 52 he cowed the Germans, invaded Britain, and made Gaul a new province of the Roman Republic. He kept the Roman people aware of his activities by sending back spirited reports of his military successes that were read to the population. He later combined these reports into *De Bello Galico* (On the Gallic War), one of the greatest classics of Roman literature. His "take" from the conquest of Gaul left him fabulously wealthy: he stole enough from the Gauls to pay off a 75,000,000 denarii debt, bribe the entire electorate of Rome to vote for him in the election of 45 B.C. (at a cost of 20,000,000 denarii), and still have enough left over to treat the Romans to the biggest gladiatorial show in history. According to various reports, the amount of gold that Caesar brought back to Italy was so great that it flooded the market and made silver temporarily more valuable than gold.

Caesar and Pompey now squared off for the final contest—which would leave one of them in absolute control of the Roman world. With Caesar in northern Italy, then called Cisalpine Gaul, with his army, Pompey controlled Rome and the Senate. In December 50 B.C., Pompey's supporters in the Senate succeeded in having Caesar declared an outlaw and took away his legal right to command the armies. Caesar appealed to his troops, and on January 10, 49, they crossed the Rubicon River, the stream that formed the boundary between Italy and Cisalpine Gaul. He then swept into Rome, forced the Senate to accept his action, and forced Pompey to leave Italy.

This attack was a brilliant military move. Pompey, not expecting a winter attack, had neglected to raise any new legions. His entire defense force consisted of two legions that had served with Caesar in Gaul; Caesar hoped—correctly, as it turned out—that these legions would desert Pompey and come over to him. As his army swept south toward Rome, Caesar's reputation, enhanced by the propaganda he had sent from Gaul, preceded him. City after city declared its allegiance to Caesar, and Pompey was forced to abandon Italy and move to Greece.

During the rest of 49 B.C., Caesar defeated Pompeian forces in Spain and gathered men for new legions while Pompey built an army in Greece. On August 9, 48, the two armies met at Pharsalus in Thessaly. Although Pompey's army was twice as large as that of his adversary, Caesar won the day; Pompey immediately fled, hoping to find refuge in Egypt. When he landed, however, the Egyptians killed him and stuck his head in a jar of honey to preserve it for Caesar. Caesar arrived three days after Pompey's death, and soon after, he had his fateful meeting with Cleopatra VII.

Of all the women in history, Cleopatra VII is probably the most famous. Although not a famous beauty—her portrait on coins reveals a hooked nose and a jutting chin—

she apparently had a real style and intellect that appealed to Caesar. She was, after all, an accomplished politician, having grown up in the deadly environment of her father's court. In her lifetime, she killed two brothers—also her husbands—and ordered the murder of her younger sister. In short, she was just the sort of person who could appeal to Caesar's ruthlessness and political savvy. In any event, he took her back to Rome with him, and she remained there until his assassination.

During 46 and 45, Caesar eliminated the last vestiges of Pompeian power in north Africa and Spain. This accomplished, he became the undisputed master of the Roman world and returned to Rome in triumph. By now, Romans wanted peace. Sixty years of civil war, conscription, and high taxes had bankrupted the population, both economically and socially. It was time to rebuild.

Ironically, that did not happen. On March 15, 44 B.C., barely a year after achieving peace, a group of some sixty senators, led by Gaius Cassius Longinus and Marcus Junius Brutus, stabbed Caesar to death in the Senate house. They correctly assumed that Caesar was maneuvering to establish an absolute monarchy. They thought his death would save the old republic. Instead, their action plunged the already exhausted Roman world into another thirteen years of civil war that left the Roman population even more worn out and willing to follow anyone they believed could deliver peace.

Left: Gnaeus Pompeius Magnus (106–48 B.C.), known as Pompey the Great and once the father-in-law of Julius Caesar, was another of the Roman politician/generals who emerged out of the Roman civil war to vie for power. In 49 B.C., Caesar and Pompey fought a huge battle at Pharsalus, and Pompey lost. He fled to Egypt where Ptolemy XIII (63–47 B.C.) ordered him beheaded as he stepped ashore.

Below: The four round structures in this street in Pompeii are mills for grinding flour. The miller poured grain into the rotating catillus (the hourglass structure on top); the flour emerged on the horizontal lower surface.

Marcus Junius Brutus (85–42 B.C.) was the principal conspirator in the assassination of Julius Caesar. Although the treachery of the act has been condemned, it seems clear that Brutus murdered Caesar out of the purest of motives: a desire to remove a man he thought was a potential tyrant and to restore the old republican government of Rome. Brutus died in battle at Philippi, Greece, fighting Gaius Octavianus Thurinus, Caesar's adopted son, who became Caesar Augustus.

The Second Triumvirate and the Reign of Octavius

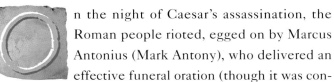

On the night of Caesar's assassination, the Roman people rioted, egged on by Marcus Antonius (Mark Antony), who delivered an effective funeral oration (though it was considerably less dramatic than the one Shakespeare later put in his mouth). He enhanced his presentation with Caesar's bloody toga and a wax replica of the martyr's body that emphasized the stab wounds. Later, at the funeral, the mob mistakenly tore an innocent bystander to pieces because he bore a resemblance to Marcus Junius Brutus and then burned down the Senate house. The assassins quickly left Rome. For a time, it looked as if Marcus Antonius would win the leadership of the Roman people and of the Roman Republic by default.

On April 28, 44 B.C., a rival for the people's affection arrived in Rome from Greece: Gaius Octavianus Thurinus, the grandson of Caesar's sister Julia and the adopted son of Julius Caesar himself. Octavianus, more commonly known as Octavius, was eighteen years old at the time and

not an impressive figure. He had a handsome face atop a sickly, skinny body, and he was noted for his calm (not to say dull) personality combined with a plodding but thorough way of getting things done. His favorite aphorisms were "Festina lente" (Make haste slowly) and "Bis das si cito das" (You do it twice if you do it quickly). Despite his perceived flaws, this plodding scarecrow of a young man would create a new form of government that would last for nearly two hundred and fifty years.

When Octavius reached Rome, he set to work using his only two assets: the fact that he was Caesar's legally adopted son, which assured him the support of Caesar's veterans, and his possession of a considerable part of Caesar's fortune. In July 43 B.C., he marched eight legions of Caesar's veterans into Rome and demanded election to the consulship, although legally he was too young to hold the office. The Senate, eyeing the troops, granted a special dispensation to accommodate his election. Once in possession of this office, Octavius ordered the Roman treasury to pay his troops a bonus, forced the Senate to issue a condemnation of Caesar's assassins, and made a political alliance—the Second Triumvirate—with Mark Antony and Marcus Aemilius Lepidus, Caesar's chief of cavalry. This was a very wise move on his part, for these two were the only politicians likely to challenge him (and vice versa). Forming the triumvirate gave everybody time to stop, think, and plot.

This trio's first action was to draw up proscription lists of people they considered dangerous to the state, that is, to themselves. Prominent on that list was Marcus Tullius Cicero. Although Octavius initially objected to the legal murder of this great orator, he finally relented when he saw the depths of Mark Antony's hatred of the man who had publicly insulted him in his famous First and Second Philippics. There Cicero had called Antonius a drunken, brutal coward who showed his lack of class by scandalously kissing his own wife in public.

The proscription lists called for the deaths of 130 senators and two thousand other Romans. Whatever the official reasons on the lists, the actual reason was that Lepidus, Octavius, and Antony needed money—money they could raise by selling the estates of condemned Romans. With these revenues and money they forced out of the Roman people by taxation, they could pursue their war against the assassins of Caesar.

By June 42 B.C., the three triumvirs were ready to begin this war. The assassins, calling themselves Republicans, wanted to restore the original form of the Roman government; they correctly saw the Triumvirate as a crude grab for power by a group of tyrants. Despite its good intentions, the Republican army lost at Philippi in September 42; Brutus and Cassius committed suicide rather than face capture, and most of their higher officers were slaughtered. The lower-ranking soldiers, including a young officer named Quintus Horatius Flaccus, were spared.

Following this triumph, Octavius, Antony, and Lepidus, realizing that none of them could beat the others, declared a truce and divided the Roman world between them, hoping to gain some time and build up their individual strength for the struggle that was certain to come. Octavius received Italy, Gaul, and Spain, in addition to Sicily, Sardinia, and Corsica; Antony took Greece, Asia, Syria, and Egypt; Lepidus, the weakest of the three, ruled in north Africa. To cement the alliance, Antony married Octavius's sister, Octavia.

With peace thus assured, at least for a time, Octavius began to repair his reputation in Italy. First, to secure his position with the Roman aristocracy, he divorced his first wife, Scribonia (on the very day she delivered his

daughter Julia), and made a politically expedient marriage with the eminent noblewoman Livia Drusilla (whose son from a previous marriage would later become well known as the emperor Tiberius). Next, to win the hearts of the people, Octavius reduced the price of grain, the staple food of the Romans, and assured a regular supply by defeating the pirates who often attacked the grain fleets. Finally, after he consolidated his rule over Gaul and Spain and raised taxes in those regions, he lowered taxes on the Romans and Italians. In 36 B.C., he felt strong enough to take on Lepidus; he marched an army to Africa, handily defeated his former ally, and declared an end to the civil wars in the west.

Mark Antony, however, still maintained his control in the east. While Octavius consolidated his rule in Rome, Antony did the same in the eastern part of the empire. He reformed the Roman administration there, carried on successful wars against the Parthians, and turned the area into a successful, peaceful part of the Roman Empire. He relied on his partisans back in Rome to protect his interests there. For the time being, Octavius had to tolerate him because Antony was immensely popular with the

Marcus Antonius, or Mark Antony (83–30 B.C.), was another of the political wonks who hovered around Julius Caesar during his life and tried to profit from the chaos surrounding his death. After Caesar's death, Antony tried to appeal to both the assassins and Caesar's supporters to gain power. In 43, he became part of the Second Triumvirate, made up of himself, Octavius, and Lepidus, that tried to jointly rule Rome. In the end, however, he alienated the Roman people and committed suicide along with his lover Cleopatra.

Below: Marcus Tullius Cicero (106–43 B.C.) was the greatest orator of ancient Rome. Cicero was an active politician who distrusted Caesar and supported the attempts to restore the republican government of Rome. He was not, however, a part of the conspiracy to murder Caesar. In 43 B.C., Marcus Antonius ordered his murder.

When Alexandre Cabanel's portrait of Cleopatra VII (69–30 B.C.) was painted in the nineteenth century, many saw her as an evil temptress and opportunist. Most likely, she was simply a patriot who tried to make the best deal possible for Egypt, then a small and weak nation caught between powerful Roman forces.

Roman people, who saw him as the avenger of the murdered Caesar and—strangely—as the champion of Roman liberty. Octavius soon realized that he could never rule Rome by himself as long as the Roman people revered Antony. He needed some way to diminish the hero in the eyes of the Roman mob. Fortunately for the young would-be emperor, Antony himself provided the means.

While in Egypt, Mark Antony had fallen under the spell of Cleopatra. In 42 B.C., she was still only twenty-seven, and Antony found her even more irresistible than Caesar had. Her astute political mind and grasp of eastern Mediterranean politics helped Antony in solidifying Roman control over that region. Perhaps in gratitude, Antony divorced Octavia in 34 B.C. and married Cleopatra.

This was what Octavius had been waiting for. Back in Rome, he launched an intensive propaganda campaign against Antony. His propagandists used Antony's disgraceful divorce of a noble Roman wife, conveniently forgetting Octavius's divorce of Scribonia a few years before, and exploited the suspicion Romans felt for everyone who was not a Roman. They focused on Cleopatra's foreignness, describing not only the religious practices of the Egyptians, with their strange animal-headed gods, but also Cleopatra's alleged excessive and perverse sexual practices, chief among which was a supposed preference for dozens of sexual partners in a single night. When Antony later gave her political control of Armenia, Parthia, Cyprus, Palestine, and Media, the propagandists

insisted that he was her unwilling sexual slave, had lost his manliness, and had forfeited his good Roman sense. Then as now, people are always perversely interested in the weaknesses of their leaders—the Roman citizens were willing to believe the worst of Antony. Consequently, when Octavius felt strong enough to attack Antony in 31 B.C., the people of Rome rallied to his support, ignored their earlier disgust with war, and readily approved of a huge sum to punish Antony and his evil Egyptian queen.

The subsequent naval battle at Actium, on the west coast of Greece, was a complete victory for Octavius. Some sources claim that Octavius spent the battle throwing up over a ship's railing; whether or not this is true, we do know that his brilliant admiral Agrippa led Octavius's fleet to a stunning defeat over the combined fleets of Antony and Cleopatra. After the battle, Antony and Cleopatra deserted their troops and fled back to Egypt, followed by Octavius. When their troops refused to fight, the two lovers committed suicide rather than face the disgrace of capture and public display as prisoners in Rome. This victory gave Octavius control of Egypt's huge treasury, which he used to rebuild Rome and to establish himself, at the age of thirty-two, as the unquestioned ruler of the Roman Empire.

The basis of his success was his ability to cleverly disguise his absolute, dictatorial rule as a fully functioning republican government under the control of the Senate, the *Comitia Centuriata*, and the other traditional organs of Roman government. To create this facade, Octavius, on his triumphant return to Rome from Egypt in 29 B.C., confirmed the Senate and the other governing bodies of Rome in their traditional powers. At the same time, however, he assumed other offices and titles that made him the actual power behind the government, because these assumed powers quietly undercut the traditional powers of the Roman government. For instance, he took direct control of all the militarily significant provinces of the empire, appropriated the right to veto any act or legislation passed by any branch of the Roman government, and made it sacrilege for anyone to threaten him with violence. Most important, he assumed personal command of twenty-two of Rome's twenty-eight legions (army units). To safeguard his power further, he saw to it he was elected sole consul every year from 33 to 23 B.C.

On January 13, 27 B.C., after quietly arranging all this behind the scenes, he appeared before the Senate and dramatically resigned all of his powers, claiming a desire to return to private life now that the Republic had been restored. Certainly this was staged, for the senators immediately rose as one and begged him to reconsider and to remain as *princeps civitatis*, or "leader of the state." After a tactful moment of hesitation, he agreed to stay on. This event reinforced the general illusion that Rome was a free republic and Octavius its loyal servant. Four days after this "performance," the Senate conferred on Octavius the title of Augustus, meaning "consecrated or sacred one." After a suitable show of resistance, he agreed to take the new name, and he stopped using the name Octavius. The Senate also encouraged him to add "Caesar" to his new name to draw attention to the "martyred" Julius Caesar; thus Octavius "died," and Caesar Augustus, the first Roman emperor, was born.

Traditionally, it is these events that mark for historians the date of birth of the Roman Empire. Caesar Augustus ruled under this system for the remaining forty-one years of his life; after his death, the Augustan Settlement continued, with some changes, as the government of the Roman Empire in western Europe until A.D. 192. It took only one man—and some extraordinary circumstances—to determine a form of government that would endure for nearly two and a quarter centuries.

A seventeenth-century Flemish painting by Frans Francken II (1581–1642) shows Cleopatra meeting Mark Antony for the first time in Tarsus. Legend has it that she arrived in a ship painted gold with purple sails, and rowed with silver oars. The crew of the ship, according to Plutarch, the famous ancient Greek writer, consisted entirely of Cleopatra's most beautiful serving women. The whole arrival was enhanced by music and perfume wafting on the breeze from ship to shore. Antony was enchanted.

Although Gaius Octavianus Thurinus, or Caesar Augustus (63 B.C.–A.D.14), as he is usually known, was physically frail, he had a robust mind. He reorganized the whole Roman Republic as an absolute monarchy with himself at the top, while preserving the appearance and trappings of the old republican city-state.

As concerned as he was with creating a workable system of government, Caesar Augustus was equally concerned with marking his reign as a period of intellectual and artistic growth throughout the empire. As such, the Augustan Age stands as the pinnacle of Roman cultural achievement and one of the most dramatic golden ages in the history of mankind. Perhaps in no other period of ancient history, with the exception of Periclean Athens, did artists, architects, and writers shine with such brilliance and originality. It seems as if the Romans wanted to celebrate their freedom from the chaos of civil war by taking the energy that had gone into fighting and turning it toward more wholesome activities. And the Romans had the economic means to do so, for after years of civil war and backbreaking taxes, the conquered wealth of Egypt was suddenly available to them; these monies were used to pay for building, paintings, and sculpture and to support a tremendous outpouring of literature.

The Humanities in Rome

 n numbers of writers alone, the reign of Caesar Augustus rivals the era of Pericles and the reign of Elizabeth I a millennium and a half later. Poets such as Ovid, Sextus Propertius, Virgil, Horace, and Tibullus wrote for an audience that appreciated the grandeur and subtleties of Latin. In other fields, the geographer Strabo and the historians Diodorus Siculus, Asinius Pollio, Dionysius of Halicarnassus, and, of course, Titus Livius (Livy) flourished during Augustus's reign. There was even time to support technical writing, for during the reign of Augustus, the venerable octogenarian Marcus Terentius Varro completed his monumental three-volume work on Italian farming.

HORACE

One of the giants of this period—of any period in fact—was Quintus Horatius Flaccus (65–8 B.C.), otherwise known as Horace. Horace's career shows how socially fluid and open to talent the new society was under Augustus, for surely no Roman writer ever started from humbler beginnings. Horace was born in Venusia, a squalid town near the top of the high heel that forms the boot of Italy. Even more discouraging than this was that he was the son of an ex-slave. Romans considered slaves and ex-slaves to be sullied by the experience of bondage and somehow less than fully human. Nevertheless, Horace's father must have been a remarkable man to rise above this prejudice, for he not only bought his freedom, but became, economically at least, a comfortable member of the Roman middle class.

Horace's father was determined that his son would have advantages he had not had and spent as much as he could to give his child a good education, first in Rome and then in Athens. In Rome, Horace was a rebellious student who was often late to school. He apparently spent too much time on the way to school watching the interesting people who inhabited Rome's streets. He received numerous beatings for this from his sadistic teacher Orbilius, but he gained his revenge by writing a satiric poem called "Orbilius Full of Whacks," thereby imprinting the cruel Orbilius on the minds of hundreds of thousands of Latin students throughout the ensuing centuries.

In Athens, he fell under the influence of gentler teachers who instilled in him a love of philosophy and idealism. This idealism was nearly the death of him, for while he was in Greece, he determined to take the side of the Republicans under Brutus and Cassius against Octavius. He fought at Philippi, but in the last moments of the battle, he threw away his shield and sword and ran. Dishonored both as a rebel and as a coward, he returned to Rome to find his father dead, and his patrimony confiscated. Fortunately, he still had good friends who were willing to intervene on his behalf. Surprisingly, he got a good portion of his property back; even more shocking, he got a job as a minor bureaucrat in the very government he had rebelled against. During the day, he shuffled papyri in a cubicle, and at night he went home to write poetry that has lasted through today.

Horace started to hang about the fringes of literary society and soon attracted the attention of Publius Vergilius Maro, known today as Virgil, who was already an established poet as well as a good friend of Cilinus Maecenas, the right-hand man of Caesar Augustus. Maecenas was a patron of the arts who, with Virgil's help, soon recognized Horace's talent. Maecenas supported Horace with a small stipend that allowed him to quit his job and wander the streets of Rome, observing people and writing poems about them.

Woe to the man or woman who earned Horace's censure, for at this early stage of his career, he delighted in writing verse in which he attacked, brilliantly but caustically, his enemies. In one scathing example of such verse, Horace wrote about a woman slightly older than himself (he was twenty-seven at the time) who had had the bad form to question his sexual powers at a party. He called the woman "a black toothed hag" whose "gaping anus protrudes from between shriveled buttocks

like a cow's ready to defecate." Her "breasts flop like a mare's udders," he said, and point downward to "a rounded belly atop swollen legs." She is the kind of woman "who must work all day to coax anything from a young man's groin."

Most of Horace's poems, however, are not like this, for he was usually not a man of violent or harsh passions. His love poems are usually light and cheerful. Even when he has been "dumped," to use the modern expression, he seems mostly concerned about drawing a lesson from the event and being able to laugh at both the experience and himself.

> What simple boy dripping with scent
> And intrigued with your golden flowing hair
> Courts you, Pyrrha, in some secret hideaway?
>
> Soon he will tearfully curse your faithlessness
> And blame it on the haughty and fickle gods
> Whose deeds ape the sea with its many moods
> From beauty to treachery.
>
> This boy is bewitched by your golden beauty
> Just as I was, who now hangs this poem
> On a temple wall, like clothing
> Drenched by the cruel sea.

Horace was a genius at evoking a mood, taking a pleasant moment—or, less often, an unpleasant one—and describing it in gentle fluid detail. In Ode 1.9, one of his most famous poems, he takes the reader through several different moods and several scenes, from a harsh view of a heavy winter storm threatening to break branches from the trees to a warm room with a glowing fireplace and a jug of fine wine and finally to a pleasant scene of young men and women gaily courting in the streets of Rome.

The great Roman poet Quintus Horatius Flaccus or Horace (65–8 B.C.), shown on a medallion, was the most reflective and controlled of the great Roman poets. Although there are some exceptions, most of his poems show a quiet, contemplative spirit who was more likely to sit back and observe events instead of participating.

Thaliarchus you seem worried by the snow
That covers the mountain, breaks the trees
And chokes the rivers. So what!

Forget the cold! Pile on the logs and
Bring forth the four-year-old Sabine wine,
Leaving all else to the gods.

For it is the gods who, at the same time
They calm the great winds and mighty oceans,
Preserve the ancient cypress and the mountain ash.

Don't seek to discover what tomorrow will bring,
Just count as a gain whatever the gods
Give before peevish old age takes your bloom.

Seek love and dancing; listen at night
To the soft whisper of lovers—
The lurking maid on the Campus Martius

Who fears her lover may not find her
And giggles lightly, scarcely resisting as he
draws the prize from her pretty finger.

Horace was blessed, for not only was he a great poet, but he also had, by and large, a gentle, pleasant personality that attracted people to him and got them to do what he wanted. When Rome, with all its noise and frenzy, became too much for Horace, he asked Maecenas for someplace else to write, and Maecenas put up the money to send him off to a private estate at Tibur (today called Tivoli), less than 19 miles (30km) from Rome amid the Apennine Mountains. There Horace composed more poems and corresponded with his friends back in Rome via poetic letters. His fame grew, and he had a near-constant stream of admiring visitors. At the same time, Maecenas kept hounding him to come back to Rome and appear at one or another social gathering, for Maecenas liked to be surrounded by brilliant people, because it enhanced him in his own and others' eyes.

Finally, desperate for the solitude a writer needs, Horace told Maecenas, "Enough!" He needed another place and he needed to be left alone. This was a daring move, for it takes either a very stupid or an incredibly self-centered person to demand more from a person who had already given as much as Maecenas had. Maecenas apparently was impressed, or at least not offended, by Horace's forthrightness, and the poet was packed off a further 8 miles (13km) into the mountains.

This time he found a farmhouse—though house may not be the right word—with twenty-four rooms, three baths, and a formal garden. It was surrounded by plentiful farm land, with eight slaves and five tenant families to farm it. Horace stayed here for the rest of his life, happy to write letters, help his slaves clear rocks from the fields, and dally with the local peasant girls. Here he wrote the *Second Book of Satires* and finished his *Odes*. When he died at fifty-seven, even the emperor wept at the news.

VIRGIL

Caesar Augustus, as it turned out, loved poetry, especially poetry that celebrated his achievements, and in Publius Vergilius Maro (70–19 B.C.), he found a poet who could do that better than anyone else. Certainly Augustus's fame for posterity has been enhanced not only by his creation of the Roman Empire but also by the fact that he recognized and encouraged the genius of this most famous Roman poet.

Publius Vergilius Maro, or Virgil, as he is best known, was born on October 15, 70 B.C., at a place called Andes in Cisalpine Gaul, near modern-day Mantua. His father was a common laborer, who improved his condition in life by marrying the boss's daughter. Because of this, he was able to give his son a good education, first in nearby Cremona and later at schools in Milan and Rome. Virgil took no part in the civil wars of the period, but his estates, inherited from his father, were confiscated by the leaders of the Second Triumvirate for distribution to their soldiers. Virgil, like Horace, appealed to his friends about this injustice, and two of them—his fellow poets Gaius Cornelius Gallus and Asinius Pollio—tried to help him. They arranged a meeting between the young poet and Octavius. What happened in this meeting nobody recorded, but soon after some of Virgil's land was restored to him; Virgil became devoted to Augustus and remained so for the rest of his life.

His friends also recognized his talent, demonstrated in an early work called the *Bucolics*, and encouraged him in his career by introducing him to the right people. However, they laughed among themselves—good-naturedly—at his awkwardness. Virgil was small, skinny, and shy, and he suffered from an awful stammer. He was a prude, and he took little romantic interest in women or men, which led his friends to call him "the virgin." All this combined to make him a social disaster in the rarefied world of Roman society. He avoided public life and lived for a while in Naples, where he wrote his *Georgics* (roughly, *The Farming Life*). In the *Georgics*, his finest work, he praised the glory of the countryside and the simple life of the farmer, while at the same time cursing and making fun of the city with its strictured social life, insincerity, and confusion.

> Happiest is the fellow who knows
> The country life and counts the
> Temptations of this hellish world as
> Fit for his feet to stamp on.

> Who knows best the country gods
> Like Pan, Silvanus, and the Nymphs,
> And who ignores society's strictures,
> The wealth of the court, and petty discord.

> Neither affairs of state, nor political crisis
> Nor compassion for the poor nor even
> Envy of the rich distracts the happy man
> From the fruits which branches and fields produce.

> The farmer with his crooked plow
> Labors throughout the year and so supports
> both his country and his children
> With his oxen and his worthy bulls.

> There is no rest for the farmer,
> But the year brings forth fruits,
> Good meat, straw, and vegetables
> That overload the barns before the winter comes.

> Meanwhile the happy family prospers,
> The children thrive on kisses.
> The heifers suffer heavy udders
> And the kids butt horns on the grass.

> Such a man enjoys his feast days,
> Stretched long upon the grass

> Around a fire with a full cup,
> Praising Bacchus, master of the flocks.

Octavius loved this type of poetry that celebrated the rural, country life, and when he returned from his victory at Actium, his friends arranged a meeting between the poet and the conqueror at Atella, near Naples. When Virgil read Octavius some selections from the *Georgics*, the Roman consul was transfixed. He spent four days listening to Virgil read his works. At the end of this period, he gave Virgil a suggestion, really an order, to write a great national epic about Rome, something that would celebrate not so much the recent history of the Republic, but

Renaissance artists delighted in portraying classical Romans in medieval dress, as this bust of the poet Publius Vergilius Maro, or Virgil (70–19 B.C.), from the Minster at Ulm demonstrates.

the spirit, fortitude, and power of the Roman personality. The result, of course, was the *Aeneid*, the poetic rendition of the origin of the Roman people from the remnants of the Trojans led by their mighty leader, Aeneas, across the Mediterranean after their treacherous defeat by the Greeks at Troy.

Was Virgil delighted with the assignment? We do not know, but there is every reason to suspect that he was not. First, there is the fact that the *Aeneid*, although it is great poetry, is not as great as his other works, the *Georgics* and *Bucolics*. He struggled long and hard over the poem,

This Renaissance engraving of the victorious Greeks before Troy appears in a 1502 edition of the *Aeneid*, published in Strasbourg, France.

despite the constant prodding of Augustus. His difficulties may have been caused by the fact that he was writing about warriors and conquest when he himself had had no experience with either. He didn't like soldiers or the army; his only experience with them had been when the ex-soldier who had received Virgil's inherited land through confiscation nearly drowned the poet when he protested the takeover.

In fact, most experts believe that the best parts of the *Aeneid* are not those that deal with battle but those which treat the relationships of people and the wonderful adventures the Trojan heroes had on their way to Italy. In Virgil's hands, Aeneas, the ultimate soldier, is not a nice man. He not only is cruel and ignoble but also has no real will of his own—he is constantly pushed around and buffeted by fate and the will of the gods. He is unable to make up his mind, and so the gods make it up for him. Much more appealing are the minor figures in the poem: Queen Dido of Carthage, for instance, or Prince Turnus, king of the Rutulians. Virgil does a wonderful job painting Dido's emotions when, having won her love and made a shambles of her rule by alienating her subjects and her neighbors, Aeneas determines to leave her. She moves from sorrow to anger, to a desire for vengeance, and finally to her ultimate vengeance in suicide. Even more effective is the picture of the brave Turnus, who would rather face death than dishonor. Although he knows he is doomed to die at Aeneas's hand if he engages the adventurer in battle, the Rutulian king still determines to fight him.

> Shall this land see Turnus fleeing?
> Is it really so dreadful a thing to die?
> Oh, gods of the underworld be merciful to me
> Since the gods of this world have been false to me.
> I descend to you with spotless soul,
> Unstained with cowardice
> And not unworthy of my ancestors.

One of the best parts of the *Aeneid* is in Book Six, when Aeneas descends into Hades in search of his father, Anchises. It was the belief of the ancients that the souls of the dead had knowledge of the future, and Aeneas's goal in going to Hades is to find out what is ahead of him. His guide is the Sybil of Cumae, Deiphobe, who tells

Aeneas how to descend safely to the underworld. This he does, through a medley of monsters and demons, across the River Styx, and into the Realm of the Dead. It is here that Virgil shows the reader the breadth of his imagination. As Aeneas descends into Hades, we are given descriptions of the various realms of Hades: the Realm of Minos, where Minos, one of the great kings of ancient Crete, presides over the souls of stillborn children and those who die falsely accused; the realm of Rhadamanthys, where Rhadamanthys, the son of Zeus and Europa, judges more serious sinners—those who hated brothers, struck parents, cheated friends, murdered, violated the marriage vows, and did not share their wealth with the poor; and, at the very bottom of Hades, Tartarus, a dark abyss where Aeneas finds the greatest villains—Tityus, who raped Leto, the mother of Artemis and Apollo; Tantalus, who tried to trick the gods into eating human flesh; and the severed body parts of Cronos, forever separated but still quivering with life. The great numbers of sinners in Hades and the various punishments inflicted on them make clear the strictness of the ancient Romans' moral code, for Virgil did not create all these punishments—he merely brought to life in dramatic poetry the beliefs of Roman religion.

After traveling through the realms of the sinners, Aeneas reaches Elysium, the land of the Happy Dead; this is the home of the souls of brave warriors and the righteous dead who have followed all the rules and lived good lives. These spirits may look forward to rebirth as a new soul after memories of their past lives have been erased through drinking water from the river Lethe, which flows through Elysium. In Elysium, Aeneas meets his father, Anchises, who tells him about the future—how he will triumph over the enemies he will meet; how his yet unborn son Silvius will found the great city of Alba Longa, from which, after eight generations, will come the twins Romulus and Remus, who together will found the great city of Rome. Anchises also gives Aeneas a thumbnail sketch of Rome's history, from its foundation through the unification of Italy, the great wars against Carthage, the rise of Julius Caesar, the victory over Antonius, and finally the foundation of the empire by Caesar Augustus.

Book Six is Virgil's masterpiece; it is not surprising that when Augustus demanded that Virgil read him some of the poem he had been working on for three years,

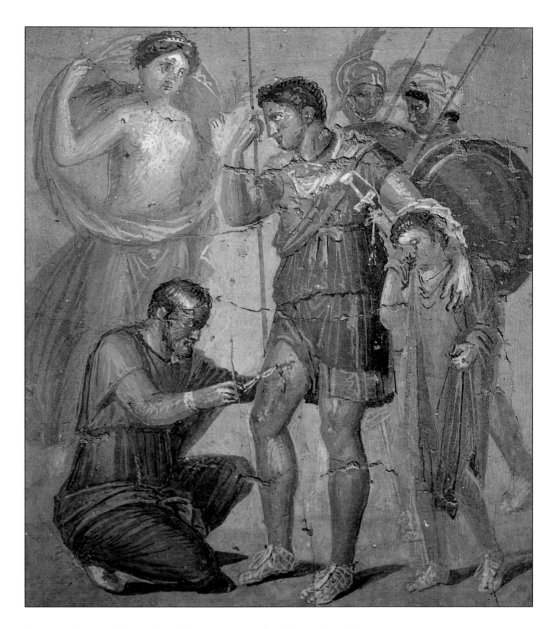

it was Book Six and a few other selections that he chose to read. He did not share with Augustus the majority of the work, filled with dreary battle scenes that are not altogether convincing. Virgil agonized over the *Aeneid*, and he was apparently never satisfied with it. As an artist who knew the greatness of which he was capable, it no doubt grieved him to produce work that he felt was inferior. Nonetheless, he struggled for eleven years to complete it. During this time, Augustus repeatedly asked to see the work, and time and time again Virgil put him off. When Virgil fell ill in Greece, he ordered that the manuscript of the *Aeneid* be destroyed if he should die. He did not die at this time, but when the time of his actual death did draw near, on September 21, 19 B.C., he ordered his friends to burn the work. Fortunately for the history of literature, his friends

In this ancient Roman wall painting from Pompeii (first century A.D.), Aeneas is strapped into his armor before battle, while his son Ascanius (Iulus) and his wife Creusa look sadly on. Caesar's family, the Julians, took their name from Aeneas's son Iulus (there was no J in ancient Latin).

did not comply with this wish, and Augustus forbade it by imperial decree. Today, although experts do admit that parts of the *Aeneid* are inferior, the work is a considered a classic of western literature, and for good reason: the vast majority of it is exceptional poetry that accurately portrays the spirit of the ancient Romans.

LIVY

In prose, the Augustan writer who best exemplifies the spirit of the Romans at this time is Titus Livius (59 B.C.–A.D. 1), who is generally called Livy. When Augustus came to power, one of his chief concerns was to stress and encourage the old Roman virtues, what people in the United States of the 1990s would call "family values." Like the Republicans of today, the Republicans of ancient Rome, whom Augustus claimed to represent, felt that many of the problems of Rome could be solved by a return to the standards of conduct stressed in the old legends about Rome's beginnings. Livy made it his personal crusade to reacquaint Romans with the standards of the past: the sacred character of the family, keeping one's word, self-control, and dignity in the face of adversity.

In his work *De Urbe Condita* (From the Foundation of the City), Livy covered the history of Rome from 1200 to 9 B.C. In this chronicle, he told legends of the early Republic that stirred the blood of patriotic Romans. He wrote of Gaius Mucius, the young boy who, in 506, during the Etruscan siege of Rome, determined to save his city by sneaking into the Etruscan camp and killing their king, Lars Porsena. Mucius planned to kill the king with a dagger, in full view of everyone, and take whatever punishment the Etruscans devised. Unfortunately, he killed the wrong man, and when he was seized and dragged into the presence of the real Lars Porsena, Mucius boldly lied. "King Porsena, I am the first of a hundred young men who have sworn to come at you one at a time, until one succeeds in assassinating you. I came first because I am judged in Rome as the most cowardly, and so if I fail no one would count my death as a loss." With that, Gaius Mucius thrust his right arm into a brazier full of glowing coals, and held his hand in the flame, revealing no sign of pain on his face, until the hand burned completely away. When he displayed the charred stump to King Porsena, the king declared that he had never seen a braver act and that if this boy was considered a cowardly Roman, he had

no desire to meet the brave ones. He sent Gaius Mucius back to Rome loaded with gifts. The grateful citizens of Rome granted Gaius a special epithet to honor him; from that day on he was known as Gaius Mucius Scaevola (*scaevola* is Latin for "Lefty").

This kind of story, illustrative of Roman courage, was just what Augustus was looking for. But Augustus also wanted stories from the Roman past that encouraged morality, and Livy was only too happy to comply. One of these tales takes place in 510 B.C., during the siege of Ardea, a town a few kilometers from Rome. Having had a bit too much wine, two cousins, Sextus Tarquinius and Tarquinius Collatinus, began to argue about which of them had the most virtuous wife. The debate grew heated, and observers feared it would end in blows, until somebody suggested a quick trip to Rome, in the middle of the night, to spy on their wives and see if their actions gave any indication of who was the most virtuous. They both thought this suggestion grand, and they set out for Rome. When they arrived, they went to Sextus's house and found his wife involved in a riotous party. Then they went on to Collatinus's house, where they found his wife, Lucretia, busy knitting socks for her husband. The question of virtue was therefore easily settled. But Sextus, upon seeing the virtuous Lucretia, became filled with desire for her, and a week later, he sneaked back to Rome and raped her in her own home. Immediately after Sextus left, Lucretia summoned her father and her husband, told them what Sextus had done, and extracted oaths of vengeance from both. She then rose to her feet, pulled a dagger from under her stolla, and drove it into her heart. With her dying breath, she explained to her shocked father and husband that although she was innocent, by killing herself she removed forever a subterfuge that unchaste wives in the future might use to conceal adultery.

Livy, however, was no mere propagandist, doing the will of his emperor blindly; he genuinely shared the emperor's concern over the decline in morals and values and believed that any period of history received its character from the kind of people living in it. Ancient Rome was more virtuous than the Rome of his day because it had better, more virtuous people in it. He hoped that his writings might inspire the current inhabitants of the city to emulate the ancient Romans. Apparently, many agreed with him, for his books were very popular. There were

Opposite: Aeneas appears before Queen Dido of Carthage with his son Ascanius, or Iulus. Dido was originally from Tyre, but she was exiled by her brother Pygmalion. Venus and Hera conspired together for Aeneas to fall in love with Dido, but Aeneas, as befits the character of the "Father of the Romans," was true to his quest to found a new city in Italy.

The *Rape of Lucretia* was painted by Jacopo Negretti in about 1570. Lucretia was the epitome of Roman female virtue. In Livy's account, she kills herself after being raped. Her death is the spark that ignites the Roman revolution against the cruel Etruscan ruler, Lucius Tarquinius Superbus, an act that ultimately results in the founding of the Roman Republic in 509 B.C.

even "pocket" editions of his works—small scrolls that presented only a few of the most dramatic tales. Livy wrote 142 books on Roman history, of which only 35 survive. In large part, the popular image of Romans as noble, long-suffering, stoic, and brave comes from Livy's stories.

OVID

But not all the great writers of the Augustan age shared Livy's vision and his desire to please the emperor. Existing side by side with Horace, Virgil, and Livy were half a dozen or so writers who disturbed Augustus greatly because they rejected the emperor's vision of a more moral Rome and even openly criticized his attempted reforms. Their rage was directed specifically at the *Leges Juliae*, or Julian Laws, which Augustus passed between 18 B.C. and A.D. 9. These laws attempted to encourage morality by decree. They ranged from mild to severe, with the most severe being a law that punished adultery by allowing a father to kill his daughter and her lover if he found them committing adultery and his own wife if she was found committing adultery in his house. At the other extreme were laws punishing widows and widowers who did not remarry. A widow was not allowed to inherit her husband's estate unless she remarried in six months, and a widower was forbidden to attend the public games until he remarried. Other laws rewarded wives who bore three or more children and punished adultery with exile.

One particular group of young poets—really rebellious adolescents, to judge by their age and manners—delighted in thumbing their noses at Augustus and his laws. When the emperor threatened punishment and death for adultery, they wrote poems extolling infidelity. Albius Tibullus (54–19 B.C.), for instance, wrote brilliantly crafted poems extolling his mistress Delia and delighting in the ways that he and Delia confounded her husband. His poems spoke of magic potions that would render Delia's husband incapable of believing any gossip's suggestions of infidelity and outlined secret hand signals that the lovers used at dinner parties to carry on their affair right in front of the poor cuckold. Sextus Propertius (50–16 B.C.) delighted in much the same thing. His special love was a certain Cynthia, and his poetry outlines a love-hate relationship between himself and this woman that seems more appropriate to modern seventh-graders than to adults of Augustan Rome. First she rejects him, and he consoles himself with another (actually two others at the same time). Cynthia discovers the group of lovers in the act, screams, throws the other women out, sobs and wails, and begs Sextus's forgiveness; the two reconcile. Then Sextus rejects her, and the whole sorry mess starts over. These kinds of petty affairs would not merit attention were it not for the fact that both Tibullus and Propertius were superb poets whose skill was the talk of Rome.

The most famous of these "anti-establishment" poets was Publius Ovidius Naso (43 B.C.–A.D. 17), best known as Ovid. Even though he was from a noble family, with all kinds of prospects before him, he refused to take his rightful place in society and the Senate. Instead, he determined to spend his life writing poetry. In 14 B.C. he published his *Amores*, a book of poetry about love. Many of the poems extol his beautiful mistress Corinna, the wife of a fellow noble. He declares his faithfulness to her, calling himself "a monogamous adulterer." *Amores* covers the usual round of lover's spats and reconciliations that is typical of this type of poetry, but its style and grace made it a best seller in Rome at exactly the time that Augustus was trying to encourage morality. The emperor was not ignorant of Ovid's work, and he was greatly displeased with it, but there was nothing illegal in writing about adultery and so there was nothing he could do.

Ovid's "unacceptable" works did not stop with *Amores*, however. In 2 B.C., he published *Ars Amatoria* (The Art of Love), a textbook on the seduction of women—both unmarried and married—a complete manual for the young middle-class or noble Roman on the "make." Its message was not aimed at the lower classes but at young men of good families who had a strong education and a good social background, exactly the future leaders of Rome that Augustus most wanted to influence to be good examples. It points out the best places to meet eligible women, how to initiate a conversation, what to talk about, how to act around their husbands, what clothes to wear, and how to wear your hair.

Ovid recommends art museums as the best place to meet the right kind of girl, for these places are frequented by women of the "right" class. Ovid stresses the need for sincerity in conversation: "Don't be afraid to show emotion, tears will impress a woman with a man's sincerity, and if you can't cry easily, then secretly poke a finger in your eye or yank out nose hairs to start the tears." He advises young Romans to bathe frequently but avoid makeup. "Dress simply, brush your teeth, get a tan, wear expensive shoes, keep your beard trimmed, and file your nails," he wrote. At dinner, dote on her every word, "Let your hand 'accidentally' touch hers when she passes a plate, and stare into her eyes. Be quick to flick a crumb off her breast, and if there is no such crumb, act like there is." When you finally have her alone, be bold and forthright—declare your love simply and directly. When you

In an ancient wall painting from Pompeii, two couples dine in the *triclinium*, or dining room, of a Roman house. Romans dined formally in a reclined position, as they thought this aided digestion. The triclinium was not necessarily a specific room in a Roman home. The couches and tables were often moved around the house to take advantage of different seasons: in the summer, for instance, Romans might eat in the *peristylum* (porch) because of the light; in the winter they might choose a room closer to the warmth of the kitchen.

have finally won her, ignore her for a time; this will make her anxious and more accommodating when at last you condescend to meet with her again.

Ars Amatoria was a literary sensation. Booksellers couldn't keep their copy slaves busy enough making more. Unfortunately for Ovid, Augustus's daughter Julia and his granddaughter, also named Julia, read the book and raved about it. It was one thing to have poets reciting bawdy verses in the streets, but it was quite another to have indecent books brought into the emperor's own residence. Augustus marked Ovid for destruction, but that destruction did not come right away. Legally, Ovid had done nothing wrong . What was needed was an overt act of immorality, and Augustus was willing to wait.

The emperor waited ten years for his opportunity. In the meantime, Ovid married for a third time, finding happiness with a woman named Fabia. According to all reports, the poet stopped his former philandering behavior and settled into peaceful domesticity. The famous writer of seduction manuals turned his skills to other things. First he wrote *Heroides*, a book about the love lives of famous women, and then in A.D. 7, he published his *Metamorphoses*, two hundred and fifty mythological tales of transformation. Like *Ars Amatoria*, this book took Rome by storm. Ovid then turned his attention to the religious festivals of Rome, and he wrote *Fasti*, or *Calendar*,

a poetic presentation of the main religious festivals of Rome. He dedicated this last work to Augustus himself, apparently forgetting—if he ever knew—about the emperor's anger over *Ars Amatoria*.

In A.D. 8, the emperor finally acted on his oath to destroy Ovid. Charged with immorality, the poet was exiled to the frontier port of Tomi (modern Constantsa in Rumania) on the Black Sea coast—surely the end of the earth to a Roman. The emperor said that the poet had participated in (or at least been present at) a debauch involving the emperor's granddaughter Julia. Julia was a disgrace, apparently a drunk and a libertine, who time and time again disappointed her grandfather, who referred to

her as "his boil." The details of the debauchery are not known. For the rest of his life, Ovid denied that he had been involved in this party. And for the rest of her life, his faithful wife, Fabia, tried to clear his name. Augustus, however, never relented, and Ovid died in exile, a sad and ironic end for this libertine turned gentleman.

Architecture

ext to literature, the most impressive achievement of Augustus's reign was in architecture. When Augustus stated that he "found a Rome of brick and left it covered in marble," he was speaking only of the official buildings of the city. At the time of his death, the most common buildings in the city were still the ramshackle slums of brick and wood that the great mass of urban poor lived in. These areas were fire hazards filled with crime and dirt. All Augustus could do with these was to organize an efficient fire department of thirty-five hundred fire fighters and create an urban police force. When it came to the official buildings of Rome, however, Augustus wanted to make major changes. He had the money—the staggering sum he had looted from Egypt—and he had the impetus, for the people of Rome wanted to forget the brutality and want of the civil wars and celebrate their new peace with visible signs of success. Augustus realized that by building lavishly he could not only celebrate his victory but also give the Roman people diversion and entertainment so that they would have ready access to pleasure instead of revolution. During his forty-one year reign, he built many temples to awe the people, as well as amphitheaters and baths to entertain them.

Roman temples were shaped like Greek temples, with a central rectangle surrounded by columns of various styles supporting an architrave and a frieze that in turn supported a sloping roof with a triangular pediment at each end. The pediment and the frieze beneath were often decorated with scenes from mythology. Inside would be a sanctuary and a statue of the god. Despite these similarities, however, Roman temples did differ from their Greek counterparts in at least two key ways. Whereas Greek temples were constructed on a base of

Although the Flavian Amphitheater in Rome was completed 61 years after the death of Augustus, it was a worthy successor to the great building programs of the first emperor. It was built in the valley between the Palatine, Caelian, and Esquiline hills by the emperor Vespasian (A.D. 68–79). As the largest public building in ancient Rome, it quickly became known as the "Colossus," hence the more popular name Colosseum.

Although some of the build-ings shown in this recon-struction of the Roman Forum about A.D. 200 were not in there during the reign of Augustus, both he and Julius Caesar began a program of adding to and beautifying the Forum. Both Julius Caesar and Augustus rebuilt the Rostra, the low plat-form in the center of the picture. It was decorated with the bronze beaks (*rostra* in Latin) taken from captured enemy ships. Caesar restored the Temple of Saturnus on the left edge of the illustration, and Augustus did the same for the Temple of Concord, the temple behind the Triumphant Arch. This arch, the Arch of Severus, was not there in the reign of Augustus.

two or three courses of stone, the Romans built their tem-ples on raised platforms. Although a Greek temple could be approached from any side, visitors to a Roman temple could gain access from only one direction, by going up a flight of stairs.

Before Augustus, most Roman temples were built of brick with some marble facing, but under Augustus, the building material of choice became the beautiful Carraran marble from northern Italy. In A.D. 2, Augustus began the construction of the Temple of Mars the Avenger; he used only this fine, white stone. The front of this gleaming white temple was decorated with eight 50 foot (15.3m) columns. This temple was basically Greek in appearance, but it had a semicircular apse at one end. This innovation would become progressively more popular in Roman ar-chitecture and would in turn become a basic element in the design of Christian churches centuries later.

Augustus built the Temple of Mars the Avenger to fulfill a vow; before the Battle of Philippi, he had promised to reward Mars, the god of war, with a temple if the god helped Augustus to win the battle. This temple, however, had other functions besides the religious ones.

The Senate met there to discuss questions of war and to reward victorious generals. In everyday use, the temple served as a law court and a place where juries were se-lected by lot; the apse was built to give the court more room to conduct its business.

This temple was built on the east side of another of Augustus's new constructions, the Forum Augusti, or Forum of Augustus. Augustus ordered it built to relieve pressure on the other two forums in Rome, the Forum Iulium (the Forum of Julius) and the Forum Romanorum (the Roman Forum). Each Roman town of any size had a forum, and Rome was so large that it needed three to con-duct all its public business. The addition of the Forum of Augustus satisfied the needs of Rome in this regard for the next century.

Outside the Forum of Augustus and next to the famous Temple of Castor and Pollux was another of Augustus's temples, the Templum Divi Iulii, or the Temple of the Deified Caesar. Augustus built this temple to commemorate the site where Caesar's body had been cremated after his assassination. Although nothing remains of the temple but the base, one can see that the podium, as the front base of the temple was called, was recessed to accommodate the altar to Caesar, built years before to mark the exact spot of Caesar's cremation. Augustus decorated the podium of this temple with the beaks from the prows of ships sunk during the Battle of Actium.

The most impressive temple constructed during Augustus's reign was the Pantheon. The original Pantheon, built in 27 B.C., was destroyed by fire in A.D. 80; the current Pantheon is a reconstruction built by the Emperor Hadrian (r. A.D. 117–138). All that remains of the original temple is the front portico, which is marked with the legend: M. AGRIPPA L. F. CO. TERTIUM FECIT. The temple was paid for by Marcus Agrippa, Augustus's chief advisor. Pliny the Elder (A.D. 23–113), who saw the original temple before it burned, wrote that it had bronze capitals on the columns, caryatids on the roof, and a mosaic floor that was a marvel of the time. This temple was built to commemorate all the chief gods of Rome, so its interior was originally filled with larger-than-life statues of gods. It later became a Christian church.

Other such buildings constructed by order of Augustus included the Temple of Apollo built in 24 B.C. near the Tiber River and across from the Theater of Marcellus. The location of this building was determined by lightning: Augustus had promised Apollo a temple but was uncertain where to put it; when he sat down near this site to consider the problem, a bolt of lightning struck the spot, and he took this as a sign from the god. Augustus placed a Greek and Latin library in the temple and used the library as a personal retreat.

Atop the Capitoline Hill, Augustus restored the temple of Jupiter Optimus Maximus, which had been neglected during the civil wars. He spent sixteen thousand pounds of gold on the interior decorations of this great temple and encrusted its walls with jewels. At the entrance to this temple, he built another temple to Jupiter called Jupiter Tonans (Jupiter Thundering) to serve as an entryway to the grander temple. Augustus claimed to have had a dream that designated the Temple of Jupiter Thundering as the watchman for that of Jupiter Optimus Maximus.

Augustus dedicated the Forum Augusti, the Forum of Augustus, in 2 B.C. to relieve the crowded conditions in the Roman Forum and to fulfill a vow he had made on the battlefield at Philippi. Young Roman males received the *toga virilis*, or the symbolic clothing of manhood, in this forum.

Augustus knew, however, that the people needed more than temples—they wanted places to go for entertainment. In 11 B.C., Augustus built a theater in honor of his nephew, Marcellus, directly across from the Temple of Apollo. Most of this theater survives today as the base of an apartment house, and from these remains historians have been able to calculate the tremendous size of the place. With a seating capacity of 20,500, it was the largest theater in Rome. Its three stories of seats built in a huge semicircle were supported by three tiers of vaults and arches, with a colonnaded and vaulted gallery at the top. Only the stage had a roof, but there was a linen awning 548 feet (167m) wide to protect the audience from rain or sun. The stage curtain did not rise when the plays started but was lowered into a slot at the front of the stage. By today's standards, the scenery was sparse, although it was much more elaborate than that of the Greeks. Behind the stage was a marble building with wings that helped to project the actor's voices toward the audience. Clever mechanical devices allowed changes of scenery to rise up atop the roof of the stage. During his reign, Augustus

built numerous theaters, including a 7,700-seat theater in the Campus Martius, and restored Pompey's theater on the Palatine Hill, which seated 17,500.

By the time of Augustus, the age of classic Roman drama typified by the plays of Terence and Plautus had died out, and the boisterous Romans had no patience for heavy Greek drama. What they wanted were musical extravaganzas, somewhat akin to a modern musical comedy, and slapstick comedy with stock villains and heroes. Roman audiences were notoriously impolite, and at any lapse in action, they would immediately start to talk.

Undoubtedly, the architectural achievement of Augustus's reign that pleased his subjects most was the famous Thermae Agrippae (the Baths of Agrippa). The first major public bath in Rome, the Thermae Agrippae became the prototype for the many that came after. To a large degree, Roman social life revolved around public baths, and Roman emperors after Augustus spent huge sums building these social centers to enhance their reputations. But *thermae* were much more than mere bathing

The Theater Tectum Odeion, a small theater built about 80 B.C. in Pompeii, could hold about 1500 people and at one time had a cover or awning for rainy weather, hence the name *tectum odeion*, or covered theater.

areas. They were huge complexes with vast interior spaces, and they were decorated with marble floors, walls, and ceilings. Scattered throughout were large wall paintings, brilliant mosaics, and statues of gods, muses, and heroes. Any Roman could spend an entire day at the bath for only a *quadrans*, a quarter of a penny, though each bather was expected to bring his or her own towels and body oils. In some baths, women were charged twice the price that men had to pay.

For formal Roman bathing in the Baths of Agrippa, the bather first entered the *apodyterium*, or dressing room, where there were niches to hold his or her clothes and a slave to watch them. Then the bather proceeded to the *tepidarium*, or warming room, where the temperature was kept high so that bathers would work up a sweat, which would prevent a shock to the system when they finally went into the *caldarium*, or hot room. Here the customer could spend as much time as he or she wished before exiting to the *frigidarium*, or cold room, for a cold bath. Finally, there was the *unctorium*, where bathers would lie on benches and be rubbed down with oil. The Thermae Agrippae even had a *laconium* to accommodate those who wished to take a sweat bath.

But this was not all. The Thermae Agrippae had an exercise yard with a track and other equipment, plus a pool that hot, dusty individuals could dive into to cool off. There were snack shops for lunches and libraries for reading. There were often singers, jugglers, and mimes for entertainment. It was customary for food, bathing, and entertainment all to be available at the baths. For this reason, the baths formed an important social outlet for most Romans; they were places where friends met, business meetings were held, and plans for the rest of the day were laid. However, each bath was strictly segregated by sex, for during the puritanical rule of Augustus, no respectable woman would be found in a male bath.

The architectural developments within the city of Rome were matched by similar massive building programs throughout the empire, for it seemed that the energy the Romans had previously put into fighting their civil war was transferred to the more positive activity of enhancing the empire's reputation through building. In all, Augustus restored eighty-two temples to heights of magnificence that certainly exceeded those they had enjoyed before the war, and he built twenty entirely new

ones. In addition, his engineers built giant aqueducts to carry fresh water into the major towns and equally impressive bridges to span rivers. The Pont du Gard outside of Nîmes, France, which rises 160 feet (48.78m) into the air, is a combination of road and aqueduct built on three tiers of arches. There were similarly impressive works at Reims and Orange. In Rome itself, the engineers created advantages for the general citizenry; by the end of Augustus's reign, every house in Rome had its own water supply, which was distributed in lead pipes from new aqueducts built by the engineers to bring water from the hills into the city.

A view of the ruined public baths, Thermae Stabiae, which once housed medicinal springs at the small resort town of Stabiae near Pompeii. The eruption of Vesuvius buried these baths with Stabiae, Herculaneum, and Pompeii in A.D. 79.

Art

ugustus's artistic encouragements did not end with architecture; sculpture and painting also flourished during this period. With sculpture, Augustus's reign marked the launching of a new artistic trend toward idealized representations. Sculpture before Augustus had been of two types: either outright copies or direct purchases of Greek statues, or busts that preserved the exact likenesses of ancestors. Hairs, wrinkles, moles, and frowns were all rendered with such precision and realism that for the first time in ancient history, historians know exactly what the people they are studying looked like. These kinds of sculpture did not die out during Augustus's reign, but they were submerged in favor of a new, generalized type of statue that hoped to remind people of the new spirit engendered by Augustus; in other words, Augustus changed the nature of sculpture for propaganda purposes. This new style is best demonstrated by the statue of Augustus traditionally called the Prima Porta, a sculpture created about 10 B.C.

The Prima Porta, which stands about 7 1/2 feet (2.3m) high, depicts Augustus in the act of addressing his army. His right arm is stretched out as if gesturing to his listeners, and in his left hand, he holds a military staff of authority. He wears a cuirass, or breastplate, on which symbolic figures are carved: the goddess of dawn drawing forth a new day with her chariot under the outstretched arms of Jupiter; Tiberius, Augustus's chosen successor, receiving the military standards that Crassus lost to the Parthians in 53 B.C.; and, at the bottom of the armor, Mother Earth holding up a horn of plenty. The symbolism is obvious: Augustus's reign heralds a new day under the protection of mighty Jupiter; he has restored the prestige of Rome that had been threatened during the civil wars and inaugurated a new and lasting reign; and his successes in this regard promise a new period of peace and plenty.

The most famous example of sculpture from the reign of Augustus was the Ara Pacis Augustae, or Altar of the Augustan Peace, which stood in the Campus Martius on the Via Flaminia, a sacred precinct where members of the Roman aristocracy made sacrifices. The walls around this altar were of white Carraran marble on which were depicted in relief the extended family of Augustus, along with various members of the Roman Senate, as they prepared to offer sacrifice on July 4, 13 B.C., at the dedication of the altar. The anonymous Greek artists who sculpted these reliefs captured every possible subject in every possible pose, from bored children to anxious matrons to dignified senators. The relief figures are cut higher in the foreground than in the background, lending a natural perspective to the piece. There is extreme detail in the depiction of clothing and hairstyles. There is great dignity in this relief, making it entirely consistent with the seriousness with which Augustus regarded duty to the state.

Throughout his new Rome, Augustus commissioned other sculptures to stress generalized concepts that he wished citizens to associate with his rule. Near the Senate house, for instance, he set up statues of Salus Publica (Public Well Being), Concordia (Harmony), and Pax (Peace); unfortunately, these statues are now lost. Wishing to stress the unity of the empire, he built the Porticus ad Nationes (Portico to the Nations) near Pompey's theater and filled it with fourteen idealized representations of the people who made up the empire, from the Celts in the north to the Ethiopians in southern Egypt.

In considering the generalized virtues that he wanted the people of Rome to value, Augustus soon realized that some were represented in a number of the classic Greek statues of deities. He therefore had statues of Apollo, Leto, Artemis, the Nine Muses, Pan, and Olympos brought to Rome from Greece. A great many of these statues were set up in the Portico Octaviae, near the Tiber, and Augustus ordered copies set up in each of the fourteen wards of the city to serve as good examples for the people; he was convinced that good examples would help create virtue in his subjects.

This concept of generalized sculpture did not long survive Augustus, for soon after his death, the old style of portrait sculpture made a triumphant return—the Romans felt that the spirit of their empire was best reflected in the harsh, craggy faces of their leaders.

With painting, Augustus sought to repeat what he had done with sculpture: he tried to use it as a means of impressing upon people the old-fashioned, solid virtues that Augustus felt had made Rome great. In his new forum, he commissioned paintings entitled *The Visage of War*,

Triumph, *Victory*, and *Castor and Pollux*. Although these painting have not survived, writers who saw them tell us that they presented figures that personified each of the titles. For instance, the picture of Castor and Pollux, the twin sons of Tyndareos and Leda and the brothers of Helen of Troy, represented warlike youth, skill at fighting, and devotion to the family. Augustus also commissioned paintings on the walls of the new Senate house he had built.

Opposite: The most famous statue of Augustus once decorated the villa of Livia, his wife, which was at Prima Porta; the statue has been called the Prima Porta Augustus ever since. Livia was Augustus's advisor and confidante. At the time of her marriage, she was pregnant with Tiberius Claudius Nero, the son of her first husband. Augustus adopted the boy and he became the second emperor of Rome, Tiberius (A.D. 14–37).

Left: A bronze statue of the god Apollo, who, until the time of Augustus, was a god that Romans revered mainly for his healing powers. But Augustus made Apollo his special god because he believed that Apollo had helped him win both the Battle of Philippi (42 B.C.) and Actium (31 B.C.).

A Roman fresco found on the wall of Livia's villa at Prima Porta is considered by art historians to be the finest example of extant Roman painting, although paintings from Pompeii certainly rival it. The painting is nearly 10 feet (3m) high.

One of the few stories of Augustus's sense of humor revolves around his artistic customs. At dinner parties, he often held auctions of paintings and supervised the bidding himself. During the bidding, he would keep the painting's back to the audience so that the people participating could not know what they were bidding on. Augustus found it amusing to note the expression on a person's face when he or she viewed the piece.

Augustus's emphasis on paintings displayed for the public, not to mention the styles and subject matter of these paintings, may have had an influence on the increase in the popularity of painting to decorate the homes of the wealthy. Excavations at Pompeii, 124 miles (200km) south of Rome, have led to the discovery of Augustan paintings preserved in a condition close to their original state; the volcanic ash of Vesuvius buried and preserved nearly thirty-five hundred wall paintings.

In Augustan Rome, the walls of the houses of the wealthy were covered with paintings done in bright colors.

The famous Roman historian Gaius Plinius Secundus (Pliny the Elder) credits the artist Spurius Tadius with popularizing this tradition of wall painting. According to Pliny, Spurius Tadius's particular talent was to reproduce elaborate landscapes and garden scenes framed in detailed representations of windows, doors, and balcony railings. These paintings had the effect of enlarging a room, because a person inside who viewed them felt as if they were gazing outward through a window. The most exciting thing about these paintings is that some of them achieve true perspective, as figures seem to be approaching or receding from the viewer. This perspective continues within the pictures themselves, where the viewer sees corners, niches, shelves, and arches filled with tendrils, baskets of flowers, and birds. That Augustus himself enjoyed these artistic flights of whimsy can be inferred from the fact that one of the most spectacular surviving scenes, named *The Garden of Livia* by archaeologists, comes from his wife's villa at Prima Porta.

Everyday Life

here was a vast gulf between the people who enjoyed paintings on their walls and those who lived in houses with bare plaster walls, between a senator like Gnaeus Lentulus, with a personal fortune of 400 million sesterces, and a common workman who earned only fifteen hundred sesterces a year. For one group there was a life of unimagined luxury and for the other a life filled with great hardships.

In ancient Rome during Augustus's time, a comparatively few people with a great deal of money lived very well, while the vast majority of people paid high prices to barely survive. On the Palatine Hill were the homes of the wealthy—large, beautifully furnished, and decorated houses, with thick doors and a staff of slaves for safety's sake—while down in the city proper a man might pay two thousand sesterces a month for a tiny room in a ramshackle apartment building called an *insula*. The wealthy man on the Palatine would have an interesting variety of food to eat and beautiful clothes to wear, while the poor man in his insula would be content with clothing he changed weekly and a steady diet of wheat porridge.

The homes of the wealthy were similar to one another in design and had little variation. The Roman house had in fact changed little in two hundred years, and increased personal wealth was seen as an opportunity only to expand that basic design, not to alter it.

A visitor entered the house of a wealthy Roman through the *ostium*, a massive double wooden door that opened directly onto the street through a small entryway. The floor of this entryway might be decorated with mosaics and include a warning or a greeting: CAVE CANEM (Beware of the Dog) or SALVE (Welcome). On either side of the door, the visitor would notice small shops selling any number of things. These shops were small rooms that had no direct entryway to the main house, and which the thrifty Roman rented out as an extra source of income.

Immediately through the door was the *vestibulum*, either a short hall that connected the doorway to the *atrium*, the main room of the house, or, in, the most sumptuous homes, to an unroofed area in which flowers and plants grew. The atrium was a roughly square room whose roof sloped downward and inward to the center of the room, leaving an opening (called a *compluvium*) to the sky through which water might fall during a rainstorm. This water dropped into the *impluvium*, a square marble pool in the center of the floor, where it was stored for later use in watering the plants and cleaning the interior. Romans were discouraged from drinking this water by the presence of vast numbers of pigeons on their roofs. The atrium was the formal greeting room for the house; it was decorated with walls of fine marble or with paintings of garden or mythological scenes. Opening onto the atrium were rooms called *alae* in which the owner kept the wax or marble busts of famous ancestors who had held public office. To clarify things for visitors, there might be cords connecting one bust to another to show relationships and small signs under each one to give other pertinent infor-

Most Romans lived along narrow streets, like this excavated and partially restored one at Herculaneum, that were pitch black at night. Travel at night along these streets was dangerous, and people of means did not venture out without hired bodyguards.

The Roman cook would cover the top of his stove with a bed of hot coals and then set bronze pots on trivets above them. The arch underneath this "range" was used to hold fuel.

mation. One of the *alae* would also be home to the *lararium*, a cabinet where the figures of the family gods, or *larae*, were kept.

At the end of the atrium was a covered area called the *tablinum*, or office, where the master of the house conducted his business. This area looked directly out into the atrium. For privacy the owner could close the tablinum off with wooden shutters. Behind the tablinum was the *peristylum*, the family area of the house. This was where the owner of the house kept the *arca*, a huge wooden chest in which he stored his money and important papers. Like the atrium, this area was open to the sky, but unlike the atrium, it did not have an impluvium; instead, there was a garden in the center. Opening onto the atrium were the *cubicula* (bedrooms), *culina* (kitchen), and *triclinium* (dining room). Every wealthy family's house had a *bibliotheca*, a library that housed books in the form of papyrus scrolls arranged in cabinets. Although these books often went unread, a bibliotheca was considered a necessary item for the successful Roman. Farther back in the house and separated from the peristylum by a wall, there was often another garden.

Many homes, even of the wealthy, had no heating, except for the fireplace in the kitchen. For heating during Rome's short winter, the family had slaves carry small metal braziers from room to room. The most expensive homes had a hypocaust system of heating, a series of ceramic or brick tunnels under the floor of the house that connected to a furnace. In the winter, the furnace would be kept stocked by a slave so that heat would flow through the tunnels and warm the stone or marble floors by conduction. Roman houses were notoriously cold, and the polite host met his guests at the door with a supply of warm woolen socks.

The dwellings of the vast majority of Romans were much different from those of the wealthy. The insula in which most Romans lived were poorly built, extremely flammable wooden and brick buildings full of tiny apartments, and a tenant might rent a whole floor, a single room, or any amount of space in between. By law the insula could be no taller than 70 feet (21.3m) and were built around a central shaft to admit light into those apartments which did not face the streets. Such rooms had no safe means of cooking or heating, and one suspects that most people who lived there bought food outside and carried it home to eat. Although there were laws against doing so, garbage and human waste were simply dumped out into the street. To escape detection and a fine, most Romans waited until night and then poured a shower of waste onto the street. It was these cascades that inspired the poet Decimus Junius Juvenalis to write that walking the streets at dinnertime was dangerous and "only a fool goes to dinner without first making a will." For the resident of an insula, keeping oneself clean would have been a challenge had it not been for the public baths. Every morning insula residents went straight to these beautiful places for their morning scrub.

The diet of the average Roman varied with his or her class. For the wealthy, dinner was the stuff of gourmet legend, while for the poor it was pure monotony.

Regardless of class, however, mealtimes were standardized. Immediately after rising at dawn, the Romans would eat *jentaculum* (breakfast). For rich or poor alike, this meal consisted of watered wine and a wheat pancake or two. The only difference arising from the class of the individual lay in the dressing used for the pancake: a rich person would dip his pancake in honey, a poor person in olive oil. The main meal of the day, called *cena*, would occur between 1:30 and 3:30, depending on the season; it was held earliest in winter, to compensate for the shorter day. It was this meal that separated the rich and the poor.

The average Roman ate a simple wheat porridge for cena. If he had some money, he might be able to add some flavoring or other ingredients, such as cheese, various herbs, olives, mushrooms, chunks of fish, or, more rarely, meat. All this would be washed down with a little

A Roman husband and wife are seated at the table for an informal family meal. Eating while reclining on couches was reserved for formal affairs. It was not unusual for Roman children to stand at the table during meals.

A fresco from a wall in Pompeii shows a typical Roman street scene. On the left-hand side, two men discuss a piece of cloth while one of the men's wives looks on. On the right, a man and his son talk to a salesman selling cooking pots.

watered wine. Again, for those with a little money, apples, plums, quinces, or grapes were available; however, fancier fruits such as pomegranates, apricots, peaches, and figs were restricted to the wealthy. Pork was the favorite meat of the Romans, and sausages called *botuli* were sold on the streets. Finally, there were commercial bakeries where citizens could buy bread, but bread was expensive enough that for many a daily diet of this food was out of their reach.

For the wealthy, dinner could be a vastly different experience. A wide range of exotic foods was available to Romans who could afford it, along with an impressive selection of wines. Unfortunately, wine at this time did not age properly and was astringent, because the cork had not yet been invented and wine jugs could not be made airtight. To compensate for this, Romans heated their wine in small lead-lined containers that "sweat" lead residue into the wine, imparting a slightly sweet taste (along with a dose of lead poisoning). Astringency was further reduced by mixing wine with generous amounts of water.

Exotic foods were available from all over the empire, and the wealthy could also afford to pay for cooks who knew how to use these foods. These cooks prided themselves on their sauces, which well-to-do Romans used liberally on their foods. One especially favorite sauce was called *liguanmen*. This concoction was made from tuna fish and internal organs placed in a heavy brine water and left to sit for six weeks. Other means of flavoring foods included honey, which was thought to bring out the flavor of meat and applied like barbecue sauce, spices such as pepper, pine nuts, vinegar, and lovage, a relative of the parsley family.

A number of recipes have survived from this era, giving historians a fair idea of the kind of cooking the rich could afford. For instance, the famous Roman orator Cicero, a well-known gourmet, especially enjoyed halibut or cod cooked in oil, filleted and mixed with cow's brains, chicken livers, hard-boiled eggs, and cheese. This concoction was cooked together and flavored with pepper, lovage, marjoram rue, honey, oil, and cumin. If a pregnant woman was a dinner guest, the host had to omit the marjoram rue, for popular opinion had it that this herb was sure to cause an abortion.

Wealthy Romans often ate too much of foods that were unhealthy. Consequently, the poor, who subsisted mainly on grain porridge and a few vegetables, generally were healthier. However, both rich and poor were plagued by a steady diet of spoiled foods, because they had no way to prevent bacterial contamination, and there was a lack of hygiene in food preparation. Without a

doubt, these were major factors in the low life expectancy of Romans. The few Romans who are known to have lived into their seventies and eighties were almost all known for their abstemious habits and simple food tastes.

Differences in clothing between rich and poor were differences of quality, not style. All Romans, no matter what their class, wore garments that draped over or around the body. The Roman tunic was basically two pieces of cloth sewn together along their edges with holes for the arms and head and sometimes short sleeves. On men, this basic garment reached to about six inches above the ankle; on women, a tunic reached to the ground. It looked much like an elongated Mexican serape with short sleeves attached. For Roman males, the other basic article of clothing was the *toga*, a large, roughly triangular piece of cloth measuring 13 by 8.2 feet (4 x 2.5m) that was wrapped around the body. Anyone could wear a tunic, but the toga was strictly for Roman males over the age of sixteen. Romans of the wealthiest classes had togas with a wide band of garnet running along the edges, and Romans of what we would call the middle class had togas with a narrower band of garnet.

The female counterpart to the toga was the *stolla*, which was worn over the tunic and reached all the way to the ground. In Augustus's time, women were allowed to wear some color on their stollae, but they were muted colors—browns, grays, rust, or light yellow. Only after Augustus did women begin to wear more brightly colored clothing. Sometimes, when she went outside, a woman would wear a *palla*, or shawl, over the stolla. Generally, the woman wrapped the palla around her, flung one end over her shoulder from behind, and carried the excess hanging from her arm.

Instead of a toga or palla, men and women often wore over their tunics a cloak called a *lacerna*, which was often colored. This garment saved the toga or palla from risk of stains and dirt, but Augustus, feeling that this was somehow improper for men, forbade them to wear the lacerna without a toga underneath; he did not, however, restrict its use by women.

Formal party wear for both sexes was called a *synthesis*. This garment, which was worn over the tunic, was most commonly made of linen or cotton. It is often difficult to tell from written sources what exactly the syntheses were made of because Romans used the same word, *carbasus*, for cotton and linen. A very few syntheses were made of silk; this extremely rare fabric, which had to come all the way from China, was a luxury item enjoyed only by the very wealthy. In general, the wealthy restrained themselves, for during the reign of Augustus,

A Roman woman applies perfume. Then, as now, perfume was expensive and came in tiny glass jars with a glass applicator. Perfume was an important item for the Roman party-goer, as Romans believed that the scent of perfume and flowers delayed the intoxicating effect of alcohol.

excessive display of expensive clothing was discouraged and sure to win the emperor's displeasure. Only later did Romans begin to wear the elaborate and colorful clothing that the popular imagination credits them with.

An observer could estimate the relative wealth of a Roman by both the cleanliness and the stitching of his or her garments—white was the usual color for clothing, and because cleaning a toga or tunic was an expensive and time-consuming business, wealthy people's garments were the cleanest. The Romans had no soap. If a person wanted clean clothing, he or she would send it to a fuller's shop. There the garment would be bleached by being

submerged in a tube of water where slaves stomped on it. The garment would then be suspended over a framework of reeds with a smoking pot of sulfur underneath. After this, the garment would be "washed" again and combed. Finally, the nap would be sheared off with scissors. This process was extremely hard on fabrics, and if clothes were cleaned often, they did not last long. The wealthier Romans could afford a number of tunics and togas and so could avoid cleaning the same piece over and over; the poor, however, were lucky to have one extra to wear while the other was being cleaned, so they often wore dirty tunics. The whitest and finest togas were called *candidae togae*, and politicians who wore them to make a good impression when running for office were called *candidati*, which has given us the word *candidate*.

The stitching on a garment also told an observer a great deal about the relative wealth of a Roman. Because the Romans had no way to temper steel, their needles were dull instruments made of bronze or bone. Sewing with a dull needle was a long and laborious process and produced uneven stitching, except in the hands of a real expert who had plenty of time. The wealthy could pay for the labor of an expert slave tailor who could spend long hours sewing, but a poor Roman had no such option.

Under their outer garments, the Roman man wore *subligaculum* (underwear), a piece of cloth wound around the waist. The subligaculum was loose enough to be worn comfortably while working outside, and farmers, slaves, and athletes wore subligacula as their only garment during work or training. Women did not wear subligacula, but they often wore a broad band of fabric wrapped round their tunic and under their breasts for support.

On their feet, Romans wore sandals or shoes; only slaves and the poorest Romans went barefoot. Generally, only women wore sandals in public; men confined their use to the home. On the street, men wore shoes that covered the upper part of the foot but left the toes exposed. Inside, at a social gathering or dinner party, men and women never wore shoes; footwear was removed at the door and returned when the guest left.

As for washing, the Romans were the cleanest people in the ancient world, with the possible exception of the Egyptians. Every day started with a bath, either at home, for the very wealthy, or at the public baths. Shaving, however, was another matter. Because of the poor quality of

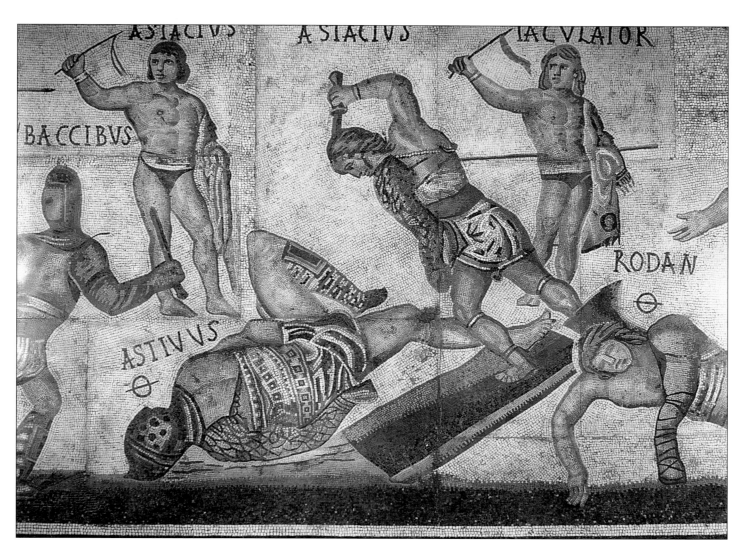

Gladiators had their admirers among Roman sports enthusiasts much as some modern people revere professional athletes. One wealthy Roman went so far as to have his favorite gladiators immortalized in a mosaic. Each man is identified by name.

Roman metalwork, it was just too difficult for the average citizen to keep a bronze or iron razor sharp enough to shave himself without great pain and suffering. If a man could afford it, he went to a barber to be shaved; if not, he went about his business with stubble on his face. Beards were considered proper attire only for philosophers, an attitude that did not change until the Emperor Hadrian began to wear one in A.D. 117.

Cosmetics, which were a vast and expensive industry in Rome, were available only to wealthy women. The wealthy Roman woman was convinced that sleeping with a mixture of flour and water on her face would decrease wrinkles and make her skin fresh. Other women swore that bathing the face with the milk of an ass was a much better treatment. Women were also extremely concerned about their teeth, and so they began each morning with a vigorous brushing. Discolored teeth, which were a constant worry for these women, could be replaced with false ones made of powdered bone or ivory.

The Roman concept of beauty demanded the removal of excess body hair, and the favored method—once again because it was the era of bad razors—was to scrape it off with a pumice stone. This not only removed hair, but also gave the skin a healthy look. For makeup, women used both black and green mascara. According to the fashion of the day, pale skin was most desirable, and many women powdered their faces with chalk, accenting this pale look with saffron eye shadow.

Roman women also took great pains with their hair, and many employed specially trained slaves to keep their coiffures looking stylish. Curling irons were used by a number of the wealthier women. During Augustus's reign, most Roman women were brunette, but many were fascinated with the idea of being blond. Wealthy women spent a great deal of money on dyeing their hair with "German soap," a kind of bleach, or buying blond wigs made with blond hair purchased from German girls across the Roman frontier.

For men of Augustan Rome, much like for modern men, baldness was a major concern. For whatever reason, this was a major worry during the last part of Augustus's reign, and quacks recommended the wildest remedies. One of the most popular consisted of rubbing the hair with a concoction made of deer bone marrow and bear fat. Another consisted of rubbing the hair with a paste made of crushed buttercups, rat feces, and pepper.

No matter whether they were rich or poor, whether they ate well or poorly, whether they wore clean clothes or dirty ones, there was one thing that united all Romans—the Games! The games included not only the famous gladiatorial combats, but also fights between men and wild animals, athletic contests, chariot races, and even mock naval battles. Because of the chaos of the civil wars, Augustus and his advisors were well aware of the potential of the Roman population for violence and trouble

making. Their decision to expand the number of spectacles and entertainments was undoubtedly rooted in an understanding or hope that this would decrease the risk of riots. Augustus was proud of the number of times he organized games. In a document called the *Res Gestae Divi Augusti* (Deeds of the Divine Augustus), he wrote that during his reign he had sponsored 8 gladiatorial combats, during which 10,000 gladiators fought; 23 athletic contests; 26 beast fights, in which 3,500 animals were killed; and one huge exhibition of a naval battle fought in a specially constructed excavation that measured 1798 by 1198 feet (548 x 365m) and in which 3,000 sailors did battle. It is no wonder that the crowd loved him.

Until Augustus built an amphitheater, most of the games took place in the Circus Maximus, a huge racetrack between the Aventine and Palatine hills that measures 1798 feet (548m) long and 597 feet (182m) wide. The

A mosaic shows gladiators fighting with a variety of animals, including an ostrich, a lion, an ibex, and a bull. Fights between men and animals, or *venationes* (hunts), were popular attractions, and were a way of showing the strength of the empire over faraway places by displaying exotic animals. When the Colosseum was dedicated in A.D. 80, 9,000 wild and tame animals were killed.

games were open to all married citizens, and admission was free as long as men wore their togas. People bet huge sums on the outcome of games, and successful charioteers and gladiators became as famous as modern athletes—and just as rich in their society.

The gladiatorial contests were the bloodiest and consequently the most popular. The most popular of these contests were those between the *retiarius*, armed with a trident and a net, and the *secutor*, who wielded a short sword and a small round shield. The retiarius would try to catch the secutor in his net, and if he failed, he would beat a hasty retreat until he could prepare his net for another cast. Meanwhile, the secutor would follow the retiarius around the arena and try to kill him with his sword. But the warriors of this particular pairing were only two of the many specialties available. Some gladiators fought as a Thrax, or Thracian, armed with a shield and a sickle and wearing greaves on the legs for protection. The traditional opponent of the Thrax was the Samnis, who was armed with a square shield and sword and protected by a helmet, a leather guard for the right arm, and one greave on the left leg. There were also horsemen. The *essedarii* fought in a chariot, and the *andabatae* fought on horseback with a lance and in full armor. Gladiators were usually slaves, although there were free men who fought for pay or adventure. There were even female gladiators. Stratonici, the most famous female gladiator, once killed three men in a row armed only with an iron chamber pot.

Second in popularity to the gladiators were the charioteers. Traditionally, there were four teams of charioteers—the reds, greens, whites, and blues—and each had its own loyal fans. The race course consisted of seven laps, about 6 miles (9.5km), and during the day there would be a dozen races. Most races consisted of either two

This Pompeiian fresco shows couples gathering for a banquet. Banquets were extremely important to Romans because they were practically their only social occasions, since they did not hold dances, receptions, or other events.

or four horses, the drivers controlling the animals with reins wrapped around their bodies. The most exciting part of the race came during the turns at each end of the Circus Maximus, for that was where a driver could easily lose control, turn his chariot over, and be trampled by the other vehicles.

A great deal of ink has been used by historians trying to justify the brutal games of the Romans. Usually, they excuse the brutality of the games by reminding us that gladiators were prisoners of war who were given a chance to live a little longer by fighting in the games. This, however, would indicate that this kind of brutal "entertainment" would be accepted in other societies as well. In reality, the brutality of the games disgusted other ancient people, especially the Greeks, who often released their prisoners and allowed them to go home. It is clear now that there was a brutal and ugly streak in Roman civilization that is totally at variance with the admirable triumphs of their civilization and that no amount of explanation can excuse.

Another brutal factor of Roman civilization was slavery. Rome exploited this system of labor more than any other ancient society; slaves were much rarer in Mesopotamia, Egypt, and Greece than in Rome. Before the time of Augustus, the military successes of the Roman armies had flooded the empire with prisoners of war. Successful military commanders enhanced their fortunes by selling the men and women captured during their campaigns; it became customary for thousands of slaves to be sold daily at the slave markets in Campania, Calabria, and Sicily. Although there were scattered voices among the Romans who objected to the harsh and brutal treatment of slaves, none questioned the existence of the institution itself.

Prices of slaves varied greatly. An ugly girl with no specific skills might be had for six hundred sesterces, while a pretty young boy or girl slave purchased for immoral purposes might bring ten thousand. A Greek slave trained as a scholar might be sold for 150,000 sesterces. Like prices, treatment varied with owners and the type of labor expected. Agricultural slaves and slaves used in mining were treated the worst. These men had little to recommend them except brawn and were therefore cheap. They were purchased cheaply and literally used up in a few growing seasons.

Roman literature is filled with stories about cruelty to slaves. In one tale, for instance, a Roman aristocrat crucified her female slave for burning her hair with a curling iron. Punishments for slaves were generally harsh, but this example seems to have been extreme even for Romans. If a slave murdered his master, the law dictated that every slave in the household be crucified as an example. Despite these tales and laws, there are an equal number of incidents where slaves and their masters showed real concern and genuine affection for each other. The great Roman orator Cicero, for instance, treated his slave Tiro as a member of the family.

If anything favorable can be said about Roman slavery, it is that a vast number of slaves were freed every year. During and after the reign of Augustus, a large number of the aristocracy were influenced by the philosophical movement known as Stoicism, which taught, among other things, that all men were brothers in that they all contain some spark of divinity. For some, it became difficult to reconcile the brutality of slavery with the behavior due a brother. Therefore, more and more masters began to free their slaves.

The same impetus that led to the freeing of slaves also persuaded some Romans to press for laws that protected slaves from harsh treatment. Augustus began this movement with a law forbidding the sale of slaves born within the empire to fight as gladiators, unless they had committed some civil crime. Another law severely limited the torturing of slaves to extract information in criminal investigations. Succeeding emperors passed other laws forbidding such practices as selling a female slave to serve as a prostitute and killing a slave without a trial. The emperor Hadrian even banished a woman for excessive brutality toward her slaves, and Antoninus Pius made killing a slave an act of homicide. By the beginning of the fourth century A.D., the humanizing movement toward slaves begun by Augustus had resulted in the virtual elimination of slavery in the western part of the empire, certainly one of Augustus's most impressive legacies.

The End of an Age

 lthough life in Augustan Rome was harsh and brutal by modern standards, it represented a great improvement for the majority of Romans over the chaos of the civil wars. Although Augustus had certainly curtailed the democratic institutions of the empire, he had replaced them with a benevolent rule made possible by his own moderate nature and, most important, the immense wealth he had won during the wars. Not only did the life of the common man improve, but creativity flourished. Centuries later, Renaissance writers characterized his rule as the golden age of Rome and represented the history of the empire after him as merely a silver age that gradually degenerated into an age of bronze.

Augustus built two temples to Apollo during his reign; the one in Pompeii is shown here. Apollo was not only the god of healing, but also the god of music, poetry, and learning in general. The second temple, on the Palatine Hill, was near Augustus's home, and the emperor supposedly used its library as a retreat.

Conclusion

Why Do Great Empires Fall?

Why do great empires fall? On Monday morning, October 15, 1764, the great English historian Edward Gibbon thought he had found the reason as he was sitting atop the Capitoline Hill overlooking the Roman Forum. From a nearby monastery he heard a group of monks singing a hymn, and suddenly linked the ruins before him at least partially to their religion. In that moment, so Gibbon tells us, he conceived the thesis of his great book, *The Decline and Fall of the Roman Empire*. He attributed the fall of that great empire to three things: first, the eviscerating activities of the Christians, who discouraged participation in government and society by fixing man's gaze on a better life in the future; secondly, an unwholesome Roman preoccupation with luxury, pleasure that led in turn to vice and corruption throughout Roman society; finally, the overwhelming military pressure of the Germans against the Roman frontiers.

In proposing this theory Gibbon unconsciously began a fad that has lasted up to the present day of seeking the causes for the fall of Rome and other great civilizations. In 1918, for instance, another great historian, Oswald Spengler, wrote *The Decline of the West*, in which he tried to project the impending fall of western European and American society due to corruption, decadence, and depravity. Current religious leaders (conveniently forgetting Gibbon's inclusion of Christianity's part in the fall of Rome) have thundered from the pulpits that American society is traveling down the same foreordained path to destruction as Rome.

In their zeal to find the causes of decline in sin, depravity, luxury, and vice, people have forgotten the third of Gibbon's reasons, which is really the simplest and most convincing—the Germanic attacks on the empire. Starting in A.D. 160 , and continuing almost without interruption for the next three centuries, hundreds of thousands of German warriors assaulted the borders of the empire, trying to break in and share the splendor and wealth that was Rome. While the Roman army put up a gallant resistance that temporarily held back the hordes and even reached accommodation with some, in the end there were simply too many Germans and not enough Romans. This argument of the fall is simple and inescapable; no matter how grand a civilization, no matter what its accomplishments, brute force unceasingly applied will topple it. "Rome was," in the words of the great French medievalist Ferdinand Lot, "murdered."

In the preceding chapters are recorded the triumphs of four other great ancient civilizations besides Rome that reached exceptional heights of accomplishment during their golden ages. Yet in the end they too fell. The reason is not some moralistic assessment of decadence and sin, but rather the simple fact that their success was envied by their neighbors, who took what they wanted because they had the military might to do it.

Hammurabi's empire on the banks of the Euphrates was the most powerful state in the region for a time, and his work of consolidation and economic hegemony continued for two centuries after his death. Yet throughout these two centuries the empire was constantly harassed by the less-civilized barbarian Kassites, who sallied out of their mountain vastness to the east to raid and steal. Finally, when the eyes of the Babylonian generals were fixed on the Kassite menace to the east, a surprise hammer blow fell suddenly from the north as thousands of other barbarian raiders, the Hittites from Asia Minor, rolled south in a fabulous new weapon, chariots, and sacked Babylon in 1595 B.C. The world was stunned, for nobody expected trouble from the north. When the Hittites withdrew, the Kassites fell on the remnants of Babylonia in a feeding frenzy.

The story was much the same with the New Kingdom of Egypt. Up to the reign of Rameses II (r. 1279–1213 B.C.), the Egyptian Empire had funneled the untold wealth of Asia into the Nile Valley, and had built with it the most spectacular architectural monuments anyone had ever seen. That same wealth created the leisure to write great literature and produce stunning art, but this luxury and splendor tempted people outside the empire to steal it. From the beginning of the thirteenth century B.C., Egypt faced wave after wave of invaders.

First, there were sea raiders from Syria who invaded the Nile Delta in the 1250s B.C., and although these were beaten back by Rameses II, his successor, Merneptah, faced them again, plus an invasion of Libyans from the west. Continually for the next two centuries, Egypt faced attacks from the north and south, but in the 1190s B.C., new threats appeared from Asia across the Sinai, and from the revolting Egyptian provinces to the south in Kush. In the end, around 1090 B.C., there was no great mystery about the fall of Egypt's New Kingdom; it was simply battered to its knees by overwhelming force applied from all sides.

With Assyria it was much the same, although the period of decline and fall was much shorter than that of Babylon or Egypt. Perhaps this was because the Assyrian Empire had not had as much time to develop as its more vigorous counterparts. In 744 B.C., King Tiglath-Pileser II suddenly expanded the Assyrian borders west to the Mediterranean and south to the Persian Gulf. But by 612 B.C., just under a century and a half later, a coalition of Babylonians and Medes, anxious to share Assyria's wealth and power, took Nineveh, the Assyrian capital, after a two-year campaign, and utterly destroyed the city.

The Temple of Isis on the Island of Philae marks the end of the classical Egyptian civilization, for it was there, in the year A.D. 394, that the last hieroglyphic inscription was carved.

Finally there is Athens, considered by many historians to have been the crowning cultural achievement of the ancient western world. Here again, in an incredibly short time, Athens had built a rich empire—mainly on the backs of its subjects scattered throughout the Aegean world. In her expansion, however, Athens frightened the Greek world and excited its envy. Sparta was willing to harness this fear and envy and lead a coalition of Greek states and Persians against Athens in the twenty-five-year Peloponnesian War.

The Athenians put up a good fight, but in the end, with most of Greece and the Persians allied against Athens, the Spartans blockaded the city and forced a surrender. The Spartans quickly assumed leadership of Greece, and were in turn defeated by another Greek coalition.

However, while all great empires end, at least some of them—certainly the five in this book—leave particularly inspiring examples for succeeding cultures to emulate and build upon. It is hoped that at least some later civilizations learn from both the triumphs and the failures of past civilizations and go on to create their own, better glories in much the same vein as expressed by a medieval cleric, himself inspired by Rome, who wrote that we "were like dwarfs on the shoulders of giants, we see farther than they because of their stature."

Timothy R. Roberts
November 9, 1996

SUGGESTED READING

The following books represent many of the sources used to write this book. Furthermore, they are highly readable in their own right.

General

James, Peter, and Nick Thorpe. *Ancient Inventions.* New York: Ballantine Books, 1994.

Riddle, John M. *Contraception and Abortion from the Ancient World to the Renaissance.* Cambridge, Mass.: Harvard University Press, 1992.

Babylon

Lloyd, Seton. *The Archaeology of Mesopotamia*, rev. ed. London: Thames and Hudson, 1978.

Oates, Joan. *Babylon*, rev. ed. London: Thames and Hudson, 1979.

Oppenheim, A. Leo. *Ancient Mesopotamia*, rev. ed. Chicago: University of Chicago Press, 1977.

Postgate, J.N. *Early Mesopotamia: Society and Economy at the Dawn of History.* London: Routledge, 1992.

Egypt

Aldred, Cyril. *The Egyptians*, rev. and enlarged ed. London: Thames and Hudson, 1984.

Budge, E.A. Wallis. *The Egyptian Book of the Dead.* New York: Dover Publications, 1967. An unabridged reissue of the original 1895 edition.

Desroches-Noblecourt, Christiane. *Tutankhamen.* New York: New York Graphic Society, 1963.

Mertz, Barbara. *Red Land, Black Land.* New York: Coward-McCann, 1966.

Nunn, John F. *Ancient Egyptian Medicine.* Norman, Okla.: University of Oklahoma Press, 1996.

White, John Manchip. *Everyday Life in Ancient Egypt.* New York: Peter Bedrick Books, 1991.

Assyria

Curtis, J.E., and J.E. Reade, eds. *Art and Empire: Treasures from Assyria in the British Museum.* New York: The Metropolitan Museum of Art, 1995.

Olmstead, Alfred T. *History of Assyria.* Chicago: University of Chicago Press, 1923. This is still one of the best books on Assyria, despite its early date.

Parrot, Andre. *The Arts of Assyria.* New York: Golden Press, 1961.

Saggs, H.W.F. *Everyday Life in Babylonia and Assyria.* New York: G.P. Putnam's Sons, 1965.

_____. *The Might That Was Assyria.* London: Sedgwick and Jackson, 1984.

Athens

Hammond, N.G.L. *A History of Greece to 322 B.C.* Oxford: Clarendon Press, 1959. Still the best general history of ancient Greece in English.

Hanson, Victor Davis. *The Western Way of War: Infantry Battle in Classical Greece.* New York: Alfred A. Knopf, 1989.

Kitto, H.D.F. *The Greeks.* Harmondsworth: Penguin Books, 1951. Still in print after forty-five years, this book remains the classic introduction to Greek culture.

Robertson, D.S. *Greek and Roman Architecture.* London: Cambridge University Press, 1971.

Sealey, Raphael. *A History of the Greek City States: ca. 700–338 B.C.* Berkeley, Calif.: University of California Press, 1976.

Rome

Cowell, F.R. *Life in Ancient Rome.* New York: Perigee Books, 1980.

Finley, M.I. *Ancient Slavery and Modern Ideology.* New York: Viking Press, 1980.

Grant, Michael. *The World of Rome.* New York: New American Library, 1960. An older book, but Grant's writing style makes for easy, informative reading.

_____. *The Twelve Caesars.* New York: Charles Scribner's Sons, 1975.

Hamilton, Edith. *The Roman Way.* New York: W.W. Norton and Company, 1932. Still the most readable book on Roman culture.

Highet, Gilbert. *Poets in a Landscape.* New York: Alfred A. Knopf, 1957. A marvelous collection of anecdotes about the famous Roman poets.

Robertson, D.S. *Greek and Roman Architecture.* London: Cambridge University Press, 1971.

Gaius Suetonius Tranquillius. Michael Grant, trans. *The Twelve Caesars.* Harmondsworth: Penguin Books, 1957.

INDEX

PHOTOGRAPHY CREDITS